HC
IN DEPTH

HONG KONG IN DEPTH

AN A–Z GUIDE

Chris Pomery

Distribution in the United Kingdom, Ireland, Europe and certain
Commonwealth countries by Hodder & Stoughton, Mill Road, Dunton
Green, Sevenoaks, Kent TW13 2YA

British Library Cataloguing-in-Publication Data.
A catalogue record for this book is available from the British Library

Editor: Don J Cohn
Series Editors: Anna Claridge and Tom Le Bas
Designer: David Hurst

Front Cover Photograph by Ray Cranbourne/The Guidebook Company

Production House: Twin Age Limited, Hong Kong

Printed in China

For my mother, Mary Pomery, who explored Western
Market without a word of Chinese and who had many
fine conversations with old men nonetheless;
and for Charlie Goddard and Helen Glover
who shared many of the funnier moments

CONTENTS

MAPS

WITH THANKS

Hong Kong has changed almost beyond recognition since I arrived in September 1983, a few days before Typhoon Ellen. This book catches one view, one incarnation passed on to me by many people with whom I've worked and whose ideas I now reflexively claim as my own. I am profoundly grateful for their friendship and their love.

A few cannot be left unnamed: my office partners Charlie Goddard and Ian Lambot, photographer Greg Girard, Helen Glover at the British Council and young Mathew, Joan Law, Yvonne Chang, Paddy Booz, Derek AC Davies, Pauline Dallas, Fred Scott, Brenda Turnnidge, Amanda Thow, Annie Edwards from South Africa, and the Sunday rambling group of Nici Dahrendorf, Elisabeth Mayer-Rieckh, Sarah Sargent and Lorelei Goodyear. My thanks are also due to many professional colleagues with whom I've been lucky enough to work with over the years, including Hamdani Milas and Keith Hawke of Hawke Films (HK) Ltd, and Amy Chan and Rory Hayden-Chan of the HKTA. The section on 'Professor Tea' (pages 86–88) was inspired by an article in Cathay Pacific's inflight magazine *Discovery* (Aug 1986) by Johnston Chang.

Any guide book is out of date even before it reaches the printers, and I guess this one is no exception. I apologise for any errors that have crept in. The good news is that the city is there to be explored: it really is very approachable and will reward you for your curiosity.

PREPARING TO TRAVEL

TWENTY THINGS TO LOOK FORWARD TO IN HONG KONG THAT YOU SHOULD NOT MISS

Most fascinating early morning encounter: *Tai chi* masters limbering up in Victoria Park. (page 94)

Most stunning breakfast: At the **Grand Hyatt** in Wanchai. It has the best view of the harbour in the early morning. (A–Z page 235)

Special Chinese breakfast: Established in 1925, the Luk Yu teahouse in Stanley St, Central, offers traditional teahouse atmosphere in very pleasant surroundings; Named after the god of tea, the place has a marvellous old feel to it, with its lacquered chairs, marble tables, mirrored cupboards, brass spitoons and old clocks. (A–Z page 253)

Typical Hong Kong breakfast: Any branch of **Maxim's** fast-food chain, which bears absolutely no relation to the chic French enterprise of the same name. Try the one on Queen's Rd, Central, near the bottom of Wyndham St. Alternatively try **Café de Coral** for the fast-food Hong Kong equivalent of a New York coffee shop.

Best Dim Sum lunch: Try one of the larger establishments like **Maxim's** in Causeway Bay, or the **Ocean City Nightclub and Restaurant** in the New World Centre, Tsimshatsui, that seats 8,000. If you need the protection of a hotel environment, try the **Conrad** in Pacific Place, Admiralty. (A–Z pages 264, 265 and 235)

Most exclusive afternoon tea: This should be taken at the **Mandarin** for discretion, at the **Hilton** for the buffet, or at the **Peninsula** for the atmosphere. (A–Z pages 234 and 235)

Best sundowner cocktails: In the foyer lounge of the **Regent** where the film stars congregate, the adjacent Sky Lounge in the **Sheraton**, or the pool bar at the **Victoria Hotel**. (A–Z pages 235–6)

Best window-shopping: The new **Seibu** department store in the upwardly-mobile Pacific Place in Admiralty, or the **Peninsula Hotel** arcades adjacent to the massive **Ocean Terminal** and **Harbour City** shopping complex in the western part of Tsimshatsui. (pages 92, 153–4)

Most interesting Saturday afternoon out: The **Happy Valley racecourse** is the place to go to smell the colony's passion for gambling. The amount of money bet here is simply staggering as the races flash by every half hour. The Shatin track is shinier but not nearly so impressive. (page 100)

Best ferry ride: The **Star Ferry** ride between Central and Tsimshatsui is Hong Kong's best bargain. Try and make it once during the day and then again after dark to catch the harbour's lights. (page 90)

Best promenade view of the city: From the **Peak Tram**, followed by a walk around the **Peak** itself. (page 103)

Best tour: A **harbour cruise** taken at sunset with cocktails, or a ride on the **tram** along Hong Kong island's north shore. (page 97)

Most interesting museum: The **Fung Ping Shan Museum** at Hong Kong University, Pokfulam, for its collection of bronzes and ceramics. (A–Z page 285)

Most kitsch tourist attraction: The **Tiger Balm gardens**, a monstrously garish concrete menagerie that is supposed to represent figures from Chinese mythology. (page 95)

Most authentic sauna and massage: The **New Paradise Health Club** in Wanchai. (A–Z page 288)

Most relaxing day trip: If you're energetic, take the ferry to **Lantau island** to visit the monastery at Po Lin with its giant

Buddha statue, and then walk back part of the way along the ridge path. (page 138)

Best out-of-town-trip: Take the jetfoil to the Portuguese enclave of **Macau**. (page 199) (A–Z page 232)

Best long walk: Anywhere along the **MacLehose Trail** which zigzags for 100km across the New Territories. This should be done only in sections for maximum enjoyment. (page 184)

Most interesting outer island: The isolated **Tap Mun Chau** in the far northeast of the colony. This tiny island is reached by a quaint twice-daily ferry. (page 126)

Best outdoor places for kids: Ocean Park entertainment and leisure complex near Aberdeen. (page 106) You can learn to windsurf on Stanley Beach, which has relatively secluded inshore waters. The **Zoological and Botanical Gardens** in Central are worth a visit, especially in midweek when they're quieter. Look for the pink flamingos, the gibbons and the orangutans. (page 88) There is also a new **aviary** in the tiny Hong Kong Park on Cotton Tree Drive.

Best indoor places for kids: The Space Museum in Tsimshatsui, across from the Peninsula Hotel, boasts a giant Omnimax film screen which gives a 360-degree feeling to the nature and space films on show daily. Tickets are often sold out well in advance here, especially during school holidays. The films are mind-blowing for adults too. The **Space Theatre** has regular shows describing man's exploration of space. English translations are available on headsets. (page 110; A–Z page 286) The permanent exhibition is often too crowded to be enjoyed fully. Try the new **Science Museum** which is also in Tsimshatsui. (A–Z page 286)

BEFORE YOU LEAVE
FOR HONG KONG

VISAS

Most **tourists can enter Hong Kong visa-free**, though ensure your passport is valid for at least an additional three months after your maximum permitted stay. **British citizens** can ask for a six-month stamp on entry; **British Commonwealth** citizens three months. European passport holders are offered between one and three months. **US citizens** receive a one-month stamp. Citizens of former East bloc countries can now get visas. Citizens of other Asian, South American and African nations generally require them too. Applications must be made through British embassies or consulates and can take six weeks or longer to process. Regulations exist demanding that visitors show proof of adequate means of support during their stay and an onward ticket.

Work permits are only granted before entry to Hong Kong. Changes in status are rarely allowed once in the territory. Visitors are not permitted to take up either paid or unpaid work, establish a business or enrol as students without a specific permit. There is some flexibility on this point compared to other Asian nations. Apply through British embassies and consulates; expect a delay of two to three months.

Vaccination certificates for cholera are only required if entering from an infected area.

An International Driving Licence (under the 1949 Berne Convention) is valid in the colony, though after twelve months you are required to produce your national **driving licence** to obtain a Hong Kong one.

Travel and medical insurance is a wise idea for all travellers. Ensure it covers lost deposits to hotel and tour companies, emergency costs, extra accommodation and repatriation in the event of serious illness. Many travel operators and credit card companies run schemes. Hong Kong's public emergency services are of a high standard for Asia, inexpensive but often overburdened. Quality private nursing is expensive.

PRE-PLANNING YOUR SHOPPING

Pre-planning is essential for efficient shoppers. Firstly, make sure you know the correct operating standards and power ratings of telecommunications and electronics items required. Make sure all your equipment is compatible. Be sure to check prices before you leave home; some goods are cheaper outside of Hong Kong through mail order or discount stores. Finally, be aware of customs regulations and levies in your own country; this can be an additional cost payable on your return. Consulates in Hong Kong will have details.

ORIENTATION

It does not take long to get your bearings in Hong Kong. The tourist area of Hong Kong island stretches west to east from Central, through Admiralty and Wanchai to Causeway Bay. Stanley and Aberdeen lie on the south side of the island's central ridge capped by the Peak which overlooks Central. The airport is located in Kowloon. The Kowloon peninsula and Tsimshatsui faces Central across the harbour. Tsimshatsui East was only recently reclaimed from the sea whilst Mongkok and Yaumatei are two of the oldest areas of the colony. Seven new towns lie in the New Territories, the land between Kowloon and the border with China, including the largest ones of Shatin and Yuen Long. The New Territories has several large natural parks and administratively includes major islands like Lantau, Cheung Chau and Lamma which all lie west and south of Hong Kong island.

THE WEATHER

Hong Kong has a subtropical monsoon climate. It has three often unpleasant and demanding seasons and about ten fine weeks during the transition from summer to winter, roughly October to late December, when you wouldn't want to be anywhere else in the world. Winter and spring can also offer unexpectedly glorious clear days.

Hot and humid summers are brought on by wet southwest monsoon winds that last from May through to August. Temperatures hover around 32° celsius, humidity around 75–90%. The onslaught is alleviated by the dry monsoon season and prevailing easterly winds bringing blue skies. Temperatures begin to drop in mid-September. A spell of cooler and wetter winter weather is heralded by the north-east monsoon winds which pick up in late December and last until March/April. Winter daytime temperatures average about 18° celsius and can dip to 5° celsius under a chilling wind from the north. Most of the rain falls in the transition period from spring to summer, picking up in April and peaking in June and July. Overall, the weather is more pleasant in the second half of the year, when conditions are generally sunnier and less humid. February, March and April are particularly cloudy and damp, with a low cover of grey stratus that can last for weeks.

Typhoons, the terrifying 'big winds', hit once a decade with devastating intensity packing 120mph winds. They can landfall along the China coast any time between May and October. There are usually a few close calls every year when a month's rain falls in a day. Listen for 'strong storm warnings' on the radio or typhoons in the Philippines. When a typhoon warning is broadcast everyone in Hong Kong knows what to do: flee in the direction of home. These days people are less shy about leaving work early to beat the rush hour. The city closes down for the minimum time, a few hours or a day at most.

CLOTHING

Light clothes are the order of the day from April to October. Sweaters and an overcoat are necessary from November to March. A light raincoat is useful all year round. Only the most exclusive venues demand a dress code these days, but protection against the fierce air-conditioning in some restaurants and taxis is often needed. In general it's your choice whether you want to dress like you have money or exactly the opposite. Style is Hong Kong's most important sartorial code, for business as well as leisure.

ON ARRIVAL

Although Hong Kong is a duty-free port, **customs** duties are levied on alcohol and cigarettes. All spirits, wine in excess of one litre, and anything more than 100 cigarettes will be taxed. Guns, fireworks and narcotics of any kind are strictly prohibited.

Hotel **accommodation** (A–Z pages 234–44) can be arranged on arrival in Hong Kong airport. There is an hospitality desk directly opposite the exit after passing through customs inspection. There can be a long queue. Hong Kong suffered from a room shortage in 1990 when the best deals were available to pre-paid package tours. Since the room glut of 1991, this has changed and discounts are sometimes available. To book your own room use the free telephones in the baggage collection area immediately after passing immigration control and before customs. Additional free telephones are located in the buffer hall after passing through customs.

Most visitors wonder whether to choose a hotel on Hong Kong island or Kowloon, and in many ways it doesn't matter. The two halves of the city crouch opposite each other overlooking the thinnest part of the harbour's channel. Central district on Hong Kong island is the colony's financial core. Upmarket shopping is evenly divided between Central and Tsimshatsui in Kowloon where there are more low-budget hostels and cheaper-priced shops. Either way the harbour is easy to cross and takes only a few minutes by ferry, MTR, bus or taxi.

Hong Kong is internationally renowned for its first-class hotels and service standards. Though high standards do not extend as deep down the pile as they used to, there's no doubt that the best hotels know how to make a guest feel pampered. The two **five-star** stalwarts are the **Peninsula** in Tsimshatsui and the **Mandarin Oriental** in Central. The Peninsula opened in 1928, has more than 600 staff for just 210 rooms and suites, and a fleet of nine olive-green Rolls-Royce Silver Spirits. The Mandarin Oriental opened in 1963 and is a regular winner of international service awards. It recently underwent a US$20 million renovation and boasts two top restaurants, the Mandarin Grill and Pierrot.

The major **Kowloon** hotels are grouped in Tsimshatsui East and along Canton Rd further west. The Shangri-La, the Royal Garden, the Regal Meridien, and the Holiday Inn Harbour View have been joined by the waterfront Nikko. The three Omni hotels—the Prince, the Marco Polo and the Hong Kong—on Canton Rd have all recently been refurbished. Newest are the Ramada Renaissance and the Kowloon, the latter managed by the Peninsula group. The Hyatt Regency has also been refurbished and now offers several attractive bars and restaurants. The Regent is a focal point for the local rich and famous; the lobby lounge offers a sweeping view of the harbour which is stunning at night. It also houses two high-class restaurants, La Plume and Lai Ching Heen.

Hong Kong island has several new luxury hotels: the Conrad and the Marriott at Pacific Place in Admiralty district east of Central, and the Grand Hyatt and the New World Harbour View which dominate the Exhibition and Convention Centre on the Wanchai waterfront. The Grand Hyatt has become the acme of modern Hong Kong with its glitzy imitation art deco interiors, a champagne bar, and nouveau cuisine Italian and Chinese restaurants. The Hilton, the first big hotel in Hong Kong when opened in 1963, has a popular ground floor coffee shop and its own converted brigantine—the Wan Fu— used for harbour tours and evening cruises.

Best value of the **waterfront hotels** is the New World on the Kowloon side which has some stunning harbour views. Next door to the the Regent, the lower tariff still includes a poolside terrace and adjacent shopping centre. On Hong Kong island, the Victoria Hotel looks east along the harbour front, a particularly beautiful view at dusk.

Of the **budget hotels**, the Emerald in Western district and the YMCA Harbour View in Wanchai, both on Hong Kong island, offer good value. The YMCA has the cheapest harbour view in town. The Ramada Inn in Wanchai is slightly more expensive than these two but also good value.

Budget travellers should head for the Tsimshatsui area where most of the cheap hostel centres like Chung King

Mansions are located, despite their reputation as insecure fire-traps.

CHANGING MONEY

Don't change large amounts of money at the airport or hotel as the rates there are noticeably lower than those offered by banks in town. If you use a streetside money-changer make sure you sign a transaction slip and get a written indication of how much currency you will receive *before* you hand over your money, as the posted rates can be misleading. Check the commission rate. Money-changers usually have high overheads such as rent and charge high commissions to cover them; however, they are open at late hours and on Saturday afternoon and Sundays when the banks are closed.

TRANSPORT TO YOUR HOTEL

Change at least HK$200 (US$30 or £20) at the airport to cover your **taxi** fare to your hotel and immediate contingencies. Remember that all dollar prices quoted in Hong Kong are Hong Kong dollars, not US dollars. A taxi ride into Central will cost a maximum of $85, inclusive of the round trip tunnel fee of $20 that is payable even for a one-way journey. Three airport coach routes provide efficient transfers to Central, Causeway Bay and Tsimshatsui.

BEFORE DEPARTING

Don't forget your **airport departure tax** of $150, payable at the checking-in counter. **Hand luggage** is limited to one piece measuring 9" by 14" by 22". Security guards at the airport can be brusque and unpleasant. They have a special steel rack to measure the dimensions of carry-on luggage and they will accept no excuses. Stay cool and remember this regulation is set by the airlines not the airport: go back and get the check-in desk's clearance in the form of a blue slip of paper.

HOW TO USE THIS GUIDE BOOK

It is tempting when writing a guidebook to try and be all things for all visitors, but it's hard! To make this guide easier to use I've set out factual information—names, addresses and telephone numbers—in a separate **A–Z Database** at the back of the book. Almost all of the subject headings and sub-headings used in the main text are cross-referenced there.

Thus, if you're looking through the 'Shopping Advice' section under 'Souvenirs' and you want the addresses of those picked out, turn to the section marked 'Souvenirs' in the A–Z Database. The same is true for the restaurants listed in the 'Dining Out' section which are sorted in the A–Z section according to their type of cuisine.

This guidebook is designed for the curious and should be sufficient to occupy you for days, or even weeks! However, since it can only be a starting point for personal explorations I've tried to indicate under the relevant chapter headings other specialist books or information sources that might supplement it. There are also several little books and maps that you really do need if you want to be adventurous. They're very easy to find and make a world of difference if you're keen to explore Hong Kong thoroughly. You won't be able to do some of the activities listed here without them. The most important are:

(1) a detailed single volume **street atlas**, called simply the *Hong Kong Guide,* which helpfully lists major buildings, temples, schools and the like with map references.

(2) for keen walkers, the six maps in the Countryside Series, available at several Government Publication Centres. Spread them out on the hotel room floor to get to know the colony.

(3) the specialist shopping and dining-out listings, updated annually, that monitor these fields. The most exhaustive are the *Gault-Millau Guide* and Dana Goetz's *Yin-Yang*

Shopping Guide. For factory outlets get Dana Goetz's *Complete Guide to Hong Kong Factory Bargains.*

(4) the Transport Department's annual services guide, also available at the Government Publications centres, lists all bus, minibus, ferry and *kaido* (mini-ferry) routes with their fares. This is really only necessary for long-term residents, but armed with it you can explore the length and breadth of the territory.

Visitors who are serious explorers should buy the street atlas and the Countryside Series maps whilst serious shoppers should arm themselves with the *Complete Guide to Hong Kong Factory Bargains.*

Other specialist information can often be tracked down through the Hong Kong Tourist Association (HKTA), the Consumer Council or the Community Advice Service. The HKTA produce a free, annual 80-page booklet listing every association and club registered in Hong Kong, which is a good starting point if you want to find specialist information. Their excellent series of shopping, sightseeing, culture and hotel booklets are available at no charge at HKTA offices.

HONG KONG FROM YOUR ARMCHAIR
HISTORY

ANCIENT TIMES

Residents may think Hong Kong's history is co-terminous with its settlement by the British in 1841, but archaeologists record traces of Stone Age occupation stretching back six millennia and contacts between indigenous tribesmen in southern China during the Han dynasty at around the time of Christ. Permanent settlement dates from the Song dynasty between the tenth and thirteenth centuries when two clans, which still have a presence in the New Territories, the Chan and the Tang, were first recorded. Invading Mongol hordes from the northern steppes, led first by Genghis Khan and later by Kublai Khan, brought about the destruction of the Song court at Hangzhou in 1276. The two half-brothers of the deposed emperor, Ti Cheng and Ti Ping, fled south. The Mongols pursued them for three years before cornering them at their final abode on Lantau and nearby Kowloon, finally killing the last pretender, Ti Ping, after a naval battle. The Mongol period didn't last long by Chinese standards, not quite a century, but it saw the emergence of the aboriginal tribes of the south as recognisably Chinese speaking groups.

THE PORTUGUESE IN MACAU

The Ming dynasty, which lasted from 1368 until 1644, didn't impinge much upon these outer reaches of the empire. The Portuguese arrived on the south China coast in 1553, founding Macau two years later and obtaining permission from the relatively weak Ming regime in 1557 to occupy Lantau, a notorious nest of Hoklo pirates, in return for their eradication. The swift highpoint of Macau's fortunes under Portuguese rule coincided with the continuing decline of the Ming dynasty and its fall to the Manchus who set up the last great dynasty—the Qing—that ruled China from 1644 until 1911. Famines racked the area and forces loyal to the Ming rulers waged sporadic raids down the coast from Formosa, now known as Taiwan. In 1622 the Manchus decreed that the entire population of the coastal provinces move inland on pain of death. When the order was revoked a few years later only a handful returned.

THE CHINA TRADERS

The Chinese finally opened the southern port of Canton, now called Guangzhou, to foreign traders in 1714 after keeping it out of bounds for the century and a half since the arrival of the Portuguese. Despite the pre-eminence of Portuguese Macau, the British East India Company established itself as the strongest Western trading group in Canton although hedged in by a range of restrictions imposed by the Chinese authorities. This was hardly a surprise as both cultures, the Chinese and the British, regarded themselves as civilised peoples surrounded by barbarians. The Chinese tried to deal with the problem by restricting foreigners' access, forbidding them from learning Chinese, from entering the city, or from trading outside specified dates. Shipping levies were imposed arbitrarily and a range of middlemen grew up to facilitate business and contacts.

THE DRUG TRADE

Trade had flowed in China's favour while Western merchants paid in silver for high-quality Chinese silk. This trend was reversed as Chinese demand for opium increased, a social problem that swelled rapidly after 1834 when the British East India Company lost its monopoly of China trade and other foreign traders, including Americans, attempted to cash in on the situation. The Chinese authorities, as modern Western governments still do, tried to solve it by interrupting the supply of the drug rather than tackling the root problems of its consumers. The trade had already been outlawed in 1799, but after nearly four decades witnessing the imperial decree being flaunted and a growing social crisis, the emperor sent a special commissioner, Lin Zexu, to Canton to stamp out the drug trade. His troops surrounded the foreign 'factories' on the outskirts of the city. After a siege of six weeks the merchants surrendered. It took three weeks to destroy more than 20,000 chests of impounded opium.

SECESSION OF HONG KONG

The British merchants, led by the Superintendent of Trade, Captain Charles Elliot RN, retired to their traditional summer retreat in Macau only to be told by the Portuguese governor that he could not allow them to stay. They took refuge instead, with their wives and families, on board their ships in the sheltered waters of Hong Kong. The British prime minister, Lord Palmerston, upped the stakes in the long-running dispute by demanding an open commercial treaty or a separate refuge under the British flag from which to trade. The emperor had already purged Commissioner Lin for daring to discuss preliminaries to a treaty which was taken as a sign of weakness. His successor, Qishen, also tried this tack after hostilities with a British expeditionary force flared up into the First Opium War (1840–42). It was the treaty at the close of this bloody spat that ceded Hong Kong island to Britain—the Convention of Chuanpi, January 1841. Captain Elliot lost no time and hoisted the Union Jack on Possession Point just six days after the signing. Though similar opportunism and pragmatism later became Hong Kong's watchword, it did neither party any good at its founding. Qishen was sent back to the imperial capital, Peking, in chains and Elliot was sacked by Palmerston, who castigated him for treating his instructions 'as if they were waste paper' and caustically described Hong Kong as 'a barren rock with hardly a house upon it'. Hong Kong's founder left Queen Victoria's newest colony under a cloud and ended up as governor-general of Texas. Today not even a side-street is named after him.

EARLY STRUGGLES

Elliot's successor, Sir Henry Pottinger, pressed hostilities ahead with vigour, advancing up the Yangtze River in central China and threatening the alternate imperial capital of Nanking, where a second treaty was signed in 1842. Although

Palmerston's government had fallen the year before and the new government's foreign secretary, Lord Aberdeen, had dropped the demand for a separate island, Pottinger freelanced beyond his official remit and secured Hong Kong a second time as well as gaining access to five Chinese ports.

The colony grew slowly at first. The Second Anglo-Chinese War erupted in 1856 in a dispute over the interpretation of the two earlier treaties and British outrage after a ship was boarded by Chinese authorities searching for pirates. This war lasted two years. Britain's treaty prize was the right to send a diplomatic representative to the court in Peking. However, the first man appointed in the post was fired on by Chinese troops as he approached the capital and hostilities broke out again. The British had been using the Kowloon peninsula to billet soldiers during the fighting in 1859–60 and were ceded it outright under the Convention of Peking in 1860. This was in line with moves by other European countries, namely Russia, France and Germany, and also Japan, which made similar depredations to secure treaty ports all along the China coast as the Qing dynasty weakened.

China weakened further after its terrible defeat by Japan in 1895. The British promptly took advantage in 1898 to gain a 99-year lease on the New Territories, the land north of the Kowloon peninsula that stretches as far as the Shumchun River. This move was aimed as much at shutting out the Russians and the French as grabbing more land from China. The British at first allowed the Chinese authorities to exercise control over the Kowloon City area but revoked this in the name of military expediency shortly afterwards. This began the decades-long wrangle over what eventually grew into the Walled City of Kowloon, over which China claimed jurisdiction for reasons of sovereign pride long after it had festered into a den of iniquity.

THE FALL OF THE QING DYNASTY

Chinese people had been flocking to Hong Kong from its very first days, much to the surprise of the British who expected them not to want to live under foreign rule. At first the British had hoped to administer them separately using magisstrates seconded from the mainland, but this parallel system never worked and broke down completely under a massive crime wave. By 1865 the colony had adopted a principle of equality, specifically prohibiting race discrimination, at London's instigation. The first Chinese person in the legislative council was appointed in 1880, though many other areas of social life remained restricted.

By the turn of the century, Hong Kong had become the principle jumping-off point for thousands of Chinese emigrants heading for the New World, a role taking on a new lease of life in the run-up to 1997. Among those who passed through the colony was Sun Yat-sen, the father of Chinese nationalism, who studied medicine in Hong Kong shortly before the 1911 revolution in China overthrew the Manchus. The prolonged unrest brought the first of several great waves of refugees flooding into Hong Kong, the beginning of its transformation from an obscure colonial outpost into an international trading city. Britain too became the target of nationalist feeling in China during the 1920s, prompted by the failure of the allied powers to strip Germany of its rights in Qingdao and Shandong province after World War I.

THE PACIFIC WAR

Anti-foreign attention in China shifted during the next decade after Japan occupied Manchuria in 1931. Open civil war broke out in 1937 and some 750,000 refugees crossed the border to Hong Kong in 1937–39 fleeing the conflict. As World War II engulfed the globe, Japanese Imperial forces launched an attack on Hong Kong simultaneously with the bombing of Pearl Harbour. The colony surrendered on Christmas Day 1941 after a brief but bloody fight. Many residents fled to neutral Macau while others were interned in camps for the three years and seven months of the occupation. Many Chinese moved back into China, propelled later by Japanese deportations to ease the colony's food shortage. At the close of the war the Americans suggested handing Hong Kong back to the Chinese nationalist government under Chiang Kai-shek, but Britain formally re-established its administration in 1946. Over an 18-month period the population trebled to reach 1.8 million as people returned after the war or fled the latest revolutionary troubles in China.

THE RISE OF COMMUNISM

This steady influx continued as the Chinese Nationalists lost their grip in the civil war with Mao's communist forces in 1948–49. Another half-million refugees arrived in Hong Kong from Canton, Shanghai and other major commercial centres creating the mix of Chinese groups and dialects that still characterize the city today.

POST-WAR ECONOMIC GROWTH

Hong Kong's post-war start on the path to prosperity was not auspicious. Hong Kong was immediately hit by a United Nations embargo extended against China for its part in the Korean War. Industrialization was promoted by textile manufacturers, some of whom had marched their entire workforce down the coast from Shanghai in 1949. Textiles still account for the lion's share of Hong Kong's domestic exports, matched these days by electronics and watches. Many of the colony's wealthiest entrepreneurs started out at this time with next to nothing, people like the Macau casino magnate, Stanley Ho, and the diversified property developer, Li Ka-shing, whose companies now make up a double-digit percentage of the Hong Kong stock exchange.

Hong Kong sputtered a bit in the mid-1960s, when it became caught in the backwash of Mao's Cultural Revolution and absorbed a fresh influx of refugees. Leftist groups mounted a series of demonstrations and attacks against the colonial government, including several hundred bomb attacks in public places, that caused a temporary paralysis of the economy. Over time the pressure subsided, largely because Chinese leaders did not call for the overthrow of the adminstration.

THE LAST DECADE

During the 1970s and 1980s, Hong Kong's economy went from strength to strength, largely because China became less of a pariah after Richard Nixon's trip to Beijing in 1972. As China has opened itself up to the outside world for foreign investment, Hong Kong has become increasingly attractive as a base for Western companies exploring the new market. Today it is as rich per capita as Singapore and second only in the region to Japan.

Hong Kong entered the 1980s growing in affluence. Public housing projects were giving many the chance to set up their own lives. Incomes and living standards were rising. The only problem looming on the horizon concerned the 99-year lease on the northernmost part of the colony which Britain had claimed during the declining years of Manchu rule in 1898. Although two decades distant, many senior people were becoming uncertain whether the existing arrangement would be able to continue after the lease became due for renewal in 1997. Most importantly, how could land continue to be treated as a valuable commodity if no one knew what China's intentions were for Hong Kong?

THE 1997 QUESTION

China's position on the Hong Kong question was well known—it wanted Hong Kong back 'when conditions were ripe'. China had even refused to allow the Portuguese to hand Macau back in the mid-1970s for fear the move would destabilize the British colony. But by 1982 the logic of the expiring leases and the extreme age of China's communist leaders (coupled with their reluctance to go down in history as the men that let this most successful part of the motherland slip from their grasp) ensured that conditions were ripening rapidly. The reintegration of Hong Kong had become diplomatically feasible following China's moves to rejoin the international community, and the British were in no mood to fight for a colony on the edge of everyone's consciousness. Western optimism ran high and overcame any doubts over China's handling of domestic human rights issues and, for example, its suppression of the Tibetan people within its own borders. China had consistently refused to register Hong Kong as a colony at the United Nations, fearing that it could then be propelled by the British towards independence. By 1982 it was obvious that China wanted Hong Kong back, a precursor to the much longed-for reunification with Taiwan.

THE NEGOTIATIONS
OVER HONG KONG'S FUTURE

Independence was never an option for Hong Kong. In fact, as the experience of the transition to 1997 has showed, Britain is reluctant to do anything that flies in the face of Chinese designs for the territory. When talks opened in September 1982 they were held behind closed doors and attended only by British and Chinese diplomats. Hong Kong's part-time politicians were excluded. Since the latter had all been appointed by the colony's governor none had a mandate from the electorate, and the Chinese government dismissed them as stooges.

Hong Kong's 5.8 million people, who had turned this tiny place into one of the richest enclaves in Asia, were pitched into an extended two-year crisis as the secret negotiations dragged on in Beijing. The talks were supposed to remain confidential. In fact, the Chinese side regularly floated its ideas in the Chinese-language press in Hong Kong to force concessions from the British. The main secret, that Britain would indeed hand over sovereignty and withdraw its administration after 1997, was kept under wraps for almost a year, though Chinese leaders continued to state publicly that it would happen if no agreement was reached by late 1984.

BRITAIN AND CHINA'S ANSWER

When the agreement was finally unveiled in September 1984, within days of the deadline imposed by China, it looked very attractive. Britain promises to relinquish sovereignty of Hong Kong on the stroke of midnight on 30th June 1997. In return, China promises to leave the colony's lifestyle and economic set-up basically unchanged for at least 50 years.

This is the theory. In practice, China and Hong Kong have been moving closer and closer during the last ten years, a process accelerated by Hong Kong manufacturers investing over the border in southern China and by mainland companies setting up offices in the colony to use its links with the outside world. So much of Hong Kong's industrial capacity has moved over the border that more people, over 2 million, now work for Hong Kong factory owners in China than in the colony itself.

This is a neat economic symbiosis. The problems, however, lurk in society. Chinese leaders believe that economics can ultimately be detached from politics. Strong political leadership can foster economic growth. It can also preserve the leading role of the Communist Party as the arbiter of Chinese society. Hong Kong has had a different experience entirely. It grew very rapidly after the Pacific War under a colonial administration that was simultaneously benevolent, unelected and generally efficient. It succeeded by minimising state control of economic activity. On the outside the colonial structure looks very appealing to China's leaders who would love to retain the colonial apparatus, and just change the name plate on the door.

IMPENDING CHINESE RULE

This hope is unrealistic. The shock of the 1997 deal was a catalyst that has forced Hong Kong citizens to examine their hopes and fears about what rule by the Communist Party of China really means. The optimism of the mid-1980s has slowly leaked away as the Chinese have mapped out Hong Kong's future.

The biggest disappointment of all is the issue of democracy. The British had suggested in the early 1980s, whilst the negotiations with China were still underway, that Hong Kong would move with vigour towards a democratic system during their final years in power before 1997. But as China's influence over the colony has grown these ideas have been watered down. Hong Kong people are prosperous enough to know that they want a greater say in their own affairs and that their politicians should be accountable to the electorate. This, however, will only partly be established by 1997.

Invisible changes may have a greater impact on ordinary life. The confidence to speak out may be curtailed by self-censorship as individuals tread more carefully for fear of stepping out of line. They are wise to be cautious for after 1997 there will be no one to help them but themselves. There are several strategies to deal with this threat which Hong Kongers, with typical resourcefulness, have been swift to implement. The most immediate reaction is to emigrate.

EMIGRATION

The first émigrés were coolies, labourers recruited in undeveloped China who passed through Hong Kong en route to the railroads of the California goldfields. Today's émigrés are a different type. The best educated and most socially mobile, their numbers have been growing every year this decade. At least 1% of the population leave Hong Kong every twelve months. (In Britain this would mean half a million people leaving every year.) This is the sort of figure that no city or economy, however dynamic or resilient, can absorb for long without a diminution in service standards. The favoured recipient countries of the exodus are Canada, Australia and the USA, although other Western countries are making it easier for local citizens who can demonstrate a connection through work or association to apply for residency and the coveted second passport. The British government also announced a scheme in 1989 to offer some 50,000 families a British passport before 1997. The Chinese government may turn this into a kind of loyalty test and have threatened not to recognize any documents issued under such emergency schemes.

HONG KONG AFTER
THE TIANANMEN SQUARE MASSACRE

Such threats by the Chinese leaders show how far mutual trust has deteriorated over the last few years. In Hong Kong, optimism now cloaks deeper uncertainty or niggling pessimism. Hong Kong's natural 'get rich quick' reflexes are sharpening. Confusions of identity seem more common in locally-made films and in everyday conversation. On the outside the city looks as successful and busy as it always has been, but in its heart it has a huge problem that it is unsure it will be able to resolve.

China's senior leader, Deng Xiaoping, once dreamt up the catchy slogan of 'one country, two systems', a formula for Hong Kong's reintegration that would guarantee its free market economic system under the political umbrella of the motherland. Today that promise feels more like a threat, a reminder that political obedience to the Communist Party is a condition of Chinese nationality and that no notion of separation can overide this truth. This is a key lesson China's leaders have reminded the nation of after their cold-blooded suppression of the student and worker protests in Tiananmen Square in June 1989. That warning was, and is, extended to include Hong Kong because the colony's population publicly supported the students' cause with massive demonstrations. Some estimates say up to a million people took to the streets on three separate occasions, around a fifth of the entire population. Millions of dollars were also collected. Those local students who were apprehended in Beijing delivering Hong Kong's donations had to undergo harrowing interrogation before being deported.

THE BEGINNINGS OF DEMOCRACY

As the clock ticks away to 1997, most people in Hong Kong realize they have a gun to their head and are behaving as sensible people do, either by walking away from the threat, keeping their heads down, or at least trying to promote a sense of identity and justice whilst the rule of law is still there to protect them. The elections in September 1991 were a turning point. Twelve out of 18 seats were won by the most outspoken pro-democratic party, including two of its leaders, Martin Lee and Szeto Wah, whom the Chinese Government have already condemned as 'counter-revolutionary subversives'. One thing is for sure, things will never be the same again.

THE STRUCTURE OF SOCIETY

As in many colonial societies, the social gap between the majority of indigenous inhabitants and the outsiders is huge. In Hong Kong these groups are generally very tolerant of each other's habits and foibles. An old colonial administrator with a lifetime of experience in Africa and the islands of the Pacific Ocean once told me that the British had had the least effect in Hong Kong of all its many colonies. In the main the expatriate community has minimal contact with ordinary Chinese people except in their office. At the highest levels English-speaking Cantonese, often educated abroad, move with ease in international business, English law and the local administration. The corollary is that Hong Kong is the last colonial playground for the expatriate, the professional foreigner who is based in Asia for several years, often extending that stay into a lifetime as curiosity becomes habit.

Today there are more North Americans than Britons living in Hong Kong—they first outnumbered them during the mid-1980s—though the largest foreign community are the 65,000 Filipinos, the majority women serving as the most colonial of workers, domestic servants or amahs. The other major foreign presence remains invisible in daily life: the sixty thousand-odd Vietnamese would-be refugees who languish in transit camps awaiting forced repatriation or resettlement.

CONSPICUOUS CONSUMPTION

Visitors are always impressed by how accessible Hong Kong is. The shops seem to be open even after dinner, taxis appear miraculously even in far-flung corners of the colony, and everything works efficiently. Foreigners rarely encounter serious crime, though beware of pickpockets on the tourist strip in Kowloon.

The flip side is Hong Kong's relentless consumerism, scarcely abated by people's conscious choice to put aside a high level of savings. The conspicuous consumption hits you in the rows of chic boutiques next to the gold shops, the advertisements for diamond-crusted status symbol watches and the numbers of sleek Rolls-Royces and Mercedes-Benzes in the crowded streets.

In truth, these days the boutiques and designer-label shops are more likely to be staffed by Japanese-speaking assistants catering to female weekend shoppers from Tokyo and Osaka. But Hong Kong remains a city where you are what you're worth in terms of clothes, jewellery and transportation. Nowhere else has the mobile telephone so quickly become an essential status symbol, snapped up initially by criminal triad gangs and real-time financial market makers, closely followed by wealthy mens' wives, and now almost *de rigueur* for any lunchtime gathering.

BUILDING FOR THE 21ST-CENTURY

This craving to embrace technological advances, especially if they have a highly visible social dimension, stretches deeper into the Hong Kong psyche than simple consumerism. Hong Kong has always got ahead by living on the edge, and nowhere is that more true than with its transportation network. Its squeaky clean graffiti-free mass transit system (MTR) operates over capacity after a decade in use. Huge fee increases are occasionally hefted onto motor car licences to deter owners from keeping them on the road, but to little avail. The container port has increased its capacity many times over in the last decade and is now the world's busiest. No visitor needs to be reminded of the breath-taking proximity of the airport's single runway to the crowded tenements of Kowloon.

This last Hong Kong experience should become history before the end of the century. A multi-billion dollar airport is to be built on the north shore of Lantau island with a host of contiguous port facilities linked by a massive suspension bridge. This is by far the most ambitious construction project ever undertaken in the colony, and in a real sense the government has portrayed it as a metaphor for the colony's future security. In a city where a five-year return can be thought of as a long-term investment, any project so huge and costly must indicate confidence in the future, they reason. Land reclamation, another Hong Kong pastime—the colony has grown by almost ten square miles over the last decade—is already underway.

SIGHTS AND SOUNDS
ON THE STREETS
OF THE CITY

Dwarfed by Central's looming skyscrapers, almost blown away by the swirl of humanity in the street, the *lap sap* lady rummages in the bottom of the orange municipal garbage bin looking for discarded soft drinks cans. The aluminium, she knows, can be sold for scrap, crushed into huge blocks of metal by a backstreet press just a few paces from the trendy night-spots on Lan Kwai Fong. Her share in the recycling process is just a few cents per kilo, yet she's always there, day after day, her body bent double with age and seemingly oblivious to other pedestrians who recognize her as a familiar local trader. She is one of a large army of trudgers and haulers, men and women pushing trolleys piled with black garbage bags up a steep hill, pulling sheaves of cardboard on a string, balancing old newspapers on a bamboo shoulder pole, in short sifting and carrying away anything that can possibly be recycled.

Hong Kong is this conjunction of rich and poor, drudgery and success side by side, the upwardly mobile and the chronically disadvantaged that have never, as yet, come into confrontation. Sorting rubbish on the sidewalk is environ-mentally friendly, but it shows the gaps in the social welfare safety net for many abandoned by their family, or simply outliving them. Yet for all that, Hong Kong has few beggars compared to London or New York. Long-term residents come to recognize them after a while, the leprous hunchback on the walkway to Swire House, or the Wanchai lady who sleeps outside the British Council.

Hong Kong has always lived its life on the streets. The sedan chairs that hauled portly Westerners up the Peak's steep hillside have long gone, but a few elderly rickshaw pullers re-tain their licences. They can be found outside the Star Ferry terminal on the Hong Kong side waiting for tourists to take a picture and a perilous trip into the surging traffic before the rapidly wiser visitor, aware that the bright red 'ricksha' is conspicuously out of place in the 1990s, cancels the tour at full price, if he has had the wisdom to fix the fare before embarking. The government issues no new licences today—an experimental tourist rickshaw service on the Peak pulled by energetic Western boys folded in the late 1980s—and yet humanely can find no reason to deprive these aging pullers of their lifetime livelihood, however outmoded.

As shop rents rocket, legions of streetside stalls still dot main thoroughfares: cobblers, key-cutters, juice makers, light-bulb sellers, plus a spread of shops that could only be store-fronts in Hong Kong, the bird-sellers, the herbal medicine men, the stores selling sweet frothy cakes. Some schoolchildren pass by, the morning shift for certain government schools have two sittings because the press for places in some districts is so intense. The buildings they learn in are hot in summer. Some are so close to construction sites that the teachers have been known to use loud hailers. If they go to a good school the girls may be called Betty, Iris or Nancy. In Hong Kong you can meet a 30-year-old with a cut-glass figure who has a Christian name from our grandparent's generation, the legacy of the post-war mission schools where emigrant teachers renamed their pupils with an English name to aid their memories. These days the kids choose for themselves, names stolen from history like Michelangelo and Hitler, or invented names from outer space or comic-land like Pancy, Clito and Davian. Sometimes they're just plain mistakes, like the bank manager I once had who had been christened by a Chinese priest as Laymond.

Be careful how you cross the busy streets. Jaywalking is a pastime, but the delivery boy pays no heed to traffic lights or 'no entry' prohibitions as he flashes by on his made-on-the-mainland iron bicycle burdened with a gaggle of silenced ducks, their broken necks lolling over the basket's metal rim and slung in bunches alongside the wheels as the bike boy nips past a ritzy Mercedes-Benz at a red traffic light. They carry anything edible, these boys, anything you or I would want to see wrapped, refrigerated or protected: huge slabs of red meat tied to the handlebars with raffia, buckets of vegetables, trays of quivering *doufu* (beancurd), plastic bags full of writhing fish and eels, and mountains of trussed crabs.

In the early mornings the markets are a cacophony of sounds and stinking smells. The ducks are honking as they're hurled in crates off the back of a ubiquitous green-tarpaulined truck. Fish gasp feebly on slabs as a blood-stained butchered bullock's head, skinned up to the horns and tossed casually into a wicker waste basket, gathers flies in the rising heat. Frogs clamber over each other inside a metal cage until one is picked, its legs chopped off in a single stroke of the blade and the skin pulled off its living back. The fish lorry is more refined, water slopping out over the sides of the blue plastic tubs that hold its cargo, kept alive by a battery of aerators. Downtown, a restaurateur leans closer to make his choice, the driver scooping the fish into plastic bags so big they have to be hauled away across the concrete. They will swim in the tanks in the restaurant's window until they are chosen for the pot or go cloudy-eyed. At the end of the day the driver opens the truck's cocks and the water gulps and gushes down the gutters.

Other vendors work directly on the kerbside, like memories from old postcards or books of faded photographs, remnants of a world seen now only in very poor places in southeast Asia like Vietnam or Burma. A street barber can still find business in Central, tucked in a back alley, a simple short-back-and-sides in a dentist's chair in front of a tiny mirror and not a trace of embarrassment by the cutter or the clipped. Calligraphers and signwriters still set up street stalls in Wanchai and Yaumatei, the large black Chinese characters on red scrolls proclaiming a family announcement, hung beneath the huge crepe-paper *fa pai* (wreathes) that signal a restaurant wedding feast. The letter writer and the *daijinjie,* the marriage broker, work still in Yaumatei, but the chop makers have moved to their own side-street in Western. Marriage one can manage oneself perhaps, but the authority of a chop, the company stamp, is still demanded by every courier deliverer or messenger boy. Only a few years ago they would be baffled if you didn't have a chop, but less so today, and anyway there are fewer messenger boys these days: why should you flog your hide around the hot streets when you can be a waiter in a uniform and work at night?

The most ubiquitous street presence are the hawkers, thousands of licensed and unlicensed street-sellers that clog alleyways and MTR entrances all over the colony, a tide of entrepreneurship that is moved back but never defeated by the sporadic patrols of the government regulators from the Urban Council. When police are spotted the illegal hawkers fling a shawl over their goods and speed away with their outsize trolleys, only to pause around the corner to wait for the officer to pass by. They're a nuisance if you're in a hurry, but the hawkers are as much a part of Hong Kong as the Peak Tram and tolerated by everyone because they're only trying their hardest to make ends meet. The most dangerous are the cooked food sellers whose carts upturned in flight have scarred children in the past in a splash of hot offal and orange-dyed squid on sticks. The most distinctive is the stinky beancurd seller with sizzling wok balanced on a cross-pole, that particular smell heralding the end of summer a week or two before the Mid-Autumn Moon festival.

In Central, a knot of people gather round the Dao Heng Bank stock monitor screens to watch the movements of foreign exchange rates, the ebb and flow of the Hang Seng Index and the ten most active stocks on the stock exchange. It has long been a truism that everyone in Hong Kong has a deal on the go, that every secretary knows the closing price of silver last night in America and the elderly Chinese servant overhears better stock tips from the master than any broker gains through his contacts. Yet a 1989 survey by the Stock Exchange found that proportionally fewer people in Hong Kong own shares than in America, so that myth must die a slow death.

Hong Kong is still obsessed with communications though. In the mid-1980s, the only people with mobile phones were tattooed triads. Then came the businessmen showing off on escalators and setting down their corporate symbols on dinner tables by fours, then the rich housewives waving them aloft during shopping expeditions. Now even shopgirls carry them, seemingly not short of the US$1,500 they can cost, as Hong Kong people save almost six times as much as the average North American. The radio pager is yesterday's technology, yet 700,000 people use them, one for every eight citizens in the colony. Instead of the pager's irritating bleeps erupting in public places people carry on full conversations via their mobile phones. I have even listened to a man launch into a long-distance discussion inside a cinema when the lights were down.

Technology is a Hong Kong fetish. The future is already here, and it works. You can do things with your bank card at an automatic teller machine that an Englishman, trapped in the dark ages of retail banking, can only dream of. You can shuffle money through a series of accounts and take out several thousand dollars cash, and unlike anywhere else in the world ATM crime is practically unheard of in Hong Kong. Crime rates are rising, though, as 1997 approaches. Violent street heists have become casually daring, though a tourist isn't likely ever to be aware of it. The guns come from China or are smuggled in from Vietnam, but the most Hong Kong touch of all is seen in local newspaper reports which simply mention that the robbers escaped by taxi. Police presence is pervasive as local officers have the right to stop and search anyone on a street and demand to see their ID card. This was originally an anti-illegal immigrant measure but the practice continues to keep everyone else in awe of authority.

Elsewhere the law is visibly flouted. In the backstreets of Mongkok the fake designer watch salesmen line up photo albums of their wares, the unwary and the trusting parting temporarily with their credit card to purchase a counterfeit for a fraction of the price of the genuine article. Throughout the territory the influence of the triads runs deep, invisible on the surface except on rare occasions when rival gangs fight it out in public. The multi-million-dollar world of petty protection, racketeering, drug running and cross-border smuggling has little effect upon the ordinary foreigner in day-to-day life. Around 50 secret brotherhoods operate in Hong Kong, including groups from the mainland and Taiwan, and as 1997 approaches they are, like everyone else, internationalizing their operations. After the Tiananmen Square massacre triad connections were used to smuggle Chinese dissidents across the border to Hong Kong, the same connections the mainland Chinese cadres are trying to foster in the run-up to the sovereignty transfer.

The Chinese obsession with numbers runs very deep. Vehicle licence plates are a prime money-spinner for charity, capitalizing on twin local fetishes, the belief that lucky numbers can corner good fortune and the chance to contribute conspicuously to a good cause. More than $70 million has been raised since 1973 when the vehicle licencing department started setting 'lucky numbers' aside for auction. The record price stands at $5 million for the luckiest number of all, the number 8, which in Cantonese has the same sound as the character for 'prosperity'. On another level, witness the ubiquitous Royal Hong Kong Jockey Club's betting shops, nothing like their tawdry English counterparts, but tiled hi-tech palaces to risk and the elusive mix of danger and opportunity. All 129 are packed on race-days from one end of the colony to the other. Down-market, old-style pawnshops are rarities these days. Just a few traditional ones are left in Yaumatei, Wanchai and Causeway Bay. Their traditional signboard shows a bat above a gold coin—the word *bat-fu* sounds like the Cantonese word for 'fortune' and is associated with luck. The gold coin is self-explanatory. One shop in Yaumatei has a symmetrical sign signifying 'double happiness', perhaps for both parties involved in the transaction, the exact opposite of the Western connotation of misfortune associated with destitution. Only a few years ago, boat dwellers in the typhoon shelters pawned their babies temporarily in the belief the transaction 'sold off' the child's evil influences and health problems.

Other beliefs die hard. A truck rolls past amid banging drums and clashing cymbals, a youth group preparing for a lion dance that accompanies all formal openings of department stores and business ventures, allowing the chairman solemnly to dot the eyes of the lion with a paintbrush so it can see its way to fortune. Other superstitions can be seen on the street. Palm readers' stalls and the ritual burning of fake bank notes in denominations of $50,000,000 drawn on the Bank of Hell during the autumnal festival of Hungry Ghosts keep the restless spirits quiet and persuade them to go back to the underworld. You can buy these notes in the supermarket in bundles.

Even Westerners believe in the *feng shui* man. The geomancer's job is to ensure that our earthly spatial arrangements, our homes and our possessions, are aligned harmoniously with the life forces that flow invisibly around us. These 'dragon lines' carry the *chi (qi),* the same force the *tai chi* masters harness every morning in Victoria Park, which brings good fortune. Every major building will be cleared by the geomancer before it opens, for having good *chi* is not enough. If you reflect bad *chi* on others no good fortune will befall your business either. In the older areas of Hong Kong you can see little octagonal mirrors called *pat kwa* (and decorated with the eight Taoist triagrams), placed high up on buildings to ward off evil influences, for *feng shui* affects the poor as well as the mighty.

In Hong Kong, in death as in life, there is often no rest. In fact, there's literally no spare space to bury the dead, and the lack of it means the municipally-interred can find themselves on the move again before even a decade has elapsed. The latest solution, which is pure Hong Kong, is a ten-storey high-rise columbarium in Tsuen Wan with room for 61,000 sets of ashes, in a building complete with skylights, murals and evil-seeking statues of a spirit guardian with the head of a dragon, the wings of a phoenix, a lion's body and a tiger's tail. A family niche costs $13,500, a cheaper pair just $1,500. This modern creation in no way outdoes the oldest 'Coffin Hotel' of them all in Pokfulam where some of the residents have been laid up in their coffins on dusty racks for almost a hundred years, surviving a dozen typhoon floods and even the marauding Japanese army's occupation. One Sinologist savant observed to me the reason Hong Kong loves noise is that it is a constant denial of mortality. A screaming table in a restaurant is just one way of keeping death at bay.

Hong Kong is alive well above street level. Advertisements hang over every possible shop frontage threatening to canopy entire streets in overlapping layers of garish plastic. Ubiquitous neon signs are uniquely still. They aren't allowed to flicker on and off anywhere within the urban area as they might confuse pilots tracking the airport's approach lights. Viewed from the harbour, signs for Chinese companies are being crowded out by Asian and Western imports advertising Korean electronics, Australian beer and Japanese cameras. Several storeys high, they cast their unearthly glow over street corners in primary reds and blues, merging yellows and iridescent greens in the sputtering electricity of their gas-filled tubes that crackle in the rain and hum at night. Watch out for them when the winds pick up, for after a typhoon passes through there are always dozens wrecked on the roadside after being swung like violent drunkards from their supports.

New buildings are encased in a striking cocoon of bamboo scaffolding. The erectors are a superstitious lot, refusing to come on site if they see someone washing their hair the night before or if they drop a chopstick over breakfast. Some bring their birdcages and hang them high up in the breeze. Most scaffolders still follow an almost feudal three-year apprenticeship, and although Hong Kong building contractors have a poor safety record, surprisingly few scaffolders slip off even though they habitually spurn safety harnesses. Workers like the bamboo because it flexes in the breeze and it gives you some warning before it collapses. Their grid-like creations are everywhere, hanging vertiginously over roads to encase new neon signs and clinging to the smooth surfaces of skyscrapers. The construction method is almost uniform, lengths of plastic twine wrapped around the bamboo's intersections to fasten the structure to the parent building. The best bamboo comes from central China, not Taiwan or Thailand. More than 3 million pieces are used every year, culled usually in the autumn and winter after the summer spurt of growth. Each piece lasts on average for two jobs, a maximum of 14 months exposed to the wind and rain, before turning a tell-tale grey-black colour. Buildings high up on the Peak don't last as long for the moisture attacks them quicker, the scaffolders say. Watch some workers dismantling a large grid if you can. It may take two hundred days to build one up, storey by storey, and just an afternoon to take it down as the scaffolders drop 20-metre lengths from 40 storeys like javelins that shatter on the ground.

A visitor should not avoid Hong Kong's poorer areas. The urban squalor here is a concrete creation, not the desperate muddiness of Jakarta's railway lines, Bangkok's klongs or Manila's shanty slums. No one will question you if you wander through the massive public housing estates in Kowloon, their numbers painted high on their outer walls and washing enough for a village dangling from poles slung out of the windows. Some of these old blocks house 50 families on each floor in buildings 30 storeys high. As families grow richer they move upmarket, taking their old habits with them. Sparkling privately-developed estates like the massive Taikoo Shing complex housing 60,000 people, have banned the hanging washing outside flats' windows so as not to lower the tone of the area. At night the estates' lights flicker like jewels as few people in Hong Kong screen their lives with curtains. You can tell the classes apart in the dark. The pale light of a million fluorescent strips demarcates the poorer public housing from the softer yellow light given off by the tungsten bulbs of the relatively wealthy.

Even on Hong Kong island you can find remnants of once-vast squatter areas, black-roofed huts clinging to the hillside. The most visible are in Causeway Bay, close to the Tiger Balm Gardens. The last few squatter areas are being cleared after a 40-year public housing programme, begun after a massive fire on Christmas Day 1953 made 50,000 people homeless. By July 1992 all huts had been removed from the most dangerous slopes and every last family will be housed by 1995. Most squatter areas have fallen victim to the relentless attrition of transport improvements like the road tunnel through Diamond Rock near Kwun Tong in Kowloon. And, of course, the biggest slum of all, the Kowloon 'Walled City' (see page 120) which was cleared in 1992. Many squatter areas were quite well appointed as improvements were made over the years to provide street lighting and sanitation. Yet occasionally a stranger does a double take when an immaculately groomed young woman emerges from a hovel that could only be described by a Westerner as dirt poor.

That insistence on overcoming limitations is a typical Hong Kong reaction. My favourite examples are the illegal façades that clutter the sides of older residential properties. These illegal extensions are literally fixed onto the outer walls and are completely independent of the architect's plans. The façades are usually disguised as verandahs, porches or balconies. Many are just three- or five-foot cages, camouflaged wrought-iron works built to support shady pot plants in a miniature hanging garden, or just to protect the washing. The most majestic are air-conditioned and look like professional extensions. The extra space of the cages increases the market value and floor area of the parent flat dramatically. A family of six might share a common area of about 30 square metres—pace it out in your hotel room to see how small it is—which a new façade can boost by about 15 percent, and at a quarter of the cost of more conventional and legal methods.

Fortunately reinforced concrete is a very common construction material in local buildings, and it is strong enough to brace cages onto outer walls, unlike masonry or curtain-wall designs. A typhoon-proof cage might only take ten days to erect, the scaffolding appearing crabwise 15 storeys up one week only to disappear the next. The cages are Hong Kong's own urban vernacular architecture, a book written on the sides of its buildings, an Asian answer to the Ponte Vecchio in Florence, the ultimate expression of *laissez-faire*. The best places to see them easily are along Kings Rd on either side of the Fortress Hill MTR station and elsewhere in North Point, or in Shamshuipo or Mongkok on the Kowloon side. Any area where the buildings are more than 20 years old will have their share as the only places the cages don't proliferate are on the skyscrapers of the upper middle-class and government-owned property. They survive simply because 600 new blocks go up every year and the government has only 16 licensing officers to maintain order.

Unlike many Western cities, only the oldest street names in Central and Western resonate with history. The names of early colonial administrators pinpoint the earliest areas to be settled, their expansion up the hillside and westwards marking the city's rapid growth. The colony's hapless founder, Captain Elliot, however, was rewarded only with a now obliterated side alley off Robinson Rd and a water pumping station in Pokfulam. The first governor, Sir Henry Pottinger, has a side street connecting Des Voeux Rd and Connaught Rd in Central, the former named after the tenth governor in the late 1870s when the street first became a main thoroughfare and the latter after the Duke of Connaught who initiated the reclamation of the waterfront. The second governor, Sir John Davis, has a forgotten lane in Kennedy Town close to where the trams turn around. The third, Sir George Bonham (1848–54), fared somewhat better with Bonham Strand in Central and Bonham Rd which carved open the Mid-Levels. The fourth, Sir John Bowring, earned his much later, a cross-street between Canton Rd in Mongkok and Nathan Rd, itself named after the thirteenth (and Hong Kong's only Jewish) governor, Sir Matthew Nathan, who opened up Kowloon for settlement.

All the later governors—Robinson, Macdonnell, Kennedy, Hennessy, Bowen—will sound familiar to modern expatriate residents, largely imprisoned in a Mid-Levels ghetto of their own making, but which makes Hong Kong one of the few major cities in the world where you genuinely can walk down the hill to work. As the years roll by the names of the governors keep spreading up the Peak—Lugard, May, Stubbs, Clementi, Peel—as predictable as the rings inside a tree. Secretaries of State for the Colonies were also honoured. The trio of earls, Granville, Kimberley and Carnarvon, who served in Gladstone's first administration (and Disraeli's second) in the early 1870s, were placed side by side in the heart of Tsimshatsui four decades after they'd left office. Administrators lower in the pecking order weren't ignored either. Shelley St isn't named after the mercurial English romantic poet but an early auditor-general. Gutzlaff St, an alleyway off Wellington St, is a memorial to the Chinese Secretary of 1845. Many others have receded even further into the mists of time. In a nautical vein the 'Iron Duke', the Duke of Wellington, has a prominent street in Central, and Lord Nelson is remembered in Kowloon.

Chinese names are less prosaic. The district of Sai Ying Pun in Western stood for the 'western encampment' of the notorious pirate, Cheung Po-chai, and was altered from the original name of *tai ping shan,* which translates as 'the mountain of heavenly peace', for the 'red light' district. The name of Hong Kong itself is thought to be a corruption of a Tanka boat-people name, *heung gong* meaning 'fragrant harbour', possibly after the delicate perfume of sandalwood trees growing nearby or, more likely, the taste of the fresh spring water. Kowloon, *gau loong,* means nine dragons, eight of whose humps can be clearly seen in the shape of the surrounding northern hills, the ninth dragon being the young emperor who fled here from the Mongols in the 13th century. Hung Hom translates roughly as 'red cliff', and was named thus when contractors hit a burst of reddish liquid during drilling in 1909, literally piercing the dragon's vein that is said to run from the mountain into the harbour and which ensures that Hong Kong remains rich. The area has seemed ill-favoured ever since. Most colourful is Tsat Tsz Mui, a street in North Point which recalls the story of seven sisters, friends who made a mutual pact never to marry. When one was forced to do so by her parents all seven drowned themselves only to be found on the shore the next day still holding hands. Their spirits are said to return occasionally as beautiful women who seduce men into mischief. In 1912 a factory worker went missing to be found buried, and alive, under a huge stone two days later. He claimed he'd been invited for a drink by some beautiful girls.

Hong Kong has to be one of the busiest cities in the world. Stress levels are tolerated here far in excess of other urban environments except war-torn places like Beirut. A worldwide opinion survey made in late 1989 found that Hong Kong people had the most extreme views of all of those polled. Twice as many as their counterparts in America or Japan felt highly stressed and almost half said it was an important ambition to own an expensive car and jewellery. Paradoxically the Hong Kongers were the most pessimistic too, more than half believing that nuclear war was inevitable in the lifetime of their generation.

Those people who do leave, expatriates finishing overseas postings or local émigrés joining the great Chinese diaspora, complain, as all addicts do, that they miss the pace of the place. Residents like to complain that it's getting harder to get things done in Hong Kong, that service standards are dropping, that waitresses seem to have no peripheral vision, that no one has any respect for personal body space when walking in the street. Like every description of Hong Kong this is all true, but only because the opposite is also equally true, that things get done, that service people are as polite to foreigners as they are to each other even if their command of English isn't good, and that the waitress is new or just a little tired from her

French evening classes. Sometimes the pressures get too much; 657 people commited suicide in 1990, stark testimony to the daily stress of overcrowding, job competition and noise. Hong Kong, like Japan, has its share of teenage suicides, school children who buckle under the pressure of authoritarian teachers and parental expectations.

And things do happen fast. Buildings rise as quickly as a storey every five days. Central and Admiralty have been transformed out of all recognition during the last decade. Hong Kong is a young city that has all but destroyed its roots and which doesn't possess either a distinctive style of architecture or sufficient space for a linear layout that makes places like New York and Paris so striking. Traditional buildings, which testify to the beauty and grace of older cities, are singularly absent. What exists is a monument to the accumulation of capital, and the sediment of this process.

Despite that lack, several buildings erected in the 1980s would catch the eye anywhere in the world, part of the new international monumental architecture that China has never had (save for the biggest wall in history). The Lippo (Bond) Centre designed by Paul Rudolph, Norman Foster's headquarters for the Hongkong & Shanghai Banking Corporation, and I.M. Pei's 70-storey Bank of China building dominate Central's skyline. Two huge buildings of 78 and 75 storeys have recently been completed; Central Plaza in Wanchai and the Citibank Centre behind the Bank of China building in Central. The Wanchai building is the fourth-largest in the world and the tallest outside America. The Citibank Centre has an imposing atrium linking its twin towers that eclipses even the Hong Kong Bank's impressive interior design.

Some buildings are plainly a disgrace, a combination of government mismanagement and chronic lack of imagination. The Cultural Centre is a travesty, a windowless freak of municipal tiles occupying the most magnificent harbour location in the world. Hong Kong could have used this project to attract worldwide attention through an international competition. Instead it chose to flatter a particular civil servant's ego. Zoning laws are lax. View Hong Kong island from the air and Wanchai looks like a dead grey canyon. The crampedness of the buildings produces its own surprises. In winter the reflected light of the setting sun bounces off the Lippo (Bond) Centre's dark blue glass and down along Des Voeux Rd, casting multiple golden shadows in the dusk. Even in random back streets you can be dazzled by the sun as it moves across the face of a far-off building, temporarily giving you two or three shadows.

Some of Hong Kong's most interesting facets are hidden, like the statistics that make sense of the city's obsession with food. Ten years ago, pundits said fast food would never take off in Hong Kong. People were too particular about buying it fresh and cooking at home, they said. They were wrong. During the Lunar New Year in 1989, the McDonald's outlet in Sha Tin recorded the largest turnover of burgers in a single hour anywhere in the world. The Café de Coral chain expanded so fast in the 1980s that it is now listed on the local Stock Exchange. Here, even Maxim's is a fast food joint, though the appropriation of that byword for luxury doesn't belie Hong Kong's other gastronomic record as the world's leading consumer of cognac per capita, a luxury tipple that dominates television advertising from early evening until late at night.

Some sights only become visible at night. Central's Pedder St comes alive at 3 am as gangs of men stack newspapers for the morning. Stalls sell magazines and Japanese-style comics on most corners, for Hong Kong has roughly one newspaper title for every hundred thousand population. Unlike Japan, Hong Kong is a modest place. Despite the plethora of girlie magazine titles, the contents are a little prudish. Some pornography only hits the streets with tiny yellow stars stuck to the ladies' exposed nipples and her pubic hair veiled from display. Hong Kong must be the only city in the world where the circulation of the local edition of *Playboy* goes down when there's a naked girl on the front cover.

There's a hint of a double standards in operation here, a failure to grapple with a complexity and contradiction in modern life. It surfaces in odd places, in the way innocuous films are still censored if there's the slightest hint of anything erotic or critical of China on screen, in the way people emigrate rather than fight for their rights and their freedom, or the way they sometimes treat their maids poorly.

The Filipina *amahs* are by far the most numerous group of foreigners in Hong Kong. At weekends they reclaim Statue Square when it is closed off to traffic and seemingly all 65,000 of them pack into it at once for a cheap meal and a chat. Their position is better than the other equally large but silenced group of foreigners, the Vietnamese boat people, who are kept tucked well away from public scrutiny and the instinctual antipathy in a city that would prefer to help its own kin across the border first and can see no reason why it should help others to flee communist rule.

BOOKS TO READ

EXPLORATION

Historical Hong Kong Walks; Baker et al; The Guidebook Company, Hong Kong, 1988. Five walks on Hong Kong island with useful historical notes.

Twelve Hong Kong Walks; Derek Kemp; Oxford University Press, Hong Kong, 1985. Delightful collection of walks throughout the colony, one for each month of the calendar, by a botanist from Hong Kong University.

Another Hong Kong, An Explorer's Guide; Emphasis (Hong Kong) Ltd, Hong Kong, 1989. Collection of essays and anecdotes by residents of interesting and out-of-the-way places in the colony.

The Hong Kong Guide 1893; Oxford University Press, Hong Kong, 1982. Originally published by Kelly & Walsh in Shanghai. Evocative.

A Visitor's Guide to Historic Hong Kong; Sally Rodwell; The Guidebook Company, 1991. Illustrated history of the colony from earliest times.

FLORA AND FAUNA

The Government Printer and the Urban Council produce a series of books in paperback that list with illustrations the flora and fauna of Hong Kong, including separate volumes for food plants, snakes, lichen and nudibranches.

HISTORY

The Dragon Wakes: China and the West 1793-1911; Christopher Hibbert; Penguin, Harmondsworth, 1984. Excellent account of China's relations with the pink-faced barbarians during the last, troubled years of the Qing dynasty.

The Opium War; Peter Ward Fay; W.W.Norton, New York, 1975. Detailed history of the 1840–42 conflicts by an American historian.

A History of Hong Kong; G. Endacott; Oxford University Press, Hong Kong, 1966. The only full-length scholarly history of the colony that's readily available. Worthy but not exciting reading. Ends after the Second World War.

Hong Kong/Xianggang; Jan Morris; Penguin, Harmondsworth, 1989. Engaging, anecdotal but scholarly account of the colony's origins written by a leading travel writer and historian of the British Empire. New post-Tiananmen Square edition now available.

Political Change and the Crisis of Legitimacy in Hong Kong; Ian Scott; Oxford University Press, Hong Kong, 1989. Well written account of the transition to 1997 and the British and Chinese governments equally pragmatic manoeuvrings. Published before the Tiananmen Square massacre in June 1989; revised edition underway.

MACAU

Macau; Shann Davies; The Guidebook Company, Hong Kong, 1990. Guide to Macau with lots of lively information by a long-time resident and author.

Macau and the British, 1637-1842; Austin Coates; Oxford University Press, Hong Kong, 1988. Interesting, lively account of British activity in the Pearl River delta before Hong Kong was seized.

Macau; Cesar Guillen-Nunez; Oxford University Press, Hong Kong, 1984. A gem-like account of the decline of Portuguese fortunes in their venerable colony of Macau.

City of Broken Promises; Austin Coates; Oxford University Press, Hong Kong, 1988. Novel by former colonial administrator.

Macau Gambling Handbook; A-O-A Publishing, Hong Kong.

Streetwise Map of Macau; simply indispensable.

NOVELS

There are no great novels about Hong Kong, save John le Carré's *The Honourable Schoolboy,* a spy thriller recounting the rise and demise of the Honourable Jerry Westerby, newspaperman and Indochina wanderer. Timothy Mo's *Sour Sweet,* an account of a Hong Kong family settling in London in the 1960s, is faithful and amusing; his epic novel of Macau and Hong Kong, *An Insular Possession,* less so. Han Suyin's *A Many Splendoured Thing* is a good read. For a book on 1997, the best so far is Kevin Rafferty's *City on the Rocks,* published by Viking/Penguin. For a travelogue of China, always a good counterpoint for any stay in Hong Kong, Colin Thubron's *Behind the Wall* (Penguin, 1987) is the best.

SHOPPING

A Complete Guide to Hong Kong Factory Bargains; Dana Goetz; Delta Publications, Hong Kong, 1991. The indispensible compendium of all factory outlets selling designer clothing, fur, furniture and more. More recently Ms Goetz has brought out a bulky reversible—'yin and yang'—shopping and city guide whose shopping notes are relevant reading only for professional shoppers.

Drummond's Hong Kong Guide to Art & Antiques; Susan Jeffrey; Hong Kong, 1986. Although dated now, this is the only specialist guide to this sector of the market. The best private collector-galleries remain hidden away and aren't covered.

The Best of Hong Kong: Gault Millau Guides; Prentice Hall,
New York, 1989. Exhaustive and bulky guide to
restaurants, nightspots, shops and hotels. Useful for
residents.

Monthly Guide

The Hong Kong Tourist Association (HKTA) produces a
monthly booklet called The Official Hong Kong Guide which
contains lots of useful information about shopping, eating out,
transportation and sights. It's included in the package the hospitality girls hand out at the airport when you arrive and can
be found in all hotel rooms. The HKTA also have an excellent
series of black-covered mini-booklets on Culture, Dining and
Nightlife, Shopping and Sightseeing, plus buying guides listing factory outlets for ready-to-wear clothes, video product
information and hints for buying jewellery.

MAPS

The Hong Kong Guide: Streets and Places; Government
Printer, First edition, 1988; a comprehensive urban
street map that includes lists and map references of nearly
all streets, key buildings, government departments,
schools and much more.

Countryside map series #1–6: Government Printer; walking maps of the colony's country parks, plus insert maps of
some urban areas;

1. Sheet 1, edition 9, 1990, $13; Hong Kong Island
2. Sheet 2, edition 1, 1986, $13; New Territories West
3. Sheet 3, edition 5, 1989, $13; Lantau & Islands
4. Sheet 4, edition 3, 1986, $15; Sai Kung & Clearwater
Bay
5. Sheet 5, edition 2, 1987, $10; NE New Territories
6. Sheet 6, edition 1, 1989, $13; New Territories Central

Streetwise Map of Hong Kong; a colour-coded and very
detailed map 'for the seriously curious' to the tourist areas of
the colony. $40 in most bookstores.

FILMS

Hong Kong-made films tend to be very patchy. None so far has really caught the full impact of the changes the city is undergoing, though watch out for directors Clara Law, Ann Hui, Allen Fong and Tsui Hark. Neither has any Western film-maker resolved the issue. Hong Kong's most successful movie export was, in fact, *The Cannonball Run,* which was made so long ago it starred Burt Lancaster. Its only internationally known star was the kung fu genius, Bruce Lee, who died an unexplained death after just four movies. His Hong Kong successor is Jackie Chan, a puckish stuntman who has yet to make it big in the West but who holds the unenviable record of using 2,000 takes to perfect a ninety-second sequence.

Hong Kong has, however, attracted a variety of deadbeat Hollywood productions and was generally synonymous for depravity and lawlessness. In *The Maltese Falcon,* directed by John Huston in 1941, the bad guy called Floyd Thursby who stole the legendary statue had it shipped from Hong Kong to the States only to be murdered himself before the film actually begins! *Love is a Many Splendoured Thing* appeared in 1955 and was a big hit. However, the movie that outstripped them all, *The World Of Suzie Wong,* made by Paramount in 1960, starring William Holden is a dull, cutesy story of a prostitute with a good heart who poses for an artist who promptly falls in love with her. Universal made A *Countess from Hong Kong* in 1967, starring Marlon Brando and Margaret Rutherford, a pursuit story revolving around a Russian émigré. Alas, neither of these great thespians were able to rescue the dull plot. The modern movie of James Clavell's epic novel *Taipan* was equally dreadful. Most amusing of all, who now remembers a Paramount B-movie made in 1951, called simply *Hong Kong,* that featured an ex-GI who rescued a Chinese orphan and a golden idol? It starred a man who later went on to greater things—Ronald Reagan.

SURVIVING THE CITY

TRANSPORTATION

GETTING ACROSS THE HARBOUR

Hong Kong's tourist areas are easily explored on foot, although the joy of this can wilt quickly in the summer humidity. Save your footwork if possible until the cooler evenings and combine it with a cross-harbour journey on the **Star Ferry**. The unforgettable seven-minute ride runs from Central to Tsimshatsui costs $1.20 on the upper deck or $1 on the lower tier (see page 90). The last ferry leaves at 11.30 pm. From the boat you can see the whole of the north shore of Hong Kong island stretching from the Victoria Hotel on the western edges of Central to the huge Citizen neon sign over Causeway Bay. Alternatively you can take the underground train (MTR) or a taxi through one of the two tunnels.

TAXIS (A–Z PAGE 232)

Local **taxis** are one of the great joys of life in the Orient. The flagfall of $9 and $1.10 for every 250 metres is spectacularly cheap for an international city and cabs are ubiquitous even in the early hours of the morning. Though many drivers' English is rudimentary, even a little Cantonese goes a long way towards inspiring friendliness. Solve the communication problem by using the city's hotels as dropping off points and then walking a few blocks to your actual destination. Written directions do not always work, especially in remote areas. Hotels are good places to pick up cabs even if there is a queue.

Cabbies will pick up and set down anywhere legal, however inconvenient. Conversely they will not deactivate the self-locking doors even if you're in a seemingly empty space if the law prohibits it. The shift change for drivers occurs at 4 pm. Do not be surprised to find them avoiding eye contact, covering their 'for hire' sign or waving at you in mock anger after 3.30 pm. They don't want a fare.

Though drivers are legally required to take you anywhere on either side of the harbour, many won't traverse the tunnels close to the end of their shift. The easy way out is to consent to a change of cab. This even works out cheaper if you bargain the second driver into accepting a one-way tunnel fee. Certain places in Tsimshatsui, Wanchai and Causeway Bay are used as waiting areas for cabs returning to the other side of the harbour. Lockhart Rd in Wanchai is a good place to look if you want to go to Kowloon. Look for a square piece of cardboard covering the dashboard flag. If it is written in Chinese it means the driver is preparing to return to the other side of the harbour; if it says 'out of service' nothing on earth will persuade him to pick up a fare. Screaming won't help. For many drivers this is their second job of the day and they don't respond to this type of persuasion. New Territories' cabs are green and restricted to certain areas north of the Lion Rock.

Cabbies seem to love maintaining the maximum noise level inside the cab, preferably with a crackling CB radio link and Cantonese opera on the radio. On two quite mysterious evenings, however, I found one with an elegant stereo system listening to Philip Glass and a second who'd lived in Colombia and spoke fluent Spanish. Complaints about cabbies' behaviour from the non-Chinese public are not common, but several women have had frights after being taken home late at night by a very roundabout route. Raise your voice if necessary.

THE MASS TRANSIT RAILWAY (MTR)

Hong Kong's underground mass transit system—the **MTR**—is one of the world's best, wonderfully clean and efficient. It has an 80,000 capacity on the cross-harbour route during the rush-hour and carries 1.7 million passengers over its 39 kilometres (24 miles) every day. Trains run every two minutes during the rush hour and at 10-minute intervals late at night, closing down around 12.30–1 am. The three main lines run along the north shore of Hong Kong island from Sheung Wan to Chai Wan, from Central to Tsuen Wan in west Kowloon, and from Jordan Rd in Yaumatei to Kwun Tong in east Kowloon connecting (after a long walk through Quarry Bay station) with the Island Line. Buy a plastic multiple-use $50, $100 or $200 stored-value ticket. Individual tickets cost $3–8.

The morning rush hour on the MTR should be avoided at all costs. A ticket surcharge barely dents the orderly 8–8.45 am crush. Mongkok station is the worst affected at this time, though stations on the Island Line rival it. Local manners have improved dramatically since rush-hour platform attendants have started coralling commuters inside the yellow ground markers. There are complaints sometimes from women passengers of eye-teasing or straightforward groping, but these incidents are not common.

THE KOWLOON-CANTON RAILWAY (KCR)

The line runs from Hung Hom in east Kowloon to the China border crossing at Lo Wu, though only those crossing the Chinese border are allowed to alight at Lo Wu. The last station on the line for regular passengers is Sheung Shui. MTR stored-value tickets can also be used on the **KCR**, although not when travelling to the border. Collect the ticket from the machine in order to pass through the turnstile. The last few cents left on your card will buy you a final ride regardless of its cost. Four 'through trains' go direct to Guangzhou from Hung Hom daily without stopping at the border. Tickets for these trains normally must be bought in advance, and passport holders need a visa for China. The MTR connects with the KCR at Kowloon Tong station on the Kwun Tong line.

The western New Territories is also served by the **LRT**, a light rail transit system linking the new town of Yuen Long to the MTR railhead at Tsuen Wan. Your MTR ticket is valid here too.

TRAMS

If you have the time, the best way to observe a broad range of lifestyles of Hong Kong island is by **tram.** (see page 97) These run every few minutes from the far end of Western district to Shaukeiwan from around 6 am–midnight. Services are infrequent late at night. There is a single main line running along the northern shore of Hong Kong island from Western to Shaukeiwan with an additional side loop to Happy Valley. A full loop out and back might take two or three hours, but you can make the journey down the island one way by tram and return by MTR as the two networks follow the same route. A ride of any length is only $1. You can't get change on board.

BUSES AND MINIBUSES

The colony is also well served by a network of **buses** and smaller **public light buses** (PLBs). Both **China Motor Bus** on the Island and **Kowloon Motor Bus** on Kowloon-side operate

POPULAR BUS AND MINIBUS ROUTES

Bus routes from Exchange Square in Central:

4	Pokfulam, or take minibus #22 from the Star Ferry terminus
6	Repulse Bay and Stanley
7	Aberdeen
11	Jardine's Lookout (circular)
12	Robinson Rd (circular)
15	The Peak, or take minibus #1 from the Star Ferry terminus
25	Causeway Bay (circular)
61	Repulse Bay
64	Repulse Bay and Chung Hum Kok
70	Aberdeen
260	Stanley

Bus routes from Jordan Rd on Kowloon-side

70	Shatin and Tai Po
70	Tai Po (then 92)
5	Sai Kung (then 92)

Minibus routes from the Star Ferry:

1	The Peak
3, 3a	Conduit Rd, Mid-Levels
6	Ocean Park
9	Bowen Rd, Mid-Levels
22	Pokfulam

cross-tunnel services. These have three-figure route numbers and are printed on a red background. **Citybus**, a private service, now operates regular routes on both sides of the harbour and to Shenzhen (Shum Chun) on the other side of the China border.

PLBs charge variable rates depending on the boarding point. Those with green destination boards are following a specified route whereas the red ones are not. Though ubiquitous, PLBs are hard to use because its difficult to read the destination in English before the minibus has flashed past in a blur. Buses have specific stopping points whereas PLBs can be hailed almost anywhere en route. Tell the PLB driver when you want to get off by yelling *yau lok!* Usually you pay him as you alight. If in doubt, watch what the other passengers are doing. As with buses, the fare is displayed on the fare box or on the window, sometimes in Chinese only.

THE PEAK TRAM

This funicular service runs every 10–15 minutes from a terminus at Lower Garden Rd in Central up to The Peak, a rise of nearly 400 metres. The return adult fare is $16, one way is $10. The last tram leaves at midnight.

FERRIES

The outer islands can be reached via **ferries** run by the Hong Kong & Yaumati Ferry Co. These quaint old tubs run along main routes from Central to Yung Shue Wan and Sok Kwu Wan on **Lamma island**; to **Cheung Chau**; and to **Mui Wo**, also known as **Silvermine Bay**, on Lantau. The three main outer island piers are west of Blake's Pier in Central. Destinations and the time of the next ferry are labelled on signboards hung over the turnstiles. If you want to go to the self-contained suburban resort community of Discovery Bay on Lantau island take the jet boat from Blake's Pier which runs roughly every half-hour. Other ferry services operate from various piers dotted around the New Territories to smaller, more remote outer islands. Check the HKTA for details or the government's Transport Guide. (A–Z page 232)

HELICOPTER TOURS AND LIMOUSINES
(A–Z PAGE 232)

Helicopter tours of the colony can be arranged through **Heliservices** which use the pad on the Wanchai waterfront. Weekday rates start at $3,705 for a 30-minute tour. There is a minimum booking period of one hour on Sundays and public holidays. **Car hire** can be arranged through local or international companies for standard day rates. **Chauffeur limousine services**, including airport transfers, are also available using the **Ace, Avis** or **Holiday Rental** firms. Avoid the vintage **rickshaw pullers** at the entrance to the Star Ferry in Central. Gullible tourists agree to a ride before realizing there's absolutely nowhere to go in them. Negotiate beforehand and don't agree to more than $50 for a photo session or $100 to go once around the block.

ON-THE-SPOT INFORMATION

The main **language** in Hong Kong is Cantonese, a form of Chinese similar in structure, but not in sound, to the Mandarin *putonghua* spoken in mainland China, Taiwan and Singapore. Most of the 98% of Hong Kong's population that are Chinese came from Guangdong province, which begins just over the border, but other Chinese dialects can be heard here, particularly in the markets, including Shanghainese, Hakka and Chiu Chow (Chaozhou).

Incidentally, Canton the city is now more often referred to by its communist-era name of Guangzhou, even though its inhabitants are still referred to in English as Cantonese and speak the Cantonese language. Just to confuse you, in Hong Kong they'll refer to their language as Chinese even though Cantonese and *putonghua* are quite different in many respects. The province of Kwangtung is today universally called Guangdong.

Cantonese is tough for a foreigner to learn because of its tones. The nine basic tones of Cantonese are applied to words with identical sounds that derive their meanings from context and combination. It's a bit like trying to learn English by memorizing syllables rather than words. A lot of Cantonese conversation is actually conducted in a slang which is very viscous and often graphically obscene, so book-learning won't get you very far on the streets either.

It is usually possible to get by in English, the other official language in the colony and the language of international trade and the senior law courts. Unlike Singapore, which maintains much higher standards of English from its multi-ethnic mix, English language skills have not been promoted so assiduously in Hong Kong. In the tourist areas most people speak passable English, but this drops off the further you depart from the beaten track. Most taxi drivers will speak enough to take you where you want, but it's always advisable to memorize the address in Cantonese to tell him anyway. As always in Hong Kong, just when you give up hope of finding someone to explain something a fluent English speaker will materialize from nowhere.

You'll also hear the educated elite discussing business and politics in a mix of Chinese and English, lapsing out of their mother tongue to use abstract words and legal concepts local society has borrowed from the British. After a while you won't even notice how you yourself are speaking a kind of *Chinglish,* a simplified English that doesn't worry too much about tenses or pronoun agreement and which bears a remarkable similarity to the pidgin language used in typecast movies involving Chinese characters.

SHOPPING HOURS

Hong Kong keeps such long **shopping hours** it appears never to take a rest from commerce. Shops open around 10 am and close some time during the evening. Those in Central close first, around 7 pm. Causeway Bay and Tsimshatsui may stay open until 9 pm. In general, the shopping centres close before the department stores or the small businesses and boutiques. Street stalls close around 11 pm, though some stay open into the early hours. Sunday is almost a normal shopping day, in fact the streets are crowded; only offices are universally closed. Recently, the large shopping centres in Central have begun opening seven days a week too.

OFFICE HOURS

Weekday **office hours** are 9 am to 6 pm, though government departments close by 5 pm and many private companies just keep going late into the night. Many people stay in their offices because living conditions at home are cramped, so odd hours are the norm. However, there's none of the formality of Japanese office life. If the boss stays in late the workers don't necessarily have to too. The morning **rush hour** falls around 8–8.45 am on the MTR and lasts a little longer on the roads, especially around the main bottlenecks of the Lion Rock tunnel and the Causeway Bay cross-harbour tunnel. The evening traffic build-up begins around 3.30 pm and can last until 8 pm. The main cross-harbour tunnel can be blocked at almost any time unpredictably, so be careful if you are staying on the Hong Kong side and need to make a tight connection at the airport.

CUSTOMS AND ETIQUETTE

These are certainly different from those prevalent in the West, but every visitor can decide for himself whether this is a result of innate characteristics or environmental adaptation. There is no word in Chinese for privacy, and it's an elusive quality in daily life in Hong Kong. Personal space, especially in public places, is not sacrosanct. As one Western friend once frustratedly observed, two Cantonese crossing the Gobi desert from opposite sides could still manage to bump into each other, albeit apologetically. Noise is similarly not regarded as an intrusion, even in places like the countryside where people might ostensibly be seeking peace and quiet.

Bargaining is a social convention well worth learning, though some shop owners display warnings against it. Tipping is an almost universal practice in Hong Kong. Most restaurants will automatically add 10 percent to your bill, though some have begun experimenting by telling you they don't. Taxi drivers will pocket the odd cents from your change, and even a dollar or two if you let them. Pushy waitresses will bring your change in small bills and hover hoping to embarrass you into leaving a larger tip: tell them to leave you in peace.

POST OFFICES AND TELECOMMUNICATIONS (A-Z PAGES 232-3)

Most district **post offices** are open from 9 am–5 pm on weekdays, 9 am–1 pm Saturdays. The main offices in Central, and Tsimshatsui and Mongkok in Kowloon, are open 8 am–6 pm, which is the last collection for ordinary mail, airmail, Speedpost express service and telefax. It is actually cheaper to post a letter in Hong Kong for delivery anywhere in England than it would be in the same English city, and with a delivery time of four days or less. Many post-boxes have Sunday collections. Poste restante facilities are available at the Central and Tsimshatsui General Post Offices and at the post office at the airport. International courier services are readily available. DHL has a series of convenient pick-up points inside MTR stations.

International **telecom** facilities are provided at Cable & Wireless offices located in Central, Wanchai, Causeway Bay and Tsimshatsui. The ones in Central and Tsimshatsui are open seven days a week around the clock for international telephone, fax, cable and telex transmissions.

Local **payphones** use the $1 coin for an unlimited conversation. As all local calls are free you can often borrow a telephone in a shop or office. Many people carry cellular mobile phones, circumventing even this inconvenience. A few local cardphones exist, but few are geared to take credit cards. If you want to call overseas and place the charge on your domestic bill you can call international operator inquiries for instructions on 013. Hong Kong shares the same **time zone** as China (itself lacking in time zones) except for a five-month period from April to September when China moves an hour ahead, and is two hours behind Sydney, one behind Tokyo, one hour ahead of Jakarta and Singapore, and two hours ahead of Bangkok. It is eight hours ahead of London GMT, 12 ahead of New York, and 16 ahead of San Francisco. Daylight saving does not operate in Hong Kong.

PUBLIC HOLIDAYS

For a hard-working place, Hong Kong has a slew of **public holidays** that blend both British and Chinese calendars. Thus the Queen's Birthday is observed on June 14th, British spring and autumn bank holidays earn two extra Mondays off work, and **Easter** and **Christmas** are official holidays. However, Christmas doesn't extend into New Year with quite the same fluidity as in Britain. The main Chinese celebration of the year is **Lunar New Year**, three days falling sometime between late January and early March when the colony literally does put up the blinds and about a fifth of the population heads back to China to see relatives. The annual grave-sweeping ceremony known as **Ching Ming** in April, the **Mid-Autumn Festival** in September and **Chung Yeung** in October are also major public holidays.

NEWS MEDIA

International **newspapers** and magazines can be collected from major hotels and a few newsstands, notably outside both ends of the Star Ferry. For local news the two English language papers are the Murdoch-owned *South China Morning Post* and the *Hong Kong Standard.* Neither are strong on foreign news. Try the *International Herald Tribune* for news, and the *Asian Wall Street Journal* and the *Far Eastern Economic Review* for regional financial news. Local entertainment is listed in the *TV & Entertainment Times* weekly magazine or a free broadsheet called *HK.*

Both English-language **television** stations show foreign news broadcasts in the morning. Local news broadcasts are always worth watching for their curious mix of day-old foreign footage and often parochial local news. Major hotels have *CNN.*

RELIGIOUS SERVICES (A–Z PAGE 287)

As befits an entrepôt like Hong Kong, a wide variety of **places of worship** can be found. Many of the smaller Chinese-speaking churches are fragments of missionary groups that were expelled from China after the communist revolution, and have usually set themselves up in districts in Hong Kong which had a regional association with the parent area they were separated from nearly 50 years ago. St John's Cathedral in Garden Rd is the head of the Anglican diocese and dates back to the 1850s. The Methodist centre is in Queen's Rd East, near Happy Valley. The Roman Catholic cathedral is on Caine Rd above Central. Services are held in English, French and Chinese. There are two Jewish congregations, an orthodox synagogue on Robinson Rd in Mid-Levels called the Ohel Leah, and reform-minded United Jewish Congregation that holds services in various hotels.

INFORMATION SERVICES (A–Z PAGE 231)

For **information** the best place to turn to is the **Hong Kong Tourist Association** which runs separate telephone hotlines for English and Japanese-speaking tourists. They also have offices to answer enquiries in Jardine House in Central, the Royal Garden Hotel in Tsimshatsui East and the Kowloon-side Star Ferry pier. Try and get hold of their excellent walking, shopping, nightlife and dining-out guides. If you need help in the street, policemen with red tabs under their lapel identity service numbers speak good English. Taxi drivers and shop owners causing a problem should be threatened with the ultimate sanction of a police report, which is usually enough to restore consumer rights over the shop counter.

Government publications can be purchased at two centres, on the ground floor of the General Post Office in Central, and in Mongkok.

GAY LAWS

Hong Kong has only just started the process of decriminalizing homosexual acts between consenting adults. The police still have on file a vast amount of information on gay activities in the colony and gay rights are not well entrenched.

UTILITY STANDARDS (A–Z PAGE 234)

Hong Kong's **electrical** system operates on 220 volts, 50 cycles AC. Tap water standards reach World Health Organization limits.

ACCESS FOR THE DISABLED

Few buildings except the most modern have special access for disabled citizens. Transport is a problem too: the MTR has no access, though the KCR does provide special gates.

EMERGENCIES (A–Z PAGE 231)

In the direst **medical emergencies**, 24-hour **casualty wards** are operated by the following government hospitals:

Queen Mary	Pokfulam Rd on Hong Kong Island
Queen Elizabeth	Ho Man Tin in Kowloon
Princess Margaret	Lai Chi Kok in north Kowloon
Prince of Wales	Shatin in the New Territories.

Private medical care, but no accident service, can be obtained from:

The Matilda	The Peak, Hong Kong Island
The Canossa	Mid-Levels, Hong Kong Island
The Adventist	Stubbs Rd above Happy Valley
The Baptist	Waterloo Rd in Kowloon

The Adventist operates an outpatients' clinic daily except Saturday, and a 24-hour dental service. Several doctors' surgeries in Central and Kowloon advertise a 24-hour call number, including the Central Medical Practise in Princes Building.

Chemist shops selling authentic brand-name Western drugs can be found throughout the territory. Prescription drugs can be bought much more easily over the counter than in Britain or America, and a pharmacist will often suggest a different brand by the same manufacturer if he cannot give you what you ask for directly. Hospitals and chain-store pharmacies like Watson's also have dispensaries, with shelves of contraceptive pills usually located next to the sweets counters.

Motoring accidents will generally attract the swift attention of policemen on their 600cc Honda motorbikes. Police stations offer helpful advice to foreigners even away from the main tourist districts. The Consumer Council is the ultimate receiver of tourist complaints against difficult traders, but go to the police for a complaint form first or call the HKTA if you want to make a report. The Community Advice Bureau is a good source of telephone numbers and general information. Everyone in Hong Kong, whether resident or visitor, is required by law to carry identification at all times, though this requirement doesn't usually affect tourists as it's designed primarily to aid the police to apprehend illegal immigrants from China.

MUSEUMS (A–Z PAGE 285)

The **Hong Kong Herbarium** in Tsimshatsui has a collection of pressed specimens of Hong Kong plants. It was begun over a century ago and now numbers over 33,000 species, including nearly 2,600 species and varieties from Hong Kong.

The **Hong Kong Museum of Art** in the City Hall, Central, hosts a series of temporary exhibits that regularly include paintings and calligraphy from the 17th century onwards, mainly Guangdong artists but also Chinese ceramics from most periods and a contemporary art collection featuring local and Asian artists. Entrance is free and the museum is open daily, except Thursdays, from 10 am–6 pm, and on Sundays after 1 pm.

The **Fung Ping Shan Museum** at Hong Kong University has several collections of Chinese art, including a large Yuan-dynasty showing of bronzes. Its ceramics date from prehistoric times and the Han, Tang, Song, Ming and Qing dynasties, plus more recent works. There is also a collection of paintings and sculptures. Entrance is free and the museum is open daily 9.30 am–6 pm, except Sundays and holidays.

The Chinese University's **Art Gallery** has four levels of exhibition space. Recent exhibits have included calligraphy and painting from the Ming dynasty until modern times, visiting exhibitions from mainland China, bronze seals, ivory carvings, stone rubbings and jade flower carvings. Entry to the gallery is free. Open daily 9.30 am–4.30 pm. On Sundays and some public holidays it opens at 12.30 pm.

Funded by mainland interests and bizarrely housed in a garish tiled setting crouching beneath an otherwise ordinary Wanchai residential tower block, the **Museum of Chinese**

Historical Relics has a permanent exhibition of Chinese cultural relics, plus occasional visiting shows. Entry is $12 and the museum is open daily 10 am–6pm.

The **Pao Sui Loong Galleries** in the Arts Centre in Wanchai house rotating exhibitions of international and local art, painting and photography. Entry is free and the museum is open daily 10 am–8 pm.

The **Tsui Museum of Art** in Lai Chi Kok is Hong Kong's first private art museum. It has more than 2,000 pieces of ancient pottery, bronzes, glassware and furniture. Open Monday to Saturday 10 am-4.30 pm.

The **Museum of History** in Kowloon Park, Tsimshatsui, houses Hong Kong's largest archaeological, ethnographic and numismatic collection covering the colony's prehistory to the present. It also has an extensive archive of photographs. Entry is free and the museum is open daily 10 am–6 pm, and on Sundays 1–6 pm.

The **Flagstaff House Museum of Tea** houses more than five hundred pieces of teaware inside the colony's oldest surviving building, now the centrepiece of Hong Kong Park mid-way between Central and Admiralty. Entry is free and the museum is open daily, except Wednesdays, 10 am–5pm.

More eccentric is the **Police Museum** tucked away up on the Peak on Mount Nicholson Rd. It has lots of law enforcement-related paraphernalia, and information on triads and narcotics that's of little interest to law-abiding citizens. Open Wednesday to Sunday 9 am–5 pm and Tuesdays 2–5 pm.

The **Old Tai Po Market Railway Museum** is quite quaint. Built in 1913, it was housed in a strange building resembling a Chinese temple. The museum contains old railway stock, uniforms, tickets and other memorabilia. Open Wednesday–Monday 9 am–4 pm.

ANCIENT MONUMENTS (A–Z PAGE 286)

A Han-dynasty tomb at Lei Cheng Uk in Sham Shui Po dating back 1,900 years and set in four barrel-vaulted brick chambers is the colony's oldest historical monument. There's an audio-visual commentary in Cantonese with an English language version on request. Admission is 10 cents. It is open

daily, except Thursdays, 10 am–1 pm and 2–6 pm, and on
Sundays and some public holidays after 1 pm. The **Sam Tung
Uk Museum** is another old walled village consisting of four
houses and cultural exhibits relating to Hakka life two centuries ago. The village was built in 1786. Open Wednesday–
Monday 9 am–4 pm. The **Sheung Yiu Folk Museum** in Sai
Kung also commemorates a Hakka village, this time with a
major brick kiln. There are four other ancient **walled villages**
in the New Territories, at Tsang Tai Uk, Kat Hing Wai, Wing
Lung Wai and Shui Tau Tsuen, reminders of times when the
clans that settled here had to defend their fertile land against
hostile marauders.

FOR CHILDREN (A–Z PAGE 286)

The **Hong Kong Space Museum** is one of Hong Kong's
few genuine interactive attractions and is always packed out,
especially during school holidays. The Space Theatre has five
showings daily (except Tuesdays) at 2.30 pm, 4 pm, 5.30 pm,
7.30 pm and 9 pm in Cantonese with a simultaneous head-
phone translation in English, Japanese and Mandarin for $5
extra. Additional performances on Sunday are at 11 am and
12.30 pm. English language performances take place at 9 pm
on Sundays, and 4 pm on Mondays and Fridays. The Exhibition Hall and the Hall of Solar Sciences are static displays with
free admission, open daily, except Tuesdays, 2–10 pm. They
open early at 10.30 am on Sundays and public holidays. The
new **Hong Kong Science Museum** in Tsimshatsui has a large
range of hands-on exhibits as well as Cathay Pacific's first air-
liner suspended from the ceiling of the aerospace hall. Open
Tuesdays-Fridays 1–9 pm, Saturday and Sunday 10 am–9 pm.

FOR ADVENTURERS (A–Z PAGE 289)

Now that it's difficult to go skydiving at Shek Kong the
only alternative is the **go-kart race track** at Mai Po in the
northwest New Territories. Charges are $100 for a ten-minute
ride. The contact number is 8070576.

Alternatively, try the nature reserve at the **Mai Po marshes** run by the Worldwide Fund for Nature, open 10 am–1 pm
and 2–5 pm (extended hours at weekends). Call 5264473 for

details. There's another reserve at Luk Keng in the eastern New Territories.

The **Hong Kong Stock Exchange** in Exchange Square, Central, can be visited between 10 am–12.30 pm and 2.30–3.30 pm. The contact number is 5221122.

CULTURAL VENUES AND FESTIVALS (A–Z PAGE 259)

The premier cultural event of the year is the **Hong Kong Arts Festival** which runs for three weeks at the end of January and early February. This brings together dance, drama and music from all over Asia and Europe. The **International Hong Kong Film Festival** runs over a similar period in April.

Hong Kong now has major venues in the Cultural Centre in Tsimshatsui and the Academy for Performing Arts in Wanchai. The **Hong Kong Symphony Orchestra** and the local **City Contemporary Ballet** give regular performances here and major international artists are gradually being enticed to include the territory on their tours to Japan and Australia. Pop stars plump for the massive 12,000-seater Hong Kong Coliseum in Hung Hom. An international jazz fest called '**Live under the Sky**' is also held every autumn at the Queen Elizabeth Stadium in Wanchai. Several civic centres around the territory host Chinese music and opera performances. Sometimes you can see these performed out-of-doors on the outer islands like Cheung Chau.

There is an active **Fringe** in Hong Kong, notably at the Fringe Club in Central which has live performances and a picture gallery. Foreign films are shown regularly at the Alliance Française, the British Council and the Goethe Institute (Arts Centre), all in Wanchai, as well as at the Space Museum.

ANNIVERSARIES

The main **Chinese festivals** of the year often have flexible dates as they are dependent on the Chinese lunar-solar calendar. The major festivals are listed below:

Lunar New Year (Jan/Feb) The largest festival of all, a time for spring-cleaning, settling debts and visiting relatives. The whole of Victoria Park is turned into a giant flower market. The following day is the birthday of the God of Wealth whose image sits in most kitchens all year round along with the Kitchen God. Wong Tai Sin temple is packed with people having their fortunes told.

Yuen Siu (Feb/March) The Lantern Festival on the 15th day of the first month marks an end to the New Year celebrations. This is very beautiful in Victoria Park. Families who gave birth to a son during the year often hang lanterns in the ancestral halls in the New Territories.

Hung Shing Kung (March) falls on the 13th day of the 2nd month. The Dragon King who rules the southern seas is worshipped in temples at Ap Lei Chau in Aberdeen, Kau Sai in the New Territories and Tai O on Lantau.

Kuan Yin (March) is just six days later. The largest celebrations are at the Buddhist temple of Ku Tung in Fan Ling.

Ching Ming (April) Spring-time grave-sweeping to pay respects to one's ancestors. It falls at the Spring Solstice, usually April 4th or 5th. The cemeteries at Aberdeen and Wo Hop Shek in Fan Ling are especially busy.

Pak Tai (April) was the long-haired King of the North who defeated the Demon King of Chinese mythology. Birthday offerings are made at temples in Stanley, Cheung Chau and Mong Tseng Wai.

Tin Hau (Apr/May) The 23rd day of the 3rd month is the major celebration to the Goddess of the Sea held all over the colony. By far the most popular deity in Hong Kong, she holds sway in more than 40 temples. The busiest is in Joss House Bay. Festivities are spread over a week or more and include Chinese opera performances, fleets of decorated boats and huge floral shrines.

Tam Kung (May) The 8th day of the 4th month is the birthday of another fisherman's god, the God of Weather. This festival is very popular in Shaukeiwan.

Buddha's birthday (May) is also on the 8th day of the 4th moon and a time for ritual cleansing ceremonies inside temples. The best place to go is Po Lin monastery on Lantau.

Bun Festival (May) Cheung Chau's own Buddhist-Taoist festival, a climax of several days' preparations. The date is decided by divination. The climax is the handing out of thousands of sweet sticky buns that were heaped up on 10-metre towers. The procession is one of the best in Hong Kong. Until a few years ago the festival ended with a mad scramble up the twin towers to grab the uppermost bun, but this was stopped after rival triad gangs reduced one race to chaos in the early 1980s.

Tuen Ng (June) The Dragonboat Festival is held on the 5th day of the 5th moon, a memorial to a poet who drowned himself in protest against a corrupt government in the third century BC. Nowadays it is celebrated with international boat races held off the promenade in Tsimshatsui East.

Lu Pan's birthday (July/Aug) honours the god of construction workers. His temple is on Sands St in Western.

Maiden's festival (August) is a day set aside for the unmarried to burn incense sticks and say prayers in search of a husband.

Kuan Yin's Enlightenment (July/Aug) falls on the 19th day of the 6th month. The largest celebration is at Pak Sha Wan in Hebe Haven.

Yue Lan (Aug/Sept) is the day of remembrance, held on the 15th day of the 7th moon, for the 'hungry ghosts' which are allowed to roam about on earth again for a day. Many Chinese operas are performed and everywhere by the kerbside you'll see families burning paper offerings to the dead.

The Mid-Autumn festival (Sept/Oct) is the largest after the Lunar New Year, a time for eating mooncakes which are supposedly a reminder of an anti-Mongol revolt that marked the beginning of the Ming dynasty. There are beautiful lantern carnivals in Victoria Park. Falls on the 15th day of the 8th month.

The Monkey God's birthday (Sept/Oct) falls on the following day. This is Hong Kong's most mystical festival and in the past included mystics in trances piercing their cheeks, drinking boiling oil and walking through fire. The largest celebration is held at the Sau Mau Ping temple near Kwun Tong.

Confucius' birthday (Sept/Oct) falls on the 27th day of the 8th moon. A remembrance service is held at the Middle School on Caroline Hill Rd in Causeway Bay.

Cheung Yeung (Oct/Nov) is the second most important

annual remembrance day for one's ancestors and falls on the 9th day of the 9th moon. Many people head for a high place like the Peak, recalling an ancient injunction to seek a high place in order to avoid the imminent fall of civilization.

The only other major dates honoured in Hong Kong are **political anniversaries**, the 'double tenth' on 10th October which is the day for supporters of the KMT government on Taiwan to hang out their blue and white flags, and 4th June which mourns the death of student activists murdered in cold blood in Tiananmen Square in 1989. Mainland businesses and other left-leaning organizations celebrate China's national day on October 1st.

Hong Kong has built up an impressive **sports calendar** in recent years. These dates are not identical every year but the annual sequence of events runs as follows:

Hong Kong International Marathon
Hong Kong Open Golf Championship
Rugby Sevens (March)
Coast of China Marathon
Dragonboat Festival (June)
Hong Kong Open Squash Championship (September)
Hong Kong Tennis Classic (October)
Hong Kong International Go-Kart Grand Prix (November)
Lawn Bowls Classic (November)
Windsurfing Championship (November)
Macau Motor-racing Grand Prix (November)

USING THE LANGUAGE

There's some good news and some bad news. The bad news is that Cantonese is as difficult as it sounds. The good news is that if you speak even a few words everyone will think you're either a linguistic genius or a Hong Kong-born foreigner, many of whom don't speak a word of Cantonese even after schooling here. Most local people speak some English—young people in the remotest villages can often surprise you with their fluency— and everyone almost without exception speaks a 'Chinglish' mix where the flood of Cantonese is peppered with English words and technical phrases. So although most of the time you'll only use Cantonese to meet people half-way as an expression of friendship, it will always go a long way.

Cantonese is a logical language with a fishwife's directness structured for bargaining with a sing-song lilt. It's also the most complex of the dozens of Chinese regional languages and has nine tones compared with the four in Mandarin, the *putonghua* people's language that is now the lingua franca of the mainland. It's important to start the tones in the right place—either high, low or median—and then ascend, descend or remain constant as necessary. Chinese is rich in homonyms. Watch closely and you can sometimes see people 'spelling' the ideograph on their hand to show which way the sound is written. And, of course, there are distinct dialects, regional accents, slang, swearwords, different vocabulary for the young and the old, slurs and shortcuts just as in any other language. Confused already? The only way out is to listen and copy, laugh when your partners laugh and don't worry too much. *They* won't.

Start by listening to the sounds around you and note how they approximate the romanizations set out here, which correspond to British English sounds and are a lot less intimidating than the academic transcriptions found in textbooks. The most common difficulties are the 'ng' sound which is really the same as in English, if you can imagine '-ing' without the 'i'. Vowels in words like *doh* for 'road' are mostly clipped short and sounded more through the nose. The personal pronoun 'I' *ngo* combines both. When you've heard it once you'll hear it everywhere.

Start with greetings. **Hello** is *nay ho,* though the 'n' sound has a bit of 'l' in it depending on whom you are talking with. On the telephone instead you'll hear a raucous *wai!* **Good morning** is *joe sahn,* **good night** *joe tau.* If you want to attract someone's attention in a crowded place just say *mmgoi,* which means everything from **wake up!** and **excuse me!** to **please** and **thank you.** Try to swallow the 'mm' sound at the beginning. To say thank you properly say *doh jeh.*

To agree with something —**yes**—say *hai!* like the Japanese, though the Cantonese stretch it by adding an extra vowel on the end so that the sound rises at the end in surprise or annoyance *hai-aaah* rather than the carefully clipped affirmative Japanese sound. To disagree just put a prefix in front; thus **no** is *um hai,* abbreviated to *mai-aaah,* meaning 'it is not.' This *um* prefix is really useful to form questions. Thus to confirm something say *dat um dat?,* literally 'OK, not OK?' It sounds a bit abrupt in English but gives the Cantonese a head start in all business situations by introducing a take it or leave it approach! Query something by asking *jun hai?* **is that correct?** and ask people if they want something with the formula *jung um jung ye . . . ?*

Any exploration starts with asking for directions. **I want to go to . . ?** is *ngo seung hoi . . . ?* If you are searching for somewhere you can say **I am looking for** . . . *ngo seung wun . . .*

Once you've established what it is you're talking about **where is it?** is *hai been doh?* and **is it close?** is *gam ghan?* If the reply is *yew yuen* that means it's **far away. How long does it take?** is simply *yau gay loi?* and the answer will come back in *chung* **hours** or *fun* **minutes.**

A more sensible question is often *day tee yau gau yuen?* **how far is the MTR?** The **KCR** is *for tse* or even *gau gong te doh,* and the **Peak Tram** is *lam tse.*

An **hotel** is always a *jau deem,* a **ferry pier** *ma tau;* **roads** are *doh,* **streets** are *gai* and **alleyways** *hong.* A **bus** is a *ba see,* a **minibus** is a *siu ba see,* literally a small bus, and a **taxi** is a *dik see.*

In a taxi you may have to give directions. **Left** is *joh,* **right** is *yau,* and **straight on** is *check hoi.* Thus, to ask for a left turn just say *june joh, mmgoi.* If you want to really try your luck you can demand *tzao-la!* **let's get going!** and then *fai dee!* **faster!**

though most drivers don't need any encouragement. Remember too *man dee!* which means **slower!** After all this **stop here!** is *hai doh teng, mmgoi.* More often it comes out as *lee doh* **over there!**

Try and introduce yourself as a foreigner. *Ngo seung ying gwok yan* means **I am an Englishman**, or **I am English**, where the words *ying gwok* stand for **England**.

You can substitute the following: *mei gwok yan* **American**, *ga la dai lan yan* **Canadian**, *fa gwok yan* **French**, *oh jau yan* **Australian**, *nau tsai lan yan* **New Zealander**, *dat gok yan* **German**, *wai yee see yan* **Welsh**, *so kat lan yan* **Scottish**, *oi yee lan yan* **Irish**, *sai ban ya yan* **Spanish**, *o dai yee lan* **Austrian**, and even *see ham dik nga wai-a yan* **Scandinavian**. As you can see, most are onomatopoeically improvised, though *mei gwok* for America literally means 'beautiful land', the émigré's promised land of riches.

In mock modesty you can add *doi mmgee* which means **I'm sorry**, *ngo um sik jung man!* **I don't speak Cantonese!** If you're really flash you can qualify this with *sik siu siu* **well, only a little bit**. The next obvious question then is *lei sik gong ying man?* **can you speak English?**

To ask a question that involves counting something the form is *gay doh . . . ?* Thus to ask someone **how old are you?** is *gay doh soi?* **What time is it?** is *gay deem-a?* And, most importantly, **how much does it cost?** is *gay doh cheen-a?*

If you make a chance encounter with a friendly face be bold enough to ask *lei gu mei meng?* **what's your name?** before you lose it. If you're cheeky you can add *lei ho leng* **you're very pretty**. You can emphasize a statement by adding *ho* in the same way you would add *um* to make a negative.

In more formal situations be careful to ask someone's name with *lei gwai sing-a? Ngo hai seung yan* proclaims your status as a businessman. *Ngo lai doh gah* means **I am here on holiday** and *ngo dai yat chee lay heung gong* adds **this is my first time in Hong Kong**.

Note the phrase *dai yat*, **number one**, which you'll see in restaurant names and other places. If you want to agree emphatically with a proposition, particularly the quality of food, you can just say *dai yat ho!*

Verbal directness isn't usually read as boorish behaviour, but rather a statement of fact. I recently returned to a restaurant I used to frequent daily during the mid-1980s to be told with disarming forthrightness by a waitress, a girl who'd once told me in front of a date that she found me cute, that she didn't immediately recognize me as I had less hair. She might even also address me, a stranger, with *lei ho chee seen-a* **you're crazy in the head**, or *lei ho chon-la* **you're out of your mind**, to which I would reply *yo mo gau chow-a!* **you're joking!** Only do this with people you feel familiar with.

Some aspects of decorum are changing. The standard inquisitive phrase of the early 1980s *lay jun hai gay doh cheen?* **how much do you earn?** has really dropped out of use now that everyone earns so much more. So has the habit of asking every stranger how big their flat is and how much they pay in rent.

The most obvious place to use basic Cantonese besides a taxi is in the market. Remember that *gay doh?* means **how many?** and *gay doh cheen?* asks **how much is it?** You can specify *lee goh* **this one**, and *goh goh* **that one**, so that to ask for **one of those, no, these!** comes out something like *lee yat goh, mo, lee goh goh!* Register amazement at the price by observing in mock horror *ho gwai!* **too expensive!** or *ho peng!* **so cheap!**

Cantonese has many measure words that are used in counting and indicating certain classes of objects. The commonest one, which will be understood in all situations even if it is not used grammatically correctly, is *goh*. Thus **one thing** is *yat goh*, **two things** *leung goh*.

Old textbooks tell you that Cantonese people habitually greet each other by asking one another whether they've eaten yet. This isn't true today, though people will often ask simply *sik faan-a?* **have you eaten?**, which literally means 'have you had rice?'

When you come into a restaurant try to indicate to the waiter or *maitre d'* how many seats you want. A table for **two people** is *leung wai*, for **three people** *saam wai*, for **four people** *sei wai*. Once seated ask *ngo day deem choi?* for **can we order please?** The **menu** is the *choi dan* or the *chan pai;* and the **bill** when it comes is the *mai dan.*

Ask the waiter quickly for *bo lay cha* if you want a black tea otherwise you'll automatically get *heung peen,* the fragrant **jasmine tea**. If someone comes to take a place that's already occupied just say *yau yan* politely. If you want to find the toilet ask *chee saw goh been doh?*

You can also ask *bei-ng ngo yit mo yan, mmgoi?* **can we have some hot towels?** if they're not immediately offered to you when you sit down. **Do you have chicken?** is *yo mo gai?* **beef** is *ngau yok,* **fish** is *yu* and **vegetables** are *choi.*

The moment of truth amongst the party when the bill arrives is *yo mo cheen?* **do you have money?**

Counting is simple. The cardinal numbers are **one** *yat,* **two** *yee,* **three** saam, **four** *sei,* **five** *ng,* **six** *lok,* **seven** *chut,* **eight** *baht,* **nine** *gau,* and **ten** *sup.* **Eleven** is *yat sup yat,* **twelve** is *yat sup yee,* **thirteen** is *yat sup sam* and so on. **One hundred** is *yat but,* and **one thousand** *yat cheen.* The only variation in ac-counting is that two objects are always accounted for as *leung goh* rather than using 'yee' though the number **twenty** is still *yee sup.*

The most important number of all is *yat cheen gau baht gau sup chut,* which is, of course, one thousand nine hundred and ninety-seven and the date **1997**. The key question then is *lei woi um woi yee man hoi ga la doi?* **are you going to emigrate to Canada?**

At the end of the evening you can say *ting yat geen!* **see you tomorrow!** Only Westerners say *joi geen* for **goodbye** these days. Cantonese people almost always say *by by!* **bye bye.**

SOME COMMON CANTONESE HOTEL NAMES AND DIRECTIONS FOR CAB DRIVERS

Hong Kong	*heung gong*
Kowloon	*gau loong*
New Territories	*sun gai*
Kai Tak airport	*fey gay cheung* (be careful as *fei jai* means 'thief')
Star Ferry terminal	*teen sing ma tau*
Outer islands ferry pier	*lay doh ma tau,* or *gong oi seen*
China Harbour	*jung wah hoi ging*
Hilton Hotel	*hee ye don jau deem*

Mandarin Hotel	*man wah jau deem*
Ramada Inn	*wa may dah jau deem*
Victoria Hotel	*hoi gong jau deem*
Excelsior Hotel	*yee dong jau deem*
Happy Valley	*pau ma day*
Central	*chung wan*
Mid-Levels	*bun san kai,* literally 'half-mountain'
The Peak	*san deng*
Aberdeen	*siu heung gong*
Causeway Bay	*tung lo wan*
Stanley	*chek chu*
Tsimshatsui East	*tsim sha tsui deng*
Caine Rd	*geen doh*
Bonham Rd	*bun haam doh*
Bowen Rd	*bo wan doh*
Stubbs Rd	*see yiu toh dat doh*
Leighton Rd	*lai dun doh*
Nathan Rd	*lei dun doh*

HONG KONG WORDS THAT HAVE ENTERED THE ENGLISH LANGUAGE

Lots of words have entered regular English usage through the colony. Only the most common are listed here. Some typically colonial words still remain in use whilst others have disappeared, or belong to another era. Thus the **amah**, the all-purpose servant and child-minder, is still spoken of even though she's now probably a Filipina with a university degree rather than a Chinese grandmother. Conversely, you'll never now hear the word **coolie**, which is of Indian origin anyway, used for a stevedore or porter. **Rickshaws** (via Japanese) the portered sedan chairs, have also fallen out of use, as has the traditional Chinese greeting of obeisance, the **kowtow**, and the bribe **cumshaw**.

Feng shui, the ancient geomancer's art of aligning space within a room or building with the dragon lines of fortune, is still very much observed, as is **lai see**, the ritual gift of money in a red envelope given at Chinese New Year, excessively for-malized these days much as the Western exchange of gifts at

Christmas has become.

The word **mandarin**, a high-ranking court official, or colloquially a modern civil servant, is not used, nor is the word **compradore** (both from the Portuguese), the old title for a go-between amongst the foreign companies and Chinese merchants. The traffic works the other way too. A business leader is often referred to as *bossee*. However, incoming goods are still stored in a warehouse called a **godown** and bills are presented at the office of the **shroff**, which is actually a word of Arabic origin. Major companies, known as the **hongs**, are still run by a chief called a **taipan**, who is not always these days a **gwai lo**, an all-purpose phrase for a white man that is best translated as something akin to 'foreign devil' or simply 'barbarian', although in Hong Kong there is little derogatory about the term. His wife will be a **gwai po** whilst a Chinese taipan's house will be ruled by a **tai tai** who will be one of those expensive looking women wandering around the Landmark shopping centre in Central with a portable phone. Only on special formal occasions will you see a real **cheongsam**, the body-hugging buttoned-up silk late-classical Chinese dress, though some restaurants get their waitresses to sport a modern version of it complete with a seam split to the upper thigh.

Colonial verbal importations from India merge in the racing scene and lend the name of **griffin** to a one-year-old horse. Its trainer is still a **seefoo** or master and the stable boy a **mafoo**. Every expatriate who can takes a **junk** at the weekends to a secluded bay somewhere around the coastline. Old ladies ply harbour taxi services in their **sampans**, which literally means 'three planks'. Slightly larger ones are called **walla-wallas**, presumably from the put-put of the engine. **Mahjong** is still a popular game. You can hear those tiles being swirled noisily in the poorer parts of town early in the morning. A few hours later the **tai chi chuan** *(taijiquan)* morning ritual gets under way. **Kung fu** is generally confined to the movies.

Morning tea is **yum cha** at which one eats morsels of **dim sum**. Only in the evening does one say **yum sing** as a toast before downing alcohol. And whatever your state the eternal verities will remain pinioned inter-dependently in the symbiotic embrace of **yin** and **yang**.

A glance through the local newspapers will throw up some unusual local usages of otherwise innocuous English words. The most obvious is **chop**. As a verb this describes the sudden homicidal behaviour of otherwise law-abiding people—the headlines in the papers read 'Man chopped by triad gang'. As a noun, a chop validates an official signature with the company name or insignia on it. Even messengers from international courier companies can be baffled if a businessman doesn't have one. Another word to master is **lapsap**, which literally means garbage but can be extended as in English to anything that doesn't work. And finally, you will never hear anyone using the novelist's cliché of **joss** to mean fortune or luck.

BEARINGS: A GEOGRAPHICAL DESCRIPTION OF THE TERRITORY

GEOGRAPHICAL POSITION

Hong Kong is a small and desperately crowded place full of uninhabited islands and country parks. A paradox, but true. Crouching on the underbelly of China, the territory covers just 1,070 square kilometres. Like everything else in Hong Kong, that figure is rising; about 2% of that land has been reclaimed from the sea over the last decade. Hong Kong's 5.8 million people live in a cramped urban environment as only 300 square kilometres is habitable. The old district of Mongkok near the tip of the Kowloon peninsula has long been one of the most densely populated urban spaces on earth. Much of the rest of the territory is deserted. Tucked into the 700 square kilometres of land that isn't strictly habitable are 21 designated country parks with peaceful walks and genuinely isolated spots. Its waters are dotted with 235 islands. Lantau, the largest, is bigger than Hong Kong island itself whilst the isolated rocky reefs in the Ladrones chain that circle the colony actually belong to China.

Hong Kong lies just south of the Tropic of Cancer on the same latitude as Mandalay, Calcutta, Riyadh, Tamanrasset, Havana, Hawaii and nearby Kaohsiung in Taiwan. It shares the same longitude as Wuhan in central China, Borneo, Bali and Perth. By rights Hong Kong should have a tropical climate, but the massive land mass of Siberia and China ushers cold air southwards in winter to cool it down. In summer, however, when the prevailing wind reverses, the monsoon breezes bring hot, humid air from the south and east (see pages 17–18).

HONG KONG ISLAND

Hong Kong island was the first area settled by the British in 1841. The earliest settlements lay in Western, just a stone's throw away from today's financial and corporate hub of the city. Most of the island's 1.2 million residents live on its northern shore, the S-curve of land that runs from **Green Island** in the west to **Shaukeiwan** in the east. This corridor is always busy and noisy, and is well served by a mass transit underground line that runs most of its length. Further south, beyond the ridge of hills that lies like a spine down its middle, are the gathering grounds of two large reservoirs, green and undeveloped areas, that cover over a third of the island. Up-market residential areas on the south side such as **Repulse Bay** and **Stanley** are increasingly popular as relatively quiet and spacious places to live, replacing the old colonial stamping grounds on the **Peak** and congested **Mid-Levels.**

Western district—its old Chinese names were *Shek Tong Tsui* and *Sai Ying Pun*—retains its ramshackle flavour. When Hong Kong was first settled, Chinese immigrants were channelled here away from the British military encampment in Wanchai and government land claims that extended up the hill towards the Peak. Western still specializes in the sale of wholesale Chinese goods and provisions. Ships' chandlers sit next door to rice merchants, purveyors of salted fish and ginseng traders. The **Kennedy Town Praya**, or waterfront, is crowded with lighters and colourful barges off-loading goods from ships moored in the harbour, mainly from China. Several old **godowns**, a Malay name for warehouses, survive, backing onto four- and five-storey **tenements** built between the two World Wars. There are traces of the **colonnaded shop fronts** that characterized the entire city a century ago. Many of these on **Des Voeux Rd West** and the adjoining backstreets still sell local favourites like **dried seafood**, **wind-cured ducks**, and **herbal medicines**. The visible history of the area is disappearing fast. **Tai Ping Shan**, the original red light district next to Sai Ying Pun, is falling under the developers' hammer and no plaque yet marks the spot in **Possession St**, now marooned several hundred metres inshore by reclamation, where the Union Jack was first planted in the colony.

Other old commercial activities survive in Western. **Man Wah Lane** is home to several **chop makers** who carve the personal seals used to verify signatures of ownership, a trade more than 3,000 years old. Most are made of soapstone or ivory with their carved inscriptions either set in relief—*yang wen*—or recessed—*yin wen.* In nearby **Bonham Strand** look for metal baskets writhing with **snakes**, a winter delicacy and alleged aphrodisiac, most popular from October to February. The Yuen Kee **cake shop** in **Centre St** is famed throughout the colony for its simple Cantonese-style confections. Nearby shops stock **birds' nests** and **funerary objects**.

Nearby in **Nam Pak Hong**, also known as **Bonham Strand East** and **West**, is the centre of Hong Kong's wholesale **medicinal herb** and **ginseng** trade. Seeds, pods, leaves, bark, flowers, insects, bugs, horns and everything else necessary for this still-thriving industry can be bought in these backstreets. The ginseng market's cosmopolitan diversity is typical: wild ginseng from central China is mixed with white ginseng grown in the American state of Wisconsin and the top quality roots from the isolated communist enclave of North Korea. These streets are also the centre of the colony's **gold and silver trade**. **Jervois St** was formerly a **silk market** and the centre of the **opium trade** until the government monopolized it in 1909 before suppressing it. **Wing On St** and **Wing Kut St** still have their **cloth bazaars**. **Wing Lok St** used to be lined by **rice merchants**. **Wing Sing St** is still a wholesale market for **egg traders**.

Pak Shing Temple on **New St** houses 3,000 ancestral tablets brought here by the first wave of Chinese immigrants more than a century ago. It was also a temporary store used to house corpses, awaiting an auspicious day to begin the last return journey to the ancestral village in China for burial. This role is still performed by the 'Coffin Hotel' in Pokfulam, run by the Tung Wah charitable foundation. **Blake Garden** above New St was the site of the colony's largest mass haunting some 50 years ago. Scores of witnesses claimed to have seen hundreds of shouting ghosts walking towards Hollywood Rd. Opposite on **Po Yan St** are **shrines** to the goddess **Tin Hau** and to **Sui Tsing Pak**, brought to Hong Kong from China to quell a plague in 1894.

   Man Mo Temple on **Hollywood Rd** is dedicated to the gods of literature and war, the figures in green and red holding the pen and the sword. The large red door is set so that people had to step around it to enter the temple. Large coils of incense with prayer tags slowly drift in the gloom inside. The drum and bell are struck by votarists to attract the attention of the gods. The bell was cast in 1847 in Canton. To the left of the main altar is a shrine to **Pao Kung**, the black-faced god of justice. To the right is **Shing Wong**, the city god. English translations are available to explain the fortune sticks cast here.

TEA SHOP

Ng Shui-wing, known simply as 'Professor Tea', holds court in his father's celebrated shop, the **Chan Chun Lan Tea Merchants' emporium** in Cochrane St. The original shop was opened in 1855 on Queen's Rd and was renowned as a gathering place for the colony's literati who were welcomed by a mahjong table and an opium bed. A chef was kept hard at work preparing food all day and the the shop's employment roll included a master pig-roaster. Many of the old men serving in the present shop have been working here all their lives.

   Tea is considered one of the seven daily necessities by the Chinese. The leaf still has an aura of mystery about it but little of the modern snob appeal attached to cognac.

   The ancient Chinese favoured powdered tea, a form still preserved in the Japanese tea ceremony, which was fashionable in China until the Song dynasty and began to fall from favour about 900 years ago. During the earlier Tang dynasty it was considered tasteful to add a pinch of salt and herbs, and admire the refractive patterns set in motion by the bubbles. Song-dynasty connoisseurs favoured a natural taste and developed a curing process that made use of steaming to arrest tfermentation, a method that later evolved into a 'stir-fry' roasting technique that captured the leaves' full flavour. By the 15th century, at a time when Britons were fighting their Wars of the Roses and the Roman Catholic church in Europe was about to spawn the

Protestant movement, Ming-dynasty tea-makers began to favour green tea, particularly *Lungching* or *Longjing*, the famous Dragon Well tea which is still produced in Hangzhou.

The many types of tea are described usually as having different colours. **Yellow teas** are not easy to come by. They are strictly a by-product of green tea experiments and undergo only a limited fermentation. **Red tea**, however, is very familiar to Western drinkers who call it black tea and flavour it with milk and sugar. It has been promoted with entrepreneurial zeal since the 17th century when Western traders introduced China to opium in exchange for red tea. Although the Dutch were the first serious China tea traders 400 years ago, red tea was first brought to the West by a Portuguese priest in 1560 just five years after the founding of Macau. Red tea leaves are left to dry in the sun to gain an orchid-like fragrance undetectable in green teas.

The best red tea is the *Kee Mun* which comes from Qimen. This was first exported to Europe in 1870 and has a rusty hue with a juicy taste. The famous red tea, *Lapsang Souchong,* still appears on the international tea exchanges. The 19th century also witnessed the invention of **cliff tea**, a half-fermented mix of green and red favoured in Fujian province. It is a verdant type, properly categorized as **black tea** or **oolong (wulong)** and created using an improved rolling technique and weathering in the sun. The most famous example is *Ti Guan Yin,* the intense Iron Buddha tea with its aggressive aroma. The most common Cantonese black tea is *bo lei (pu er)* the darker tea served in restaurants as an alternative to the lighter, more fragrant jasmine tea, *heung peen.*

The great aged teas were teased into revealing their secrets in Guangdong province a century ago. **Bo lei** is a tea for connoisseurs that purifies itself with age to leave only its essence, an accumulation of experience that feels calm, settled and focused. Another famous black tea is *Liu An,* known locally as *Luk On,* whose physical counterpart is the hard rocky landscape of the north, not the soft colours and misty mountains of the south, says Professor Ng. Both are fully fermented teas stored in brick form and derived from inexpensive teas grown in the provinces of Yunnan in the southwest and Anhui in central China. They should be left at least ten years, preferably even 35 or 40, to be enjoyed in their prime like a good claret.

Luk On is the more sensual of the two, claims the Professor, an opera star behind a mask and a child of the opium era. Sensual delight ripples through all his descriptions adding a sexual *frisson* to the regular cuppa known to Westerners. Like a wise old man, an aged tea is charged with the glowing sweetness of a maiden freshly discharged from school, firm in resolution but unconfirmed in her prejudices, the Professor muses. It dislikes humidity and chills, seeks warmth and possesses a crystalline wakefulness, mellow but unencumbered by the stillness of death.

The spirit of the present age is not for tea, the Professor continues. Tea is too gentle. It should not be drunk for relaxation like instant coffee. The mind must be relaxed for its clarity to reach you, he adds. The Professor has a theory that links the fall of Chinese dynasties to prevailing habits of tea consumption. 'Tea connoisseurship feeds on decadence. It is the final blossoming of any period, its last tango as it expends the greatest energy on the finest points of taste, a wealth of insight squandered in the frenzied appreciation of multiple flavours. The Qing dynasty was a period of great anxiety when insecurity drove people towards new levels of specialized expertise, its indulgence harbouring troubled intellects,' he once revealed as modern devotees, young and old, enter the shop front.

Central business district is as anonymous as its name suggests. Unlike most major international cities there's barely a single seat in the open air where you can rest your feet in a quiet corner. The great exception is **Blake's Pier** with its magnificent view of the harbour. Another haven is the **Zoological and Botanical Gardens** set above the colonial governor's bizarre turreted residence. In Cantonese its name is still *ping tau fa yuen*, the 'head soldier's flower garden'. Opened in 1871, it is spliced by Albany Rd into two parts, an aviary and a small zoo. In 1958 the curator described it as a motley collection crowned by a blind cockatoo, but it has been expanded since and is the only place in the world with breeding pairs of all six species of peacock pheasants, including the rare Palawan species. Some 280 species are housed amid the wrought-iron aviaries and cast-iron lampposts. The most spectacular birds are the flamingoes and scarlet ibises. The mammal section concentrates on warm climate fauna, including many endangered species like the engaging lemurs, small pandas, tree kangaroos, siamangs and huge orangutans that loll in the heat. The zoo has an unrivalled record of success in breeding all its primates.

Central is the premier location on the island for up-market boutique shopping. These shops are clustered around the **Landmark** in Pedder St, **Prince's Building**, **Alexandra House** and along the corridors of the **Mandarin Hotel**.

Most of the architecture in Central is unexceptional, predominantly cramped curtain-walled concrete buildings. The white-washed **Pedder Building** stands out in the street of the same name, flanked by columns and topped with Victorian statuary of goddesses. The modernist phase, coinciding with the economic expansion of the 1980s, is best seen in the grey aluminium-clad exterior of the **headquarters of the Hong Kong & Shanghai Banking Corporation**. Designed by the British architect, Norman Foster, 'The Bank', as it is simply known, is Hong Kong's premier institution. This building was erected during the mid-1980s, the fourth headquarters built on the site since 1865. The previous 1935 version looked a bit like the nearby **Bank of China building**. You can sometimes see it on older banknotes. The high-tech **Foster Building** uses techniques more closely associated with the construction of suspension bridges. The exterior doesn't attempt to disguise its striking cantilevered structure of five suspension trusses slung between the eight load-carrying masts. All its services are stacked at each end of the building leaving the central hall area as a free working space. A moving staircase, the longest freestanding escalator in the world, lifts you into the 170-foot-tall central atrium and the main banking counters, the city's cathedral to the god of mammon, a bargain at around $5 billion. For that money the bank gets its own massive seawater pipes to circulate water through its airconditioning units, a sunscoop slung on the southern side to deflect the sun's energy into the central hall, and an unused helicopter pad on the top. The two bronze lions—Stephen and Stitt—came from the original branch in Shanghai and were carefully relocated before the opening ceremony by the bank's geomancer. The pockmarks were caused by Japanese shrapnel during the last war.

Opposite the Hong Kong Bank is the **Legislative Council building**, formerly the Supreme Court. A statue of blind and impartial justice still tops the edifice built in 1912, a peculiar hybrid with a Chinese-style double-tiled roof and an imperial railway portico probably conjured up by an expatriate's memory stretched during the sea voyage to the East. Today some legislators are more equal than others, elected by Hong Kong

STAR FERRY

The Star Ferry is Hong Kong's most dependable sight. The twelve sturdy double-ended tubs make some 450 journeys across the harbour's waters every day, at three-minute intervals during the rush hour, with around 100,000 passengers per day paying a dollar downstairs close to the heat of the engines and an extra twenty cents up top in the saloon.

The service as it appears today started in 1898, the brain-child of a Parsi gentleman, Mr Dorabjee Nowrojee, who offered the young HK & Kowloon Wharf Company free travel for its coolies constructing the Kowloon waterfront in return for a permanent space to berth. At the turn of the century only a fraction of the present population lived on the still recently settled Kowloon peninsula and ferries docking in Central hitched up somewhere in what is now the middle of Ice House St. Only Europeans were allowed on the first class deck and a collar and tie was obligatory. Coolies in third class carried copper cash, a string of five-cent coins around their necks to pay their fare and the cargo fees.

The Star Ferry weathered the uncertainties of the colony's early days, though it nearly went bust when a clerk forged a sheaf of share certificates and ran off with the money. None of the 31 ferries that have carried the company's name have sunk on the job since the war, though the Chief Engineer opened the seacocks of two vessels alongside the Ice House St pier when the Japanese overran Hong Kong at Christmas 1941 and a third was dive-bombed to the bottom of the Pearl River by an American pilot whilst flying the Imperial flag. In the final days before the colony's surrender the ferries evacuated British troops from Kowloon to their last defence on Hong Kong island, and a few days later to the internment camps in Shamshuipo. When released four years later, the Chief Engineer's first job was to raise the two ditched hulls in Central's harbour.

Ten of the ferries now running were built between 1956 and 1965, one a year dropping down the slipway of the old Hong Kong Dockyard that is now buried forever beneath Taikoo Shing's tower blocks. The oldest still commissioned is *Celestial Star*. Two new, larger ones—*Golden Star* and *World Star*—were added in 1989 at a cost of $32 million, each licensed to carry 750 passengers in air-conditioned comfort within the confines of the inner harbour.

Around four fifths of users are local commuters, not tourists, a figure that slumps only when the driving rain dissuades all but the hardiest from avoiding the MTR. Passenger figures have dropped over the years from a peak of around 150,000 in the 1960s, falling roughly 15% every time a new harbour crossing point opens. According to General Manager John Carey, though never a money-spinner the company has never made a loss. His biggest worry looms when typhoons threaten. In the old days the first warning was a cannon fired in the harbour. Fists often flew in the stampede to board the ferry, then the only means of crossing the waters. Today the big wind can be tracked over several days and city-wide evacuations are carefully phased. Nonetheless, the ferries still operate long after the Number 8 signal goes up and the colony battens down its hatches. Boats and pontoons are gradually moved as the service winds down to the Yaumatei typhoon shelter to secure their rightful berths, which are often snatched by barges and lighters scurrying for a safe haven.

Not so much has changed over the years. In 1967, during the Cultural Revolution confrontation with China, an increase in the first-class fare sparked communist-instigated riots ending up in a month-long stoppage in June. The government's Marine Department demanded a change of ships' bells a few years back, declaring the old ones too small. The ferry's 0.8-nautical-mile run will shorten by 300 metres over this decade because of the new reclamation work in Central and the Yaumatei typhoon shelter will disappear altogether. But the ferries will still run, as always.

The Star Ferry commutes between Tsimshatsui and Central from 6.30 am to 11.30 pm every day with a reduced service on major holidays. If you hear the bell you don't have to run for the gate, another will be along in a few minutes. Other routes run between Central and Hung Hom, and between Wanchai and Hung Hom.

voters rather than appointed to the job by the British governor, but the chamber is still not noted for its brilliant and cogent speeches.

Another colonial relic is the governor's palace, **Government House**, built in 1891 and altered by the Japanese during their occupation of Hong Kong between 1941 and 1944, when the candy-floss turrets at both ends were added. The **old Bank of China building** was taller than the old Hong Kong Bank building adjacent to it, a domination re-established again only in 1989 with the completion of I. M. Pei's sinister glass-walled **new Bank of China building** at the foot of Garden Rd. **The Hong Kong Club** building next to Chater Garden used to be an imposing colonial structure. Strangely it retains a Mussolini-type balcony overlooking the **Cenotaph**, an imperial megalith commemorating the local dead of two world wars last borrowed spontaneously by local people to hang tributes mourning the Peking students and others murdered by the Chinese government in June 1989.

Central has changed a lot in the space of a generation. **Chater Garden** used to be a cricket pitch at a time when the Connaught Centre, recently re-christened Jardine House, was the tallest building in Hong Kong and named after the Duke of Connaught who laid the foundation stone for the first praya reclamation back in 1900. Even *HMS Tamar,* the Royal Navy's waterfront base, will disappear in the next phase of reclamation, much to the annoyance of Chinese military chiefs who will be banished from Central to the confines of Stonecutter's Island across the water.

From Central it is but a short walk towards Admiralty. A few years ago Queensway was a leafy interlude between Central and Wanchai, but in the last five years the developers have moved in throwing up tower blocks and hotels. Pacific Place, the Conrad and Marriott hotels, the Bank of China building, the Supreme Court block and the Lippo Centre have all been built since the late 1980s. The Lippo Centre, the most striking of them all with its twin towers of reflective blue-tinged glass, was designed by the American architect, Paul Rudolph. Hong Kong's most relaxing and tasteful department store, **Seibu**, spreads over three floors in the Mall in Pacific Place, for once earning the advertizing plaudits declaring that something new has hit the colony.

Further east marks the beginning of **Wanchai**, the old red-light district of the days of Suzie Wong in the swinging and sleazy 1960s, now rapidly being transformed into an extension of the shopping complexes of neighbouring Causeway Bay. The developers' clear-out has removed most of the old street-side restaurants and tenements, replacing them with more profitable saunas and hotels, though one or two places on **Lockhart Rd** suggest what the place was like during the Vietnam War. Yet the venerable Madam Springwater has retired from the **An-An Bar** and even Frankie, of **Frankie & Johnny's Tattoo Parlour,**, has emigrated to California. Today the bars and dance joints are tired and seedy, the girls are bored, and Wanchai's gentrification is inexorably underway. Old stalwarts favour the revamped **Makati Inn**, a disco-bar popular with off-duty Filipina maids that burned down a few years back. **Joe Bananas** goes through yuppie-ish phases and a succession of intimidating doormen to keep British soldiers at bay from its tiny dance floor. **The Wanch** is a cleaner British-style pub in nearby Jaffe Rd. More pleasant by far is the Japanese bar underneath the Golden Poppy Thai restaurant on the corner of Lockhart and Jaffe that is usually quiet, serves food from upstairs and screens videos of bizarre Japanese television game shows. The streets north of **Wanchai Rd** are worth a quick look for local flavour, remnants of the inter-war years where stallholders sell caged birds and tiny printing presses pound out bright red wedding invitations.

East of Wanchai is **Causeway Bay**. In Cantonese its name *tung lo wan* means 'brass gong bay', presumably after the shape of its original shoreline now only visible in the curve of Causeway Bay Rd. Today it is the main shopping area on Hong Kong island and the location of major Japanese department stores like Daimaru, Matsuzakaya, Mitsukoshi and Sogo, that moved into the area in the 1970s. There is little else to see here apart from legions of shops and boutiques, unless you want to struggle over Gloucester Rd to look at the **Noon Day Gun**, celebrated by Noel Coward whose 'mad dogs and Englishmen go out in the noonday sun' and where 'in Hong Kong they strike a gong and fire off a noonday gun to reprimand each inmate who's in late'. It was put there by one of the oldest of Hong Kong's major *hongs*, the trading company Jardine Matheson. The most exciting way to get across the busy road is through the unmarked Alice-in-Wonderland iron door under the Palace Cinema sign which takes you along an underground passage housing the World Trade Centre's salt water service pipes.

Some people swear by the expensive **sampan dinners** in the typhoon shelter, which is what you're being offered by the old ladies that patrol near the Excelsior Hotel in the evenings. If you want to hear an old crooner wail his way through songs from the 1960s whilst you eat seafood, marooned within sight and sound of the traffic and the stench of the shelter, that's up

TAI CHI IN VICTORIA PARK

Dawn breathes its way silently into Victoria Park in knots and eddies of rhythmic activity, the gentle motions of *tai chi*, an ancient martial art in a modern amphitheatre of skyscrapers, all standards and ages juxtaposed, if not in harmony then at least without a trace of embarrassment. A young man cleaves a wooden sword through the air. Another grunts *kung fu* punches at an invisible assailant with a rolled-up newspaper. Three women flick pairs of red fans open and shut in unison, martial coquetry with a sleight of hand. Nearby a man traces a circle in the dust. Controlling his breathing for twenty minutes, he begins to circle the enemy inside. Two old men 'push hands' together, a dexterous form of mutual *tai chi* that makes them look like a pair of graceful, underwater break dancers.

The techniques of Chinese boxing can be classified as either internal, like *tai chi*, or external, like *Shaolin kung fu*, made famous by movie stuntman Bruce Lee. Five main schools of *tai chi* co-exist. The most famous are the *Yang* and the *Wu*, but no one group can truly claim legitimacy over the others. Its origins are lost in the mists of time, but legend has it that the first set of movements were transcribed by a Taoist sage witnessing an inconclusive battle between a snake and a stork. Many movements are still named after animals—White Stork Stretching its to you. In a year or so it will all have been redeveloped anyway and the **Yacht Club**, which started life on the end of a spit in the harbour, will be marooned inland.

Students of kitsch should not miss the **Tiger Balm Gardens**, a large concentration of garishly painted concrete mythological creatures and Chinese gods stuck on the hillside overlooking Causeway Bay and topped by a pagoda nestling among the tower blocks. The gardens were built by a wealthy family of Chinese-Burmese origin whose two brothers made their fortune by inventing the Tiger Balm ointment that is a standard Asian remedy for aching bones, sore muscles and mosquito bites. **Victoria Park** is a popular venue for an evening stroll, sponsored bands, radio programmes and democracy demonstrations. It was one of the first social welfare projects

Wings, or Grasping a Bird's Tail. The old masters say you must listen not with your ears but with your heart, and then not with your heart but with your breath. The ear is limited to ordinary sounds, the heart confined to the rational. With the breath a man waits for events uncommittedly.

Despite its slow and innocuous movements, *tai chi* is a martial art form. Like Japanese *aikido,* the assailant's energy is absorbed and deflected by the practitioner; the attacker quite literally overwhelms himself. A meditation in movement and a choreography of the mind, *tai chi* is different from yoga and other static concentration exercises that seek to obtain tranquillity through inertia. *Tai chi* requires great concentration to allow the body's reflexes to work and to clear the mind. It's an anti-gravity exercise, a continuous flow of circular movements without peak or interruption, with only enough exertion to overcome the weight of the body itself. The aim is to attain perfection by moving as slowly as possible. In fact the old masters forbade pupils to take any other form of exercise. Modern medical researchers are conclud-ing that *tai chi* can genuinely alleviate psychological and patho-logical pressures. In the mainland its practice is now encouraged, or even compulsory, in some medical schools.

You can watch people performing their morning *tai chi* exercises between 6.and 8.am in Victoria Park in Causeway Bay, Kowloon Park in Tsimshatsui and Morse Park in Wong Tai Sin.

promoted by the Royal Hong Kong Jockey Club which drained the marshland back in 1951 and pushed the waterfront back from its old line near the Park Lane Radisson Hotel.

Looking eastwards beyond Causeway Bay is **North Point**, a secluded area of beaches and walks at the turn of the last century and now a fast-growing residential district. Places like **Java Rd** and **Wharf Rd** are among the oldest streets in the colony, though most of the 70-year-old four-storey housing blocks are being replaced by finger-thin high-rises. **North Point market** in Cheung Yung St, the terminus of the North Point tram, is one of the most accessible in the colony and a real eye-opener, especially in the early morning when most of the daily shopping is done. Look along **King's Rd** at the monumental slabs of tenement housing following the curve of the road and pitted with tiny balconies and verandahs literally suspended on the side of the building, Hong Kong's very own vernacular architecture and definitely illegal.

Quarry Bay and the area eastwards towards **Shaukeiwan** and **Chai Wan** show a typical Hong Kong mix of factories and public housing side by side. Apart from the obvious health hazards in the pell-mell post-war rush for growth and wealth, there are obvious ironic contrasts surviving, like the Hong Kong Tobacco Co. building that sits next door to a massive multi-storey funeral parlour. **Taikoo Shing**, which now houses 60,000 people in a massive private estate, used to be the colony's old dockyards. The estate is a Hong Kong utopia, a series of galleries and giant malls offering fast food, boutiques and even a tiny ice rink. Unlike the public housing estates, the management have banned the hanging of washing outside the windows, a Hong Kong way of protecting newly acquired middle-class values. A trace of the old times can be seen on the opposite hillside round the corner from the massive Kornhill development where some of the 300,000 **squatters** still left in Hong Kong perch on the hillside. This area is, like the rest of Hong Kong, undergoing rapid growth. The Sai Wan typhoon shelter is being filled in at Aldrich Bay, Siu Sai Wan Bay has been reclaimed and the sleepy village of **Chai Wan** has changed out of all recognition. The best way to investigate this area is to take the tram to Shaukeiwan and the MTR back.

Above Chai Wan stands a series of cemeteries at **Cape Collinson,** including the Sai Wan War Cemetery where many of the participants in the colony's brief but bloody defence against the Japanese rest. A walk to the Cape and the lighthouse at the end is possible after passing through the cemeteries, going left down a small sideroad towards the wireless station at Siu Sai Wan and turning right onto a path to the Cape.

TRAM JOURNEY

The trams are the last working relic of the **Victorian age,** tortoises that often outstrip the hares stuck in the traffic with their mobile phones, all but planned out of existence several times in recent years but still surviving. Enthusiasts come from all over the world to ride on them. Calcutta and Melbourne have their single-deckers, and Lisbon its four-wheeled bogies. Bangkok's track is still in place. But outside of Blackpool in the north of England, Hong Kong is the only working colonial-era separate-bogie double-deck trams anywhere in the world.

First proposed in 1881, it took 20 years to get the idea off the ground once local fears of unprofitability and military vulnerability were conquered. Originally intended to link Central with Aberdeen, it eventually opened in 1904, 15 years after the Peak Tram, along the northern shore of the island with single-deck cars labelled 'European' and 'Native', first and third class respectively. Legislators were forced within five years to forbid coolies from modifying their carts to run along tracks as a way of avoiding the poorly maintained roads. The trams quickly filled an important transportation need, and in 1912–13 they also ironically played a key role in the **colony's currency crisis**. The flood of Chinese immigrants to the island had boosted revenues and brought the young company its first dividends. However, local people were making a margin on Hong Kong's currency by melting down the colonial Bombay-minted silver dollars and turning them into Chinese 'silver dragons' with the same face value and a lower metal content. When the governor, Sir Frederick Lugard, banned the coins on the trams they were boycotted and forced to employ armed guards. The government retaliated by threatening to demand compensation from local traders for the trams' loss of business and gradually the situation returned to normal. The $45,000 compensation paid to the tram company was regarded as a small price to pay for establishing the soundness of the colony's currency.

The inter-war years marked the heyday of the trams. The **racecourse loop in Happy Valley** opened in 1914 and charged first class prices on race days. Regular summer excursions were laid on to the beaches at North Point. Since then the shoreline has advanced through reclamation and left the trams marooned inland. The tramlines from Central down to King's Rd, however, mark the water's edge as it was 80 years ago, and in **Kennedy Town**, the only area where the tramways still run along the waterfront, the original power-line poles are still in working order. In 1928, 26,000 Japanese sailors were given free rides during a port call by the Imperial Navy. Thirteen years later during the Japanese occupation the trams fell into complete disrepair. When the general manager, a Mr Bellamy, formerly of the Salford, St Helen's & Calcutta Tramways, was released after four years' internment in August 1945 he found only fifteen of the 109 cars fit to run.

During the 1967 strikes and disturbances the trams became a target for anti-colonial sentiment. Some 315 bombs were left on board whilst another 600 dummies disrupted services throughout the summer's turmoil. Despite their exposed position in the middle of the road, trams don't often wind up in serious accidents, though occasionally they jump the rails. The last major accident was in 1983 when number 113 got knocked over by a bus in Central. There were no fatalities.

All 163 cars are **handcrafted in teak and oak** over a solid steel chassis. Most were built in the old Taikoo dockyard, with the axles coming from Australia or China and the odd bit of control gear knocked together in a Wanchai backstreet. When new they represented the pride of British engineering: motors made by English Electric, bogies by Maley & Taunton of Wednesbury, and controller systems by Dick Kerr of Preston. More eccentrically, the bilingual destination blinds are still made by a family firm in North Wales. Two trams, numbers **86** and **91**, have been spared recent renovations and retain the old-style small adverts for local products that the whole fleet had until the mid-1980s.

It's all resolutely low-tech; there's no computerized control room, just a giant lego board listing the bogies, cars and their overhaul dates. Around 350 drivers and inspectors, a tenth of them ladies, keep the service running 18 hours a day, approximately 360,000 journeys feeding people into the MTR stations and packing out the lunchtime rush from Central to Wanchai. There have been a few concessions to changing times. Rattan seats have given way to soulless plastic, dim light bulbs to garish fluorescent strips and bells replaced by noisy air horns. Though the old depot in Happy Valley is no more, inspectors still walk the line to ensure the trams keep moving during rush-hours. **Extensions** east to Aldrich Bay and west to Green Island are planned, plus a loop into the Central and Wanchai reclamation area that will be created during the 1990s.

Only a few trams run the whole route from Kennedy Town to Shaukeiwan non-stop; most only make short hops so watch the signboards on the front of the cars. The entire route can take as little as 53 minutes to traverse before 6.am or after 11.pm; during the daytime rush-hour that stretches to 84 minutes or more. The upper deck offers a close-up view of the colony's development, layered strata from the wealth of Central's skyscrapers to Shaukeiwan's poor tenements. The flat-rate fare is $1, and the quick return on the MTR takes half an hour.

Double back towards **Happy Valley**, one of the first places settled on the island and site of the oldest cemetery in the colony, the resting place of the fever-ridden bodies of the British troops billeted in this marshy, mosquito-infested island. The **Parsee** and **Catholic cemeteries** are very peaceful places, the latter earning a mention in John le Carré's novel *The Honourable Schoolboy* where Jerry Westerby witnesses Drake Ko honouring a gravestone. Today the valley is dominated by the **Royal Hong Kong Jockey Club**'s main horse racing circuit and the headquarters of the **New China News Agency**, Peking's de facto embassy in Hong Kong and focal point of local demonstrations. The backstreets stretching up the hill are filled with motor garages, and the market in **Sing Woo St** is one of the colony's oldest and most complete, with early morning and late night food stalls. The Jockey Club's horses are led down from their special stables for early morning trackwork through the backstreets, down Shan Kwong Rd and the red-carpeted alleyway at the western end of **Yik Yam St.** As le Carré observed, the horses' hooves are muffled during trackwork to spare the residents' slumber.

Much of the rest of Hong Kong is residential. The **Mid-Levels** is an upper middle-class and expatriate ghetto area, full

RACING FEVER

Gambling on the horses is Hong Kong's most ubiquitous leisure activity, revealing an obsession with money and chance that verges on addiction. In the 1990–91 season the punters bet a total of HK$47.26 billion, $8,066 for every man, woman and child in Hong Kong, spending an average of $120 on the 67 meetings held that season, or HK$10,827 (give or take a few dollars) for every adult over 15 years of age. Put another way, after 55 race meetings Hong Kong's gamblers had bet more on the races than the government estimated earnings that year from all its direct taxes on personal income and company profits. By the end of the season they'd bet the equivalent of two and a half months of Hong Kong's merchandise exports, or around five times the annual total of Vietnam's exports or one third of India's. Even an average afternoon outstrips movements on the local stock exchange. The record daily turnover was in excess of $1 billion, equivalent to US$132 million.

Racing began in Hong Kong on marshland drained in 1846, just five years after the Union Jack was first planted. The club was founded in 1884 and quickly became the social focus of the colony. It used to be said the Jockey Club was one leg in the trio of institutions that ruled Hong Kong, less influential than the Hongkong and Shanghai Bank but more so than the Hong Kong Club. Today you could add the New China News Agency to that list, but the Jockey Club with its 12,000 members, 200 voting members and 12 stewards still typifies this side of the colony's life. The racing scene is completely integrated round the Club which purchases half of the 150 horses imported each year, including the young ones, known by an old Anglo-Indian term as 'griffins'. The Club has a monopoly of betting services throughout the colony, and in the spirit of fair play half of all owners manage to break even at the end of the season. The 700 horses don't have a bad time either, living in air-conditioned stables in Shatin complete with swimming pool and muzak.

But whatever the social dimension of the Jockey Club itself, the heart of the Hong Kong racing scene is the gambling. Twenty years ago bets were still tallied by hand. Today, 127 off-course betting shops with nearly 2,400 selling machines dispense just under 5 million tickets every race day. An average of 48,000 people attend every meeting, with a sizeable number crowding the alternate course at either Happy Valley or Shatin to watch the races on a 20-metre-wide video screen and punt their bets via 300 on-course vending terminals and over 1,000 manned kiosks. On racedays the colony's pulse beats to the half-hourly crack of the starter's pistol. Every newspaper is turned to the same page. Television and radio carry the races live. You can see the taxis pulled over as their drivers listen so intently they cannot drive. The final race of every season always breaks a betting record, the last spurt before the lean times over the summer.

The bets work on a *pari-mutuel system,* adding up all the individual wagers on each set of odds and dividing them by the number of tickets sold. The banker cannot lose while the punter gains most on more complex bets and, on average, receives about 80 per cent of his money back in dividends. Twelve types of bet are on offer with around a quarter of all takings placed on 'exotic' bets linking results in two or more races. The jackpots for these bets are huge. The highest win for a *Double Trio* stands at $32.5 million for a $10 bet. The favourite wager by far is the *quinella* —picking the first and second horse past the post in any single race—where the highest win is a more modest $12,509. Last year the club recycled $1,104 million towards charity projects. Past profits have been used to great effect to drain Victoria Park, to build both the Ocean Park recreation complex and the Academy for Performing Arts, and most recently to endow the new University of Science and Technology and the Chinese International School.

To keep one step ahead of demand, the club operates one of the most sophisticated computerized telecommunications systems in the colony. Deep in the bowels of the Shatin stadium lies the heart of the beast, the Telebet centre, several hundred operators poised over computers answering telephone calls from the 481,000 account holders—one for every four phones in the colony—roughly one person in every twelve living in Hong Kong. To play this game you have to deposit money in a special account whose balance is instantly displayed on the screen when your call is logged by the operator. To ensure probity and accuracy, every conversation is taped. The club's latest innovation are 25,000 Customer Input Terminals, miniature hand-held devices that connect directly to the club's computer via cellular phone links.

Recently the club has felt the uncertainty surrounding 1997 and the economic boom of the late 1980s. In both cases the result was the same: increased gambling. Betting levels have almost doubled over the past five years and multiplied more than four times during the decade. Since the Sino-British negotiations began in 1982, the date most people choose to mark the beginning of Hong Kong's paranoia with its own future, betting levels have trebled. With this amount of money floating around, the club is sometimes tinged with the scent of corruption. A massive betting syndicate was uncovered in the early 1980s allegedly run by one of the colony's top garment manufacturers, who fled to Jamaica before doctors testified he was too sick to travel back to face trial. With many key computer staff emigrating to obtain a second passport before 1997, the club has even transferred some of its operations to Australia so that staffers can work there and return to Hong Kong without leaving the Club's embrace.

of very expensive luxury skyscrapers clinging to the hillside and tortuous roads devoid of taxis in the early mornings. **Bowen Rd**, half way up the hillside, offers a lovely walk or early evening jog, for much of its way free of cars. It traverses the island from Admiralty to Happy Valley past several landmarks, including the Lovers' Rock, **Yan Yuen Shek**, which is more accurately translated as 'the rock of one's predestined lot in marriage'. Women come here to place pin-wheels and light joss sticks on certain days of the month. Further along is the massive round 64-storey Hopewell Centre and some other small shrines that dot the pathway.

In Chinese *Tai Ping Shan* is 'the mountain of great peace'. For the British, the **Peak** represents the pinnacle of social climbing. In the colony's earliest days the hongs reserved it for themselves and Chinese were even banned. It's also the coolest, most congenial place to live, well above the bustle and grime of the city, if you don't mind having your head in the clouds some of the time. Some of the grandest houses have been sold off recently, including the residence of the former chairman of the Hong Kong Bank, purchased by a Japanese retail tycoon.

The expatriates moved up the hillside as the colony grew. Peak Rd, which snakes to the top above the Peak, was built in the 1920s. You can take the Peak Tram to the point just below the summit, which no one calls by its name, Victoria Gap, or you can walk up. The best way is to get off the Peak Tram (or alight from a taxi) at **May Rd**, one of the most pleasant back streets left clinging to the hillside, with several fine turn-of-the-century houses now converted into flats. Look for the beginning of **Chatham Path** which hairpins its way up from the tram stop at May Rd to Barker Rd, ending next to a former hospital for women and children that was founded in 1897, Queen Victoria's Diamond Jubilee. A continuation called **Hospital Path** leads up to Severn Rd; the Peak is a ten-minute walk from there.

On the Peak itself, a tour around **Mount Kellett Rd** offers some spectacular views of Lantau island and Cheung Chau from a lookout point next to the Matilda Hospital. Lugard Rd, and its continuation into Harlech Rd on the south side of the hill, offer a splendid circular walk from the Peak Tram station. (See Walks section, page 184.) This opens with a view of Central towards Causeway Bay, moves westwards overlooking the inner and outer anchorages of the harbour with views of Lantau and Cheung Chau in the distance, and then doubles back near Pokfulam reservoir. This is the oldest water catchment in Hong Kong, built in 1877. Behind are the massive **Chi Fu Fa Yuen** and **Wah Fu public housing estates**, home for tens of thousands of people.

If you've walked all the way around the Peak, stop for a drink in the newly renovated **Peak Café**, originally a shelter for sedan chair bearers, next to the **Peak Tram station**. The latter is a disgrace to Hong Kong: cramped, dingy and full of dreadful souvenir shops selling overpriced kitsch. It was built on the former site of the governor's summer residence, which was moved to Fan Ling. The **Peak Tram** has never had an accident since it opened in 1888 and still uses its original haulage gear. Rising to 1,308 feet (339 metres) above sea level, it was almost completely renovated and overhauled in the late 1980s. Out went the old green, largely wooden tram cars in favour of new carmine-red Swiss-made 120-seaters, the first major change since steam gave way to electric power in 1926.

The Peak is also the start of the 50km-long **Hong Kong Trail** (see page 184). An alternative walk descending from the Peak towards Conduit Rd in the Mid-Levels is possible; from here you can take the #13 bus back to Central.

Pokfulam originally meant 'thin bird wood' and was the site of a waterfall used by passing ships to resupply. It has little unusual to offer today, unless you have a Chinese friend with a relative interred in the '**Coffin Hotel**' on Sandy Bay Rd. Fewer than 300 black-painted coffins rest there now, the oldest dating back to 1906, a reminder of not so distant days when Chinese emigrants wanted their remains returned to their ancestral villages. Families often deposit a deceased relative temporarily to await an auspicious day for formal burial elsewhere and modern émigrés sometimes call in to collect ancestors' ashes which are then hand-carried through Kai Tak airport to a new life in Australia or Canada. The 'hotel' isn't open to casual visitors, but you can peer at it from the Chinese Christian cemetery on Pokfulam Rd.

Aberdeen was once a quiet fishing village, one of the first places British troops landed to take on fresh water before the colony was founded. It was formally named after the Foreign Secretary in office in 1845, Lord Aberdeen. Hong Kong's first dockyard was built here in the 1860s. Though a dormitory town and industrial centre in its own right, the focal point is still the harbour, home port for the **inshore-water** and **deep-water fleets** that patrol as far as Vietnam. A boat costs about $500,000 to build in one of the shipyards around the shoreline. Some families still live on their boats inside the typhoon shelter, and though small children grow up on board the trawlers amid the potted plants on the poop deck, the TV and the cats, everyone is gradually being moved onto land. A horde of sampan ladies will be only too eager to show you around the harbour for half an hour at a cost of $30 or more. Negotiate first.

A short walk in the town is rewarding as it retains some atmosphere. The shrine at the top of **Aberdeen Old Main St** is dedicated to **Hung Shing**, the weatherman spirit invoked both for prediction and protection. Further down is a traditional wedding gown shop, a pawn shop opposite, and the renowned **Tse Kee fishball stall** which makes the ubiquitous dumplings on the premises rather than importing them from the Walled City. Continuing along the street, pop inside the **Tin Hau temple** with its green-tiled roof, then wander back through Tung Sing St, which is the first left off the continuation of Aberdeen Main Rd. At the far harbour end you'll find a Chinese paper shop selling offerings and lanterns for festivals, a pawnbroker and an herbalist. There's also a shrine to **Pak Tai** on Wu Nam St, and outside the Hong Kong Bank branch on Nam Ning St there are two shrines to **Kwun Yam** and **Kwan Kung**, the deities of mercy and war. The island on the opposite shore is called **Ap Lei Chau**, 'duck tongue islet'.

Nothing remains of the water trade, the floating brothels of 'flower girls' dating from another period and colonial imagination. As for superstition, the power station opposite originally had five towers, four real ones and an extra false tower to deflect the bad associations of the number four. The extra one was recently knocked down. Aberdeen still has a lively early morning **wholesale fish market**, open from 3 to 12 am and turning over up to 100 tonnes daily, including everything from shellfish to sharks. Permits to go in are available from the government's Agriculture and Fisheries Dept.

Kaido (boat taxi) services to Lamma can be hailed from the pier. The ride to Yung Shue Wan takes about 40 minutes and costs between $100–150 depending on the time of day or night. It is not to be attempted during stormy, typhoon-threatening evenings as the boats carry no lights crossing the main channel and the swell is mutinous.

Further south lie the opulent **Aberdeen Marina Club** and the **Aberdeen Boat Club**. Water taxi pick-ups for the three floating restaurants in the harbour—the Jumbo, Tai Pak and the Sea Palace—are located on Shum Wan Pier Drive. Well-known tourist traps, none of them offers better food than places on land and their decor is kitsch. The Aberdeen Marina Complex has a ninth-floor restaurant, the Blue Ocean, that serves good dim sum.

Further down the road on the opposite shore are several junk builders. These are still mainly family-owned concerns, the craftsmen building the boats from the keel up without written plans using wood grown in Indonesia and floated in from their shelter on the north shores of Lantau. The breakers' yards have less and less to do. Cunard's flagship liner, the *Queen Elizabeth I,* was turned into reinforcing rods here after it caught fire and sank in Hong Kong harbour in 1972.

Ocean Park is a large leisure complex entered from the end of Shum Wan Rd. Take the Citibus from Admiralty MTR station. Many of the facilities inside demand only passive participation, like watching a trained killer whale jump through hoops or cockatoos performing tricks. The walk-through aviary is stimulating, as is the 15-metre-deep aquarium and the wave cove where penguins and seals gambol and frolic, both easily viewed through underwater windows. Most challenging is the roller-coaster, nicknamed **the Dragon**, which whips you through three complete loops along its 1km journey. This is much more exciting by far than the 1.6km cable-car ride you take from Repulse Bay Rd to get to the complex. (A minimum height restriction of 1.22m operates for the **Dragon** ride.) On the way out by the Aberdeen-side exit you can stop off at the Chinese history theme park called **The Middle Kingdom**, which aims to encapsulate the passing dynasties of China's long history in a comprehensive way. If you do this then don't bother with the **Sung Dynasty Village**, something similar but a bit old-fashioned, buried a good 40 minutes from Central near Tsuen Wan.

Next to Ocean Park is **Water World** which has paddling pools for toddlers, extensive shallow water areas for youngsters, slide chutes capable of producing great velocities, and diving platforms for children over 1.22m tall.

Overlooking Aberdeen and Happy Valley is the **Wong Nei Chung Reservoir Park**, a small expanse of water perched next to the entrance to Tai Tam Country Park which has rowing boats and water-bicycles for hire.

The two major bays on the southwest shores of the island are Hong Kong's best, most accessible beaches, although the water is of doubtful cleanliness and visitors are reminded that local measuring standards are much less stringent than in Europe. **Deepwater Bay** is backed by a golf course. The water here is reputed to be the cleanest in late autumn when it reaches the lower end of its temperature range. Several of Hong Kong's leading magnates are reputed to bathe here first thing in the morning. Taxi drivers like to snooze here between shifts or wash their vehicles at all times of the day and night.

A promenade round to **Repulse Bay** is possible along the rocky shoreline. This bay is an expensive residential area with a popular beach where recent extensive sand works have given it a face-lift. The great landmark was the old **Repulse Bay Hotel** that stood on a commanding site in the centre of the bay until it was torn down in 1978 to make way for a new apartment block. Alas for the developers the profitability of the new scheme diminished. Undaunted, they eventually rebuilt the old hotel, this time as a restaurant with shops underneath. Also nearby was the site of a mock castle called **Eucliff**, built by a wealthy merchant in response to a soothsayer's threat that the man would not die so long as he kept building castles. Local people used to say it was haunted with the ghosts of men tortured by the Japanese army. The statues at the southern end of the beach are of Tin Hau and Kwun Sai Yum, the 'one who listens to human voices', the Goddess of Mercy who was originally a male deity but who later reappeared in female form. The beach here is also a favourite meeting place for the homosexual community.

Stanley was the main inhabited area on Hong Kong island, a thriving fishing village of some 2,000 when the British arrived in 1841. An old pirate lair, it was rechristened in favour of the incumbent Secretary of State for the Colonies, Lord Stanley, in 1845. During the Pacific War the Japanese built an internment camp here which is now the colony's maximum security prison. A **cemetery** along Ma Kok Rd accommodates some of the British dead, the earliest graves dating back to 1843. The area further south on the edge of the spit is off-limits for civilians and forms the barracks for British troops based on the island. After 1997 this will, of course, be turned over to the People's Liberation Army, who were reportedly favourably impressed by facilities when they looked it over a few years ago.

Today Stanley is a relatively quiet village with an expensive fresh market and a well-publicized strip of clothes and antiques vendors whose prices are not as cheap as they were when their reputations were made! However, it's still worth a stroll through to see what you can find, especially for T-shirts, overruns of designer jeans, sportswear, leather and silk, although better bargains are probably to be had in Kowloon's back streets.

A walk along Main St brings you to a **Tin Hau temple**. Originally built in 1767, villagers sheltering inside from Japanese wartime bombing were saved when a device fell nearby but failed to explode. The skin of a tiger shot by Japanese soldiers hangs on a wall inside, as does the drum and bell allegedly used by the infamous pirate, Cheung Po-chai, who used Stanley as a base for his depredations in the last century. A few paces further on lies a temple dedicated to Kwun Yum, the Goddess of Mercy. The colourful pavilion was rebuilt in the late 1970s after a local woman and her daughter claimed they saw the statue of the goddess move and a bright light shine from its forehead.

Stanley is a great place for watersports. You can get **windsurfing instruction** on the beach at Tai Tam Bay, known as Stanley Main Beach, and you can swim from St Stephens Beach to south of Stanley Bay. The village is well served by buses; the express service #260 goes through the Aberdeen tunnel, the slower #6, 65 and 63 go over the top, and #14 goes to the Chai Wan MTR station. The taxi fare is around $60 from Central.

A *kaido* trip to the **Po Toi islands** on the extreme edge of Hong Kong's territorial waters makes a great day out. Though its population has halved over the past few years, it is very popular at weekends for the superb seafood at the village of Tai Wan, notably at the Ming Kee restaurant. There are several walks across the island, including one to the Tin Hau temple amid the bulbuls, hornets and cicadas. On the 23rd day of the third month there is a big festival, once severely criticized by Luigi Tan in John le Carré's *The Honourable Schoolboy*. Some **rock carvings**, maybe 2,500 years old, can be seen on the cliff face, geometric patterns representing stylized monsters. A walk can take in the solitary point at Nam Kok Tsui before returning uphill through Ngau Wu Teng. The weekend *kaidos* run from St Stephen's beach in Stanley, and on Tuesdays, Thursdays and Saturdays from Aberdeen Public Pier too. Check with the HKTA for confirmation of this service. No camping or overnight stays are allowed on Po Toi.

Shek O beach at the far southeastern corner of the island is a popular daytime and evening haunt, small but busy with crackling barbeque joints, laughter and ubiquitous radios. It's also home to some of the richest taipans, who like the nearby golf course and who seem to have numbered their houses on the main road in the order they were built rather than their relative location. On summer weekends the place really buzzes and only calms down around 2 am.

KOWLOON

The Kowloon peninsula is synonymous with **Tsimshatsui**, the colony's ritziest shopping area that is casting aside its old back-street image of bootleg vendors in favour of glittering boutiques with high value-added prices. This is a far cry from the jibe of 'Nathan's Folly' made at the expense of the governor who first proposed developing the barren area in 1904. Though the main drag of **Nathan Rd** has changed its shopfronts several times, the towering banyan trees have been there from the beginning. The main shopping centres in Tsimshatsui are the Ocean Terminal and Harbour City complex on Canton Rd, and the New World Centre on the waterfront. Nathan Rd, the so-called 'Golden Mile', has replaced most of its tailors and camera shops with retail chains and boutiques. The small streets between **Mody Rd** and **Kimberley Rd** are good areas to prowl for bargains in clothing and electronics, and there are more camera shops around **Haiphong Rd**.

The tip of the peninsula houses two of Hong Kong's showcase cultural venues. The **Space Museum** has a permanent exhibition describing man's exploration of the universe, plus regular film showings on its giant 'Omnimax' screen. The **Cultural Centre**, a windowless monstrosity overlooking what is probably the world's finest harbour, is a good example of the lack of imagination bedevilling the colony's administrators in its dying days. It hosts regular daytime and evening shows and recitals. The **clock tower** outside dates from 1916 and once stood in front of the railway station when it was still possible to take a steam train from here all the way to Paris. The **promenade** outside the Regent Hotel leading round to Tsimshatsui East is the best way to view the harbour by day or by night. Behind it is **Blackhead Point**, also known as Signal Hill, topped by a tower built in 1907 from which a large mechanical time-ball was dropped daily at 1 pm so that ships in harbour could set their chronometers, an event halted only in 1933 when it was supplanted by radio.

The **Peninsula Hotel** is Hong Kong's oldest and most distinguished. Built in 1928, it was nonetheless used by British troops as quarters before its official opening. Since then it has sheltered the likes of Ronald Reagan, several South American dictators, the ex-King of Bulgaria and many film stars including Sophia Loren. Noel Coward stayed here for a week shortly after it opened immured in his room redrafting his most popular play *Private Lives* which he'd written in the Cathay Hotel in Shanghai on a Far Eastern trip during the winter of 1929. He also managed to have a row with the management, principally because his companion had signed his name falsely when they checked in. Within living memory the Peninsula's lobby, the social hub of the colony, used to be informally divided for the sake of public propriety, the left-hand side for non-Brits and those involved in dalliances and the right-hand side for the upright Englishmen and their lawful ladies. Heaven help anyone who tries to suborn the maitre d' by demanding to jump the tea-time queue; I have never seen it done. Ceiling fans have only recently been banished now that the lobby is comfortably air-conditioned, a keen point with the dozens of Japanese shoppers that throng its arcades laden with designer bags and serious intent.

Several landmarks in Tsimshatsui are worth highlighting, like the kitsch Chinese-style building housing the Hongkong and Shanghai Bank branch on the corner of Nathan Rd and Humphrey's Avenue. Opposite is the main Kowloon mosque and behind that is Kowloon Park, parts of it supposedly a copy of a garden in Suzhou and a peaceful place to walk amid old men playing chess. The **Museum of History** mounts a range of archaeological and ethnographic exhibitions relating to Hong Kong's distant past. A more colonial reminder is the **Marine Police station**, an imposing whitewashed mansion built in 1899, one of the oldest buildings in Kowloon, that stands marooned opposite the Cultural Centre now that Kowloon Park Drive has chopped off its once impressive lawns and trees.

Yaumatei and **Mongkok** are two of the least reconstructed areas in the whole colony. To the imagination it feels like old Shanghai minus the glamour: dingy tenements, arcades crammed with goods dangling from poles, specialist shops selling objects with purposes that aren't immediately obvious, and lots of people milling around! It's here that you'll see the real Hong Kong that people imagine from faded photographs and sepia prints, the seedy yellow and purple neon signs advertizing sex with white girls, the gut-wretching whiffs of cooked food stalls boiling big brown bowls of tripe, the tie-dyed cakes behind grubby windows, the cavernous porcelain sellers' portals stacked high with cheap china bowls and garish mythological statuary. It's a great place to wander around. Rather quaintly, the old village name of Mongkok translates as 'overlooking the cape' while Yaumatei recalls a place where sesame seed plants were grown. Bowering St is a busy street and daytime clothes market. Shanghai St is also full of life.

A good place to start exploring is the grid of streets between **Jordan Rd** and **Kansu St**. Exit from the west side of Jordan MTR station, walk up Nathan Rd and turn left into Kansu St before the flyover. Six blocks over is the downmarket end of Canton Rd; turn left and walk past #630, the Cheung Kee Marble Company, which makes porcelain pictures of the deceased by cauterizing negatives onto the stone for around $300. Near-by on the opposite side of the road at #613 is a Burmese teak wholesaler, and a charcoal wholesaler occupies #602, the building with the old-style pillars standing in the street. Almost next door is a joss-stick maker who works in a cloud of sandalwood dust. Continuing south, in the direction of the Star Ferry, #601–5 is a Youth Centre once used by the Japanese to hold and interrogate prisoners-of-war. Its distinctive art deco styling, porticos and verandahs are now marooned in the emptying street. #581 is a small factory making bamboo steamers; the baskets are mounted on top of each other for faster or slower cooking speeds. Further down the road in the pre-war tenements around #555–7 you can hear the familiar sound of **mahjong tiles** being swirled all day. Four people play against each other. The game can be played with cards, but these make no noise, an integral part of the ritual, because 'sound always denotes happiness', as a tourist brochure once described it. There are several shops in this area that make and sell mahjong tiles, including the traditional nine-dot mahjong sets.

The Mongkok **cross-streets** between Jordan Rd and Waterloo Rd are worth exploring for an hour or two, however short your time in the colony. There are pawnshops that as part of an old ritual used to buy fishermen's babies and sell off the bad spirits inside them, Chinese bakeries producing sticky moon-cakes, purveyors of herbal tea remedies from buddha-bellied brass urns, itinerant letter-writers drafting missives for illiterates and sellers of fine Swatow embroidered silks and bedsheets in different colours for various social ranks.

At night, several streets in Yaumatei are transformed into teeming markets of which two, rolled into one, are well-known. The Kowloon **Poor Man's Nightclub** has superseded the former Hong Kong version which used to set up nightly outside the old Macau ferry terminal. After 8 pm it's chock-a-block with cooked food stalls, herbalists and sellers of all types of geegaws and knick-knacks, including Nepalese jewellery. The air is cut with the piercing strains of **Cantonese operatic arias**, usually hits from the 1960s when opera was in vogue, often interspersed with recognizable modern Canto-pop tunes. Since Japanese sing-a-long *karaoke* bars became voguish the

THE JADE MARKET

The jade market at the intersection of Kansu St and Battery St is a well-established Hong Kong sight. Unlike gold, which is usually displayed and sold in Hong Kong in 24-carat form, jade has no intrinsic value. The price is determined by its cultural worth, the more translucent pieces commanding higher prices. Strictly speaking, 'jade' refers to two different stones that are easy to mistake for one another. **Jade** is a compound of calcium and magnesium, whereas **jadeite**, which we in the West also call nephrite or 'kidney stone', has traces of sodium and aluminium. The name comes from a French corruption of a Spanish word taken from the Latin. 'Nephrite' derives from the Greek and relates to its purported efficacy in dissipating kidney pain and colic, a quality of the stone also attested to by Chinese doctors since the Ming dynasty. It was highly valued by Confucius, who described it as compact and robust like the intellect, sharp-edged like justice, and producing a pure tone when struck.

Mined in Burma, China, Taiwan and Australia, jade comes in many colours and shades across a spectrum of green, red, blue and black. Thickness, purity, translucency and the intensity and consistency of colour are the four traditional tests of value. Local people favour the purest green colour most highly. Most old people wear a jade amulet or bracelet to ward off ill health, and infants often have a bracelet piece tied to them from birth by their doting grandparents. The stallholders here bargain amongst themselves by shaking their hands concealed behind a newspaper from others' eyes. The number of fingers they hold out indicates the bid offered in multiples of the decimal figure called out simultaneously, *yat* for hundreds of dollars, *diu* for thousands and *chao* for tens of thousands. The market, which moved here in 1984, has been going for nearly 30 years and has around 100 stalls and nearly 500 licences. Business gets going by 10 am and closes around 3 pm.

amateurs' routines seem less impressive. The performers here use traditional opera gestures, but not the elaborate make-up. There are **dentists** performing under pools of yellow light, **child acrobats** and decrepit **fortune tellers**—including one called Mr Cosmos—usually promising, for a small fee, that the future will offer more than the present has already brought, an insurance policy on the hopes and fears of the colony's trudgers and haulers. Some clairvoyants train small birds to pick tarot cards for their clients.

Close by is the second major market on **Temple St.** This is more of a tourist place and only opens at dusk, closing around 11 pm. Reach it by walking out of the Bowring St exit from Jordan MTR. The stalls offer bargain clothing (often overruns or defective items), fake jewellery, bootleg pop music cassette tapes, and counterfeit status-symbol watches. There's no space to try clothes on here so check it carefully before buying. Pirating a trademark is illegal in Hong Kong as abroad, and hapless Americans have been hauled up before US Customs and asked to explain the gold 'Rolex' on each wrist. You can find the watch salesmen without any difficulty—they will approach you with all the subtlety of a Peking 'change money' dealer—standing with their books of photos of their fakes like a catalogue of dishes offered in a local restaurant. It's a five-minute wait whilst a runner disappears off to the secret store-room and the watch is delivered. The going price is $400 and up, but the wholesale price to the runners, according to a friend in the Customs and Excise Department, is $200. Many fakes are excellent reproductions with reliable Russian movements. I have watched people casually hand over their credit cards to the runner without a second thought, so reliable does the system seem. One European friend did this and lived in fear for a few months that extra charges might appear on his bill. They didn't, but I don't recommend this payment method here. Mind your pockets in the crowd.

The **Tin Hau temple complex** on Public Square St is one of the most interesting temples in Hong Kong simply because it's right in the heart of the urban area. The four temples inside are more than a century old. The **main temple** is dedicated to **Tin Hau**, a Taoist figure who is the queen of the heavens and patroness of seafarers. Dozens of large spiral incense coils hang in the courtyard, each costing $120. On the right-hand side wall are **tai sui** representing every year of the zodiacal cycle. On the left-hand wall are memorial tablets and medallions intended to promote individual families' safety. The fortune-teller in the courtyard reads the **chim** sticks, each of which has a cryptic message to be interpreted. Sometimes he will also throw down two cups. If they land one up and the other down it is taken to answer a question affirmatively. If both land face down the answer is negative. If both land face up the question should be asked again, thus showing the Cantonese are fundamentally optimistic! The temple next left is given over to **Shing Wong**, the God of the City who has his work cut out reporting all the good and bad deeds of Hong Kong's inhabitants to both heaven and the underworld. On the far left-hand side is the **Fook Tak temple** dedicated to To Tei, the God of the Earth. The one on the right serves **Kwun Yum**, the Goddess of Mercy, and other community gods. The stones collected here are believed to hold spirits that are able to save worshippers. On the far left-hand side is a smaller temple dedicated to **Shue Yan**, favourite of the fortune tellers. It usually has a television blaring and festoons of paper lanterns outside. The courtyard is full of old men playing dominoes and **Chinese chess**, and a street barber who does only one style for $15, double the price at the New Year. The temple is open from 8 am to 5.30 pm.

The area around **Shanghai St** has many surprises and is a good place to stroll around. Take the MTR to Yaumatei station and walk back down Nathan Rd until you hit Public Square St and turn right; Shanghai St is three short blocks away. Turn right again. Number 280 on the right-hand side is a **shrine shop** selling special cupboards, altars and octagonal *feng shui* mirrors. Outside is an eight-foot-high dragon with flashing light bulbs in its eyes designed decades ago to attract customers to a restaurant. Next door is an incense shop. The sandalwood blocks are used to convey messages to the gods and are always burned in trios, one for the heavens, one for the underworld, and the last for yourself on earth.

Crossing Pitt St to the next block is the Wing Sing *beam balance shop* that makes wooden beam balances to a 2,000-year-old design for a unit called a *ching (jin)* which measures roughly a catty, around 1.3 lbs or 600 grams. (Hong Kong is only grudgingly going metric!) Souvenir scales and abacuses are made using a manual drill. Number 302 further up the road is a food store stocking bizarre, mostly mainland **Chinese wines**, of dubious medical efficacy and often featuring animals decomposing gently in an alcoholic marinade. These are allegedly beneficial for the circulation, rheumatism and general debility. (Chinese doctors are still unlicensed in Hong Kong.) There are also several **metalware shops** en route. Look for the tiffin-carriers holding multiple cups of tea and the charcoal hotpot-holders called *fung to* selling for around $250. Look also for the chopping blocks in the **wooden board shop** on the left-hand side of Shanghai St after Man Ming Lane. The wood comes from Thailand. Some butcher boards are up to 30 inches wide—you can see them in the markets with great hollows scraped out of them after months of being scraped clean. The thick butcher's sandals are also destined for the market place.

The **old theatre** on Argyle St was built in 1922 and still has hand-pulled curtains and the original gaslights inside, though today the screen flickers with skin flicks not newsreels. The **wholesale fruit market** opens around 4.30 am. Its two hundred stalls distribute about three-quarters of the colony's fruit. **Yaumatei typhoon shelter** nearby is full of brightly painted barges festooned with shreds of 'lucky paper' and loaded up with second-hand TVs for sale on the mainland. The shelter used to be home for several hundred boat dwellers, looked after by two burly Italian priests until four or five years ago when the former were resettled on land. As recently as a decade ago around 3,000 people lived in some five hundred boats here, the parents working onshore and leaving the infants behind on the boat tethered by lines to stop them from falling overboard whilst grandmother painstakingly assembled plastic trees from fingernail-sized parts for just $10 a sackload. The shelter is due for reclamation in the next few years.

There's not much else to explore in Kowloon, unless you get a thrill out of watching the airplanes coming in to land at **Kai Tak airport**. If they are landing from the west over the city their final approach brings them sliding over Boundary St for a last-minute 40-degree right-hand turn. If you want to take some great photographs, wait on **Nga Tsin Long Rd** or **Hau Wong Rd** as they come thundering over every few minutes. The airport is scheduled to close in 1997 when the new one

HONG LOK GAI BIRDMARKET AND THE WAN LOY TEAHOUSE

Hong Lok St, off Shanghai St, houses Hong Kong's number one caged-bird market. By 7 am the narrow alley is packed with birdsellers' cages and hordes of imprisoned grasshoppers waiting to be fed as delicacies to the birds that arrived on the pier at Cheung Sha Wan in bell-shaped baskets, hurled on shore by the stevedores in the pale early morning light. The favourite bird is called **seung see** (xiang si), the white-eye, a tiny green love-bird made up with a slash of white eyeliner that comes from the area around Guilin in southern China. It's favoured because it remains relatively chirpy in captivity. As one seller explains it, the birds are 'lovesick'. The market is very international: there are songbirds from Indonesia, mynahs from India, flycatchers from Thailand, cockatoos from Australia and finches from Africa. The brilliant red Java sparrows are the cheapest at around $150 each. Occasionally you can find an irridescent and irritated parrot twirling itself in loops on its perch to which it is connected by a metal chain. Missing are the eagles destined for the pot that you can still find in places like Guangzhou in China. Here the market is tamer, generally legal, and each bird has its own mythology. The Java sparrows, it's said, can be trained to tell fortunes through their behaviour and are good for children to play with.

The **delicate bamboo cages** can be made to accommodate individual species. The rare Mongolian skylark, which only sings in flight, has a tall, narrow cage. Thrushes are always kept within bamboo walls, never in ivory or metal cages which could damage their delicate wings. Mynah birds have their own unique barrel-shaped cages. The bamboo prisons can cost more than the birds themselves. The standard cage is mass-produced in Guangzhou and assembled in Hong Kong for a few hundred dollars, but a master-maker can charge thousands for a piece that can take a month to create. Antique ivory cages are often passed down from generation to generation as valuable heirlooms.

Bird-walking is a popular early-morning custom, and not just for old people, principally in the Wong Tai Sin public housing estate and in Victoria Park on Hong Kong island. If you stay in Hong Kong a week you're quite likely to see someone on the MTR with their caged bird under a towel.

The best place to witness the cult of the songbird in Hong Kong used to be the **Wan Loy Teahouse** at #322 Shanghai St. Sadly, this quaint old establishment closed down in early 1992. In the communal male atmosphere of the tearoom, with its special poles used to hang birdcages, the Wan Loy was a unique throwback to the old Hong Kong. It was so well known that in 1990 it formed a backdrop for a television advertizing campaign for the very popular Hennessey cognac, a drink of which was promoted as a small consolation for a man whose bird would not sing in company. The bird market is also threatened with closure, as the site is seen as prime residential land. Other bird markets will take its place, but will inevitably be smaller and with less atmosphere.

The ground floor of the Wan Loy was also the scene of regular **bird fights**. The occasional bird fight is still held in the area. It is, of course, illegal to gamble on the outcome, but you might as well try and make the sun rise in the west as stop a Cantonese with time on his hands from betting. By 10 am around fifty men can be jostling around the table. Nothing is written down as everyone knows each other. The contests are swift and bloody, the two thrush-sized birds grappling like wrestlers and looking for the first slash with their sharpened spurs before the stronger clinches the weaker into submission.

Bird culture has always been an integral part of life in Hong Kong but as the younger generation devote less time to the pursuit it must inevitably die out.

north of Lantau will open. Though it was thought the location here was unsafe even before the airport opened for commercial use, to date there has been no major accident at Kai Tak despite the flight path's precarious proximity to more than a million people living in Kowloon. **Boundary St** marks the old division between the land to the south which China ceded in perpetuity in 1842 and the New Territories to the north which were leased only in 1898. The borderline here once had a bamboo fence that extended onto the adjacent mudflats, but this was torn down when the lease was signed.

The walks beneath the **Lion Rock** include a steep climb up **Shatin Pass Rd** to a monastery overlooking the entire

Kowloon peninsula. Often a troop of monkeys will decide to come down and take bread from strangers' hands. Even better, take a walk around **Piper's Hill** east of what is now the old Tai Po Rd; there are so many monkeys here that the locals call it '**monkey mountain**'.

If you want a quick guide to **social history** in Hong Kong to see how much has changed in the space of a generation, take a walk through the public housing estates all around Wong Tai Sin MTR station. You can tell they're municipal by the huge numbers stencilled on their sides. Take a walk around without fear and try to imagine how a family of six might live in a tiny area of just a few hundred square feet, a thin balcony and all the clutter that inevitably accumulates. If you continue on the MTR eastwards towards Kwun Tong you can see the newer private or assisted-purchase housing estates, the next rung up the ladder. In fact, the journey overland from Mongkok to the eastern suburbs is a passage through the social history of the colony, 150 years of social mobility and hardworking aspirations spreading from the oldest settlements to the shiny new towns of the New Territories.

Without doubt the best temple in the colony is the **Temple of Wong Tai Sin**, just a few paces from the MTR station and marked on its exits. Religion in Hong Kong is a curious mix of tolerance and disregard for detail, a layer of superstition that allows primitive animistic beliefs that are maybe 4,000 years old to coexist with Buddhism (imported from India in the first century AD), China's home-bred Taoist rituals, and the precepts of the master sage, Confucius, who certainly isn't dead in people's hearts. Even fashionably dressed young people will come and ask Wong Tai Sin to guide the outcome of a decision favourably. The god himself is another rags-to-riches Hong Kong success story, which is perhaps why people place so much faith in him and his powers of divination. Just 80 years ago he was a nobody from Canton, but the fame of the fortune-tellers attached to his temple grew and grew. Today his temple complex has dozens of buildings, pavilions and shrines. There is respect and reverence here, but it's not expressed, as in Western churches, in silence. Instead the temple is a garish mêlée of beggars, children, old women hawking food, herbal doctors and legions of fortune-tellers. I have never seen a plan in English of the temple complex explaining it in detail, but interested readers are advised to read Paddy Booz's informative essay in Emphasis Publications' *Another Hong Kong: An Explorer's Guide.*

THE WALLED CITY

In Cantonese they call it *hak nam,* the city of darkness. For decades it was synonymous with all that was dirty, evil and uncontrolled in Hong Kong: opium dens, warring triad factions, dank and disgusting living conditions; plain anarchy, in fact. Today, its days are literally numbered; its 30,000 inhabitants, who were registered for the first time only during a surprise police operation a few years ago, have been moved out. They were offered generous compensation, but their former homes and factories have been boarded up, and the whole place will soon be razed to the ground, quite possibly in the largest controlled implosion ever attempted on the planet.

The Walled City was an anomaly from its very beginning. By far the oldest surviving settlement in what is now Hong Kong—the first record of a building here dates back to 1688— the present massive high-rise wedge of buildings is barely 20 years old. The settlement that was here in the mid-19th century when the British arrived was a small but proper Chinese town, laid out symmetrically with attention to the verities of *yin* and *yang,* water to the south and mountains to the north. However, the geomancers could neither predict nor prevent either the marauding rebels from the north or the British navy arriving from the sea to the south.

When Britain took control of the area surrounding Kowloon City under a 99-year lease signed in 1898, the Walled City area was meant to remain under Chinese jurisdiction outside the agreement. But after skirmishes between troops, Britain unilaterally extended its remit to include the Walled City area too, a move that was only partly successful and which left the city's future undecided. Since then the place has been a massive loophole, even though Chinese officials actually left the city in

1899, a sort of limbo and sanctuary from British rule.

During the Pacific War, the Japanese used the outer granite wall to reclaim land for the airport runway. After the war, waves of immigrants surged over the border from China. Arriving in Hong Kong without the right documentation, they took refuge here with others who simply wished to remain anonymous. It became an asylum, untaxed, uncounted, unregulated and generally off-limits. Miraculously the whole place has never burnt down. Factories sweated their bonded labour in disgraceful conditions using purloined electricity, moonlighting architects reproduced the city's designs without implementing any safety checks, and 77 wells reached as far as 300 feet down in search of water. And with upwards of 35,000 people crammed into just 2.25 hectares, a space only 100 metres wide and 200 metres long, the Walled City was one of the most densely populated spots anywhere on the planet.

Over the years the anomaly became a glaring anachronism as Hong Kong's colonial administration mounted a massive public housing drive, introduced mandatory identity cards to restrict the movements of illegal immigrants, and presided over a massive rise in living standards. Ironically, it was the imminent expiry of the 1898 agreement that forced Britain and China to confront the 1997 issue as early as the late 1970s. At one stage early on in the talks, China's de facto ambassador to Hong Kong, Xu Jiatun, pointedly made a walkabout around the city and praised the inhabitants for their independence. (The reform-minded Mr Xu fled China for self-imposed exile in California after the 1989 massacre in Tiananmen Square.)

As the last families were moving out, the Walled City's al-leyways still dripped water from a tangled riot of plastic pipes suspended at eye-level and rivulets of dirty gunk drifted south-wards along its gutters—the whole city is built on a slope, two storeys higher on the northern side than the south—through the solid mass of factories and flats. One of the last to leave was Jackie Pullinger, the born-again British missionary and guardian angel of the city's heroin addicts, hundreds of whom she has of-fered the earthly salvation of self-respect from a tiny cubby-hole in the centre of the city. One of Hong Kong's best-known land-marks, when the Walled City finally disappears in a huge nox-ious cloud of dust few will mourn its demise.

NEW TERRITORIES— NORTH KOWLOON

On the other side of the Lion Rock are the newest parts of Hong Kong, a brace of eight new towns begun on greenfield sites a decade and a half ago, a planner's dream to redistribute a large proportion of the colony's population from crowded Kowloon by the end of the century. More than two million people now live in the New Territories, a number that could rise to 3.5 million.

The New Territories is characterized by a range of Country Parks and beautiful walks that can be made at all times of year. Details of these are given in the section on 'Walks' (page 183).

Lei Yue Mun at the far eastern end of the harbour's entrance is a great place to watch the jets landing and taking off at Kai Tak. It is also home to over a dozen seafood restaurants where you pick your dinner whilst it's still alive. This is something of a tourist trap used by tour companies so consequently prices can be steep unless you have a good Cantonese guide to bargain for you. Take a taxi to Shung Shun St and follow the footpath on the left at the bend, or go all the way to the ferry pier next to the typhoon shelter and take the walkway and a sampan ride to the other side. Try and choose a restaurant where you can sit outdoors in the summer; there's little point coming all this way to be enclosed.

A pleasant excursion can be made to the nearby deserted island of **Tung Lung Chau**; take a *kaido* from Sai Wan Ho, or from the Lam Kee Ferry Company just west of the pier; on weekdays another *kaido* from Aldrich Bay leaves from a spot close to the afternoon fish market. The island lies in the mouth of the harbour inlet and has a fort built by the great 17th-century Chinese emperor, Kangxi, a ruler suspicious of the cussed southerners and their boats and whose autocratic decision to depopulate the area he was later forced to rescind. Now it's deserted save for a few farmers: 20 square kilometres of solitude disturbed only by the Kai Tak flightpath. The fort was made of stone bound by lime mortar and housed about 25 men and eight cannons before it was abandoned in 1810. There's a good view of the Ninepin islands and some rock carvings, possibly celebrating the arrival of the two Song-dynasty boy-emperors who sheltered in Hong Kong after fleeing from the Mongols in the 12th century. Once a year there is a huge Tin Hau festival in neighbouring Joss House Bay.

Tseung Kwan O is better known as **Junk Bay**. Most of it is disappearing under reclamation as a future home for 400,000 people, connected by the Tate's Cairn tunnel that opened in 1991. This hasn't spoilt all the views from the peninsula known as the **Clearwater Bay** area. There is a fine country club here and the beach at **Silverstrand** is frequented by swimmers in summertime.

Sai Kung is a former quiet fishing village that has outgrown itself with a ghastly marina complex. It's still well known for its fierce currents offshore and the pier-side fish market. **Sai Kung Country Park** has some beautiful walks around **High Island reservoir** and over the hills to the bay at **Tai Long Wan**. There's a pleasant little **folk museum** close to the Pak Tam Chung gateway to the park at Sheung Yiu village, just eight restored houses with a gatetower, but no outer wall. There's a central courtyard with communal kitchens, individual cocklofts and furnishings like hanging cradles, four-poster beds and even cat flaps. The village dates from the late 19th-century and was part of a brick-making concern with its own lime kiln that was abandoned in 1965. The nearby path shows labelled plants that were used in either medicine or manufacturing, like the sandpaper vine used to polish ivory chopsticks. The museum is open every day except Tuesdays.

A glance at the map tells you that there are several *kaido* routes spiralling out from Sai Kung to far-flung villages. By far the nicest is **Yim Tin Tsai**, a tiny island with a primary school run by an Italian Catholic mission based in Sai Kung. The mission dates back to 1864 when it proselytized the remoter villages. Today the school has 34 pupils who commute every day with their teachers from Sai Kung. The village is quite deserted and the pier dilapidated, but the church is a century old, not particularly graceful but quite spruce. Ten families remain on the island. The rest have gone overseas and boarded up their old homes. The school boat leaves Sai Kung pier around 7 am and returns at 4 pm; alternatively you can hire a *kaido* from Sai Kung pier. The church is also open for mass once a fortnight.

Sai Kung used to be quite deserted but has become more accessible since the Sai Sha Rd link to Shatin was improved. There's not much to see here except the massive **Whitehead detention centre** incarcerating tens of thousands of Vietnamese would-be refugees. Few are classified as genuine asylum seekers and will be dispatched by the Hong Kong government back to Vietnam as soon as it is politically acceptable to do so.

Shatin was the first of the new towns begun way back in 1973. After the Ma On Shan reclamation is finished it will have mushroomed to 550,000 inhabitants. Another 200,000 people are expected to move here before 1996. The almost obliterated village of Tai Wai, now just a stop on the KCR line, used to send its rice to the imperial dinner table in Peking in ancient times. The **Che Kung temple** commemorates a Song-dynasty general whom a villager once dreamt suppressed a plague here years ago. There are big celebrations on the second day of the Chinese Lunar New Year, one of four festivals during the year. The nearby **four-face Buddha statue** comes from Thailand and is always garlanded with pretty flowers. Nearby is the shell of the **Walled Village of Tsang Tai Uk**, the Cantonese equivalent of a castle where the Tsang family clan could live in security. It's almost 100 metres in length. Inside the interior courtyard you can see the wooden slats that functioned as a primitive security grille, and the inscription above reads 'living together from generation to generation', a mite Ozymandias-like as only distant relatives live here now. You can visit both places by walking between the Tai Wai and Shatin KCR stations.

The most impressive sight in Shatin is without doubt **Man Fat Sze**, the Temple of Ten Thousand Buddhas, actually a cluster of five very different temples and one of the most interesting sights in the colony. Less than forty years old, it is situated right above Shatin KCR station on the hillside. It was rebuilt in 1990 in a neo-folk style when the electric mini-tram was set up. You can still walk up by looking for the HKTA signposts, following the sidewalk out of the station as it curves around by the flyover, taking a left turn onto a footpath, and another left turn a few paces further onto a dirt path. The temple complex stands at the top of almost 400 steps. On the way you pass a small open-air Thai temple called **Fat Wah** with a four-face Buddha statue. Look then for the red pagoda through the trees which is where you're heading. At the top of the steps are four small temples clustered together. The left-hand one is the temple to the God of the Heavens, who is flanked by four massive guardians and Kwan Tei, the God of Righteousness whose job it is to punish the wicked and protect the poor. The Buddha inside is the mother of all Buddhas, represented with a thousand eyes and arms to alleviate suffering. The figure with downturned hands is the Goddess of Mercy, one of Buddha's ten disciples, popular among Chinese worshippers. The final figure, the massive Amita Buddha, carries a gold tower in his hand and promises to deliver the faithful to the Western Paradise after death to unbounded happiness.

On each side of the courtyard are 18 statues of the Arhats, witnesses to the truth of Buddhahood, all garishly coloured. The one perched on the blue *lohan* is Manjusri, one of Sakyamuni's ten disciples, who settled in Shanxi province. Riding the white elephant is Samantabadhra, who settled in Sichuan. The figure in the centre, facing the sea, is the Goddess of Mercy, who has the power to assume any shape to rescue those in distress. Opposite is the fiercer, armour-clad figure of the guardian of the temple. The adjacent pagoda has nine storeys and a staircase inside that you can climb.

The main temple on the lower terrace contains 12,800 miniature statues of the Buddha. It is claimed that they all have different expressions and gestures. The place is very atmospheric and, outside of weekends, quiet with only the dust and incense wafting up into the eaves. Fortune tellers wait outside and many local people come here to shake the **chim** fortune sticks. The main temple lies a little higher and further back. Inside, a 15-metre Amita Buddha stands in front of the remains of the temple's founder, a monk named **Yuet Kai**, who died in 1965 aged 87. He was a native of Kunming in southwestern China but spent most of his life in Hong Kong meditating and writing. You can buy a delightful book which tells you, with graphic black and white photographs, how Yuet Kai achieved such a degree of asceticism that eight months after his death his body had not decayed at all, turning instead the colour of gold. This is described in the book as the 'one great event after the Sixth Patriarch', and it was enough to persuade the monks to set him upright in a glass case beneath a covering of gold leaf. Lest this seem too bizarre, such happenings are recorded in other cultures, notably early Christian writings and English chronicles from Anglo-Saxon times about the lives and deaths of the saints. However, it's not often you can see one on display!

About five miles from the monastery complex lies the **Tai Po Kau Nature Reserve** overlooking **Tolo Harbour**. Unlike most parks, this is not a recreational facility—you won't see a single barbeque pit—but rather a 60-year-old reserve spread over 460 hectares. There are four forest walks which list many tree species en route, including the native sweet gum tree and imported camphor tree, paperbark and the China fir. There's also the joss stick tree *aquilania sinensis* which may have given Hong Kong its fragrant name. Cassette tapes play the bird song of nearly twenty species and many animals can be seen, including barking deer, baboons, pangolins, scorpions, porcupines and civet cats. Get there by slow bus along the Tai Po Rd. There are several footpath entrances but the main one is signposted.

Tap Mun Chau, also known as 'grass island', lies in the almost forgotten northeast corner of Hong Kong. Virtually the only way to get to it is on the **M.V. Man Sang** which makes a circuitous route of the Tolo Harbour from the ferry pier at Ma Liu Shui a few minutes' walk from University KCR station north of Shatin. The old boat travels at a steady six knots, calling in thrice daily at the island like a lost soul and stopping off at six isolated piers en route. Most of Tap Mun's families have long since emigrated to Manchester, Belfast or Amsterdam, their remittances and occasional visits keeping alive many of the 320 people left behind. Most of its inhabitants formerly lived on fishing boats. Even today the village is divided, Hakkas to the right, Cantonese to the left. No one bothers to lock their doors; the police are only there to help catch the illegal immigrants from China. The waters in the bay are filled with fish farms and small fry, waiting for the restaurants' agents to come round in April and October to select the best and the fattest for their front-window tanks. The old women sort abalone, a Tap Mun delicacy, and *uni,* sea urchins destined for Tokyo's finest restaurants. The island supported many more when there was no electricity, telephone or police station. These amenities have now arrived, but without a school the young ones go to live with relatives in nearby Tai Po or Shatin and they rarely come back.

The one street on the island is usually deserted, save for a gaggle of old women in black baggy pants and gleaming gold teeth. I asked one why she'd come here. To escape, she replied. From the city, I asked? No, she said, from the invading Japanese. There's a small temple with the veiled goddess Tin Hau, a junkyard atmosphere in a fug of incense, model junks and a ceremonial sedan chair propped up against the wall. The graveyard papers flutter in the breeze as it dries the seaweed laid out on the pathway. There's little here really, but the walk over the grassy hills to the cliffs on the far shore is a fine one and the swell rolls in from the ocean to thunder on its rocks— there's no beach on the island, which may explain why it's mercifully deserted. You can stay overnight in a guesthouse if you wish, for around $60 a night. The New Hon Kee is the island's only restaurant, and it serves the best seafood I've tasted anywhere in Hong Kong.

If you rise early you can enjoy nine peaceful hours in this deserted place, and even a late riser can spend a sunlit hour in the late afternoon as the ferry loops out to three other isolated piers on the Sai Kung peninsula before picking up passengers at Tap Mun for the last time just before 6 pm. The morning ferry leaves Ma Liu Shui at 7 am, the afternoon one at 3 pm. Take the KCR from Kowloon and get off at University station. The ferry pier is signposted from there and is clearly visible. You can go out to Tap Mun on the ferry and back via a *kaido* service to Wong Shek pier, though the helmsman will probably call it Tai Tan, the name of the nearest village; this leaves every two hours from 7 am until 3 pm with extra services at 5 pm and 6.20 pm on Sundays and public holidays. From here the #94 & 94R KMB bus connects every hour back to Sai Kung until 7.35 pm. (Check these details with the HKTA before you depart as schedules can change.) If you get up so late that you miss the ferry going out from Ma Liu Shui you can hire bicycles to ride along the towpath beside Tolo Harbour.

Ping Chau probably deserves the title as the most deserted of all Hong Kong's 236 islands. Public ferries only intermittently head out from Ma Liu Shui into Mirs Bay and the blue hills of China in the distance beyond this island, the most easterly in the colony. Ping Chau's heyday was in the 1950s and 1960s when it was the centre of several smuggling rackets to and from the mainland. As with other islands, almost all of its inhabitants have long moved into the new towns, returning only to serve the weekenders, or have gone overseas to join the Cantonese diaspora. It's been deserted for two decades. Its five villages are now largely overgrown, the tumbling shrines and temples a weekend retreat for picnickers. There's a single grassy hill, peanut plants growing wild and the pounding surf crashing in the background, a bracing landscape amid dragonflies and butterflies. You can spend the night near the ferry pier for a few dollars; the ferries run from Ma Liu Shui every Saturday at 11.15 am, returning Sunday at 1.10 pm. (Check these details with the HKTA before you leave.)

Tai Po itself is barely recognizable now that the village has been transformed into another of Hong Kong's 'new towns'. There is a small **Man Mo temple** just over the bridge, walking back from the KCR station, and also the **Tai Po Railway Museum**, located in an old railway siding nearby, which has documentary and photographic records of the railway's construction between Hong Kong and Canton. The old market at Tai Po is very colourful, one of the few places you can get a feel for the colony as it must have been 30 years ago.

The area inside the Country Parks at **Plover Cove** and **Pat Sin Leng** is amongst the loveliest in Hong Kong (see 'Walks' section, page 195). Careful scrutiny of the map will reveal lots of possibilities. One of the most interesting is **Lai Chi Wo village** on the north-eastern edge of the Plover Cove Country Park overlooking **Kat O Chau island.** You can get here by bus to Wu Kau Tang, another old Hakka village beyond Bride's Pool. The coastal area was once famous for its oyster divers. Always anti-Japanese and pro-communist, the remaining inhabitants are still cussedly independent-minded. Like many others, this whole area is now bankrolled by remittance money and littered with deserted villages like Ha Miu Tin, So Lo Pun and Sam A Chung. **Lai Chi Wo** has an imposing Hok Shan temple with a rice-drying yard in front of the old spirit screen. Before the war, more than 400 people from the Tsang clan lived here; now this community has shrunk to just a handful. There is an intermittent *kaido* service between Lai Chi Wo and the closed border village of Shau Tau Kok and **Crooked Island**.

The northern parts of the New Territories seem so far away that long-time residents rarely make it out here, unless they are avid golfers going to the links at Fan Ling or horse-riders going to the stables at Beas Hill nearby. **Fan Ling** has several sights, notably the relaxing **Foon Ying See Koon** Taoist temple, just three minutes' walk from Fan Ling KCR station. Built in 1929, the temple is the headquarters of the Quanzhen sect, the second-largest Taoist sect that was founded in Shandong province in 1167. It is also a centre for the Longmen sect in Hong Kong and honours three Chinese Taoist philosophers from different dynasties. The atmosphere can be very peaceful, but the place is busy with families at the weekend. Waterfalls and palm trees shade the forecourts of special houses that hold the ashes of the dead. The minimum charge is $3,000 with spaces higher up the wall most highly favoured. Some 15 nuns periodically chant the offices of the dead between 10.30 am and 4.30 pm. The temple offers a good vegetarian lunch at around $30 per dish. As the menu is only in Chinese you'd best point to the ones you want on other tables. The temple opens early, at 7 am, and closes at 6 pm. Fanling also has a large fresh produce market at Luen Wo, a few hundred metres down the Shau Tau Kok Rd.

BORDER PATROL

Hong Kong is the last major outpost of the British Empire and is still guarded by British troops that patrol the border on six-week rotations during each regiment's two-year stint in the colony. The garrison is currently 8,500 strong, but has been slowly cutting back its numbers for years as the immediate threat of Chinese intervention has retreated. In December 1990, local police started patrolling the border again for the first time since the soldiers took it over during the Cultural Revolution disturbances in the late 1960s. This changeover from military to civilian control, yet another part of the 1997 transition as the British army prepares to leave Hong Kong forever, should be complete by mid-1993.

The border itself is 22 miles long and snakes up the middle of the Shenzhen River along the low-water mark on the Chinese side. With marshes to the west, steep hills to the east and paddy fields in front, it is not a simple crossing to make and most illegal immigrants— known in Hong Kong simply as 'IIs'—prefer to try by sea or jumping aboard a smelly pig-train coming from central China. The sea route is controlled by criminal gangs known as 'snake heads' who operate souped-up speedboats, or false-bottomed fishing vessels laden with contraband videos and cigarettes. In one recent notorious case, several local police officers on an anti-smuggling sting were kidnapped in Hong Kong waters by mainland Chinese soldiers escorting a shipment of stolen Mercedes cars into China.

But even with 360 men guarding the land approaches at any one time, the border is not easy to seal off. There are several gates used as local crossing points and the east coast village of **Sha Tau Kok**, in Mandarin *Shatoujiao,* is actually divided down the middle of the main street. Nine points along the border are constantly manned and kitted out with state-of-the-art thermal image intensifiers and special infra-red binoculars for night-time surveillance. The main fence is 12 feet high and topped with a double roll of barbed wire with a concrete path on the Hong Kong side. Elsewhere are the remains of other fences erected since China ceded the New Territories to Britain in 1898, including a smaller picket fence and an anti-snake fence built in the 1960s. Occasionally, Gurkhas report, a huge python is found by a patrol lazing on the concrete.

Many would-be 'illegals' get picked up before they ever get to the border demarcation line. Since the suppression of the student movement in 1989, the People's Armed Police on the Chinese side has kept a closer watch on casual movements in this area. A second Chinese fence was already in place on the northern edge of the Shenzhen Special Economic Zone (SEZ) to restrict migrants drifting south from China's central provinces to look for work in the SEZ. Once there, though, minders take a minimum of $200 to guide would-be émigrés to places along the fence. Then it's a race against time as they climb or cut the touch-sensitive wire—seasoned watchers say some have scaled it in just eight seconds—or attempt to prize open a gap in a culvert grating and slide through a drain.

Once they get through, the IIs have to try and dodge the sound sensors laid every 30 metres, the dog patrols, and the irregular movements of Gurkhas patrols on their mountain bikes, unarmed save for two-foot-long nightsticks. If the IIs are spotted, a platoon can be on the scene within minutes. Though a Gurkha was murdered in 1988, the greatest risk is encountering a digesting python or a charging wild boar. While some IIs are ambushed before they've even got out of the restricted border area, others are simply picked up wandering barefoot in circles unsure how to get into the city. 'It's not fair really,' observed one officer. 'The minders tell them to head for the lights and they end up trying to get back to Shenzhen.'

Though it has never been a problem in recent years, the number of interceptions dropped around 70 per cent in 1989 after Hong Kong started jailing repeat offenders rather than immediately bussing them back over the border as before. That ritual is still held every day at 3 pm, and numbers rose again as they do every year after the harvest is gathered in China and people look for more work over the winter. Work can be hard to find in Hong Kong where every citizen is legally required to carry their government identity card at all times. On occasions, as many IIs are caught crossing back into China as coming over to Hong Kong. Many still get through. Military captures account for only a quarter of all II detentions. The rest are picked up in regular police sweeps on building sites in the colony, or just hauled in at random on the street for an ID check they cannot satisfy.

Even today the II influx ebbs and flows, swelled regularly by unfounded rumours in China of an amnesty for IIs that reach Hong Kong. It wasn't always so tough. The Hong Kong administration used to run what was called the 'touch base policy', the ultimate in British gamesmanship. If an II could cross the border and reach the urban area he was 'home' and could stay. Tensions have periodically flared, especially in 1967 when the Cultural Revolution swept China when there was a major shooting incident in the divided border village of Sha Tau Kok. The last big II influx was in 1981 when 170,000 made it through. This is a nightmare the British authorities are terrified might one day be repeated, as it might be if controls in the mainland were not so strict. When China wanted to show its displeasure towards Hong Kong officials who provided safe passage for pro-democracy activists after the Tiananmen Square crackdown, they even refused temporarily to take the IIs back.

The young men come because they can earn up to ten times more this side of the border as in China. The differential highlights one of the problems of uniting Hong Kong and China. Hong Kong, despite deporting IIs, actually has a desperate labour shortage. Unscrupulous building contractors hire illegals only to report them to the police just before payday. In another scam, labour agencies on the mainland side pocket a share of the wages from legally-admitted mainland workers whilst Hong Kong employers force them to sign 'voluntary' agreements waiving the colony's legal minimum wage.

Around 27,000 legal migrants are allowed to enter Hong Kong from China every year, in addition to several thousand brought in under the labour importation scheme. But with 60,000 people crossing every day, it's hard to plug all the gaps. Even so, officials in Hong Kong have suggested less than 5,000 IIs are on the run at any one time, whilst an estimated half million wait in the queue to come over to join family members already here.

If you want to see signs of the changes that have swept China since Mao's death, the border is a good place to start. Back in the days of Maoist purity in the 1960s, **Shenzhen** was just a single-storey town of 20,000 inhabitants. Now it houses more than 350,000 in a high-rise city with its own fledgling stock exchange, a Hong Kong clone built almost entirely with the colony's money, an example of economic expansion that ignores the political border to reclaim for Hong Kong a new economic hinterland and a reservoir of cheap labour. The best place to view the mainland is from an army helicopter; failing that the lookout point at **Lok Ma Chau** can be reached by taxi from either Yuen Long or Fan Ling.

There are several interesting ancestral homes in this part of the New Territories, large family houses that were the head-quarters of the big five clans that grew up here at the time when Europe was struggling through the Middle Ages. The best preserved is known as **Tai Fu Tai**, the lovingly restored ancestral home of the Man clan built by Man Chung-luen in 1865 to celebrate his success in the imperial examinations. '**Tai Fu**' literally means 'important person'. It is tucked away close to the border near San Tin in a village called **Wing Ping Tsuen**, midway between Fan Ling and **Yuen Long** on Castle Peak Rd. On display are high-quality pottery friezes decorated with symbols of literary attainments from a famous Guang-dong kiln. The home was abandoned during the Japanese oc-cupation, but has been restored with money from the Jockey Club to its original condition complete with nail-free joints, period furniture and family portraits.

The northwestern edge of Hong Kong is a mass of swamps, oyster beds, mangroves and mudflats. **Deep Bay** isn't actually very deep and is the favoured spot for swimmers to cross illegally from China. You can sometimes see their foot-prints on the flats in the morning, alongside those of the oyster farmers who skip over the mud on a cleverly arranged board they propel over the surface. There's a fine nature reserve at **Mai Po** which monitors migratory wading birds passing through en route north and south; details from the local branch of the World Wildlife Fund. **Lau Fau Shan** is a re-nowned seafood centre. There is an early morning fish auction and the beach is swamped with oyster shells for hundreds of metres in each direction. The largest seafood restaurant is called the Yue Wo Tong. The food is not cheap and you're advised to be wary of all marine bi-valves as local waters are not the cleanest. You can get to Lau Fau Shan by KMB bus #55 from Yuen Long, or by hailing a #34 green minibus. Near to the new town of Tin Shui Wai, which is really an extension of Yuen Long, is a three-storey pagoda at **Tsui Shing Lau**, built in the 14th century. Close at hand are the remains of an old study hall called Shut Hing of which only the impressive entrance way remains.

   Tuen Mun is a new town with little to recommend it. It's really a dormitory for the Tsuen Wan industrial area, neat and spruce with a new light rail system and not much for the visitor. The name '**tuen mun**' means 'garrison strait'. The village was originally built around a fort designed to protect the sea lanes to Canton. There are three temple complexes you can visit. The larger two are quite impressive. **Ching Chung Koon** is a Taoist temple located behind Tuen Mun's hospital on the western side of the nullah. **Miu Fat** is a Buddhist monastery, or rather a series of houses, at the top right-hand end of Castle Peak Rd heading north. Further north is **Ling To** monastery, a very peaceful spot several kilometres northwest of Tuen Mun.

   There's not much to see in the central parts of the New Territories. **Shek Kong airfield** used to be a parachuting drop zone but now hosts thousands of Vietnamese detainees waiting to be repatriated. The road over the mountains called **Route Twisk** is the best motorbike ride in the colony, and well worth a bus ride on the top deck too, for some good views on a clear day. The **Kadoorie Experimental Farm** tucked away in the Lam Tsuen valley spreads over nearly 900 hectares, devoted mainly to botanical research. A geological fault keeps the rocks warm in winter, so the area is quite enchanted. The early spring brings magnolias and citrus blossom, then the camelias and azaleas. It's also an important conservation area for orchids, and has 80 varieties of hibiscus and 20 species of bougainvillaea.

NEW TERRITORIES— OUTER ISLANDS

Ferries to the three main outer islands run from a series of piers west of the Star Ferry in Central. Weekend ferries are particularly crowded, so it's best to buy a return ticket in advance. Lamma ferries are usually small double-deckers without air-conditioning. Lantau and Cheung Chau ferries are larger triple-deckers, air-conditioned on the top deck with a sitting out area at the stern. During the week you can buy a first-class ticket on board: at weekends it must be bought at the ticket booth before boarding. Bring change for a bus fare if you're going to Lantau.

Cheung Chau means 'long island' in Cantonese, though it's more dumbell-shaped. Once a quiet fishing village and pirates' lair, the island is now a dormitory town for windsurfing Chinese yuppies and Westerners who can't afford the exorbitant rents on Hong Kong island. The crooked back streets are blocked with stallholders selling paper goods, dried seafood and other provisions. Extensive reclamation has pushed the shoreline into the harbour, though fortunately it's still limited by a three storey height restriction. Part of the character of a pre-industrial society has survived on Cheung Chau which has strong clan associations and trade guilds, and a powerful triad presence. In fact, it was recent triad rivalry during the ancient Bun Festival that led to a ban on its central feature, a mad scramble up a 20-metre pole to claim the highest bun.

The whole island takes barely an hour to stroll around. Walk along the north side past an ice-making factory that sends great blocks of ice rumbling down an overhead wooden chute onto the quayside. Nearby are the last remaining junk builders on the island. Walk around the point to Tai Kwai Wan, which the locals know as 'dead baby beach' after a number of unwanted children were once washed ashore here, and follow the road and path up to the high point of the island. Coming down you'll pass a temple to the fishermen's friend,

Tin Hau, and another to **Pak Tai**, the spirit of the north and supreme emperor of the dark heaven. The latter was built in 1793 and stands on the original waterfront. Inside is a sedan chair used to carry the god's image through the streets, and a Song-dynasty sword recovered from the sea nearby said to be a thousand years old. The prettiest features of the temple are the four stone lions guarding the entrance and the ceramic figures on the roof. Cheung Chau's other notable landmark is a huge **banyan tree** at the southern end of the village. This is the home of a spirit of fertility, still invoked by old women who pray for a grandson.

You can take a *kaido* to **Sai Wan** at the end of the island and walk back from there. On the right-hand side there is a pretty Tin Hau temple. Further over, by a separate path, is a cave named after a notorious pirate called Cheung Po Tsai. Although the last pirate attack on boats passing through the channel to Lantau was in the 1920s, the cave is nothing to look at. Walking back through Sai Wan village there's a secret place called the Western Garden, elegantly decayed and situated at the top of the path. This end of the island is dotted with cemeteries as its *feng shui* is particularly auspicious. The rocks looking south towards the Soko islands are very wild, often deserted, and quite romantic in winter. There are two bathing beaches on the island, the larger **Tung Wan beach** by the village opposite the pier and **Kwun Yam Wan**. You can rent windsurfing boards beneath the Warwick Hotel. A *kaido* service operates from Cheung Chau to **Tai Long Wan** on Lantau island and the infamous 'Frog and Toad' bar.

Lamma is the most accessible of all of the outlying islands, just 40 minutes from Central. The main village is **Yung Shue Wan**, on the north-west side of the island. Building work has boomed here in recent years but you can still see some vegetable field plots worked by villagers, and scent the sewage compost system and the ubiquitous, sweetly noxious smell of maturing shrimp paste. There is a small temple to Tin Hau at the southern end of the village, guarded by two stone lions and a red spirit screen to deflect evil spirits that can only travel in straight lines. On the left side is To Tei, the City God; on the right, Muen Kuen, the gatekeeper. The smaller of the two Tin

Hau statues is paraded through the village once a year.

There are several popular beaches on Lamma that are good for windsurfing and swimming, though unfortunately they lurk under the shadow of the power station and suffer from hordes of giant Portuguese-men-of-war jellyfish attracted by the heated water. **Hung Shing Ye beach** further south has changing facilities; a smaller and far prettier beach further on doesn't. The end beach is called **Lo So Shing beach** after a local practice of flipping mother turtles on their backs when they came ashore to lay their eggs. There are no more turtles these days. The walk up the diminutive (353 metres) **Mt Stenhouse** looks simple but the path is hard to find. By contrast, the route over to the island's other village, **Sok Kwu Wan**, is easy to follow even on a moonlit night. Just outside Sok Kwu Wan the path passes **Sun Fung Tung**, the 'god wind' cave, excavated by the Japanese during the Pacific War to house **kamikaze** torpedo boats which were mercifully never used.

Sok Kwu Wan is renowned for its excellent seafood restaurants, all side by side near the ferry pier and often full of raucous towel-throwing expatriates getting drunk on Carlsberg, Tsingtao and over-priced Portuguese wine. The harbour looks very pretty at night with twinkling lights on the fish-farm rafts that are protected by fierce guard dogs. There are ferries to both villages from Central and a *kaido* service from Aberdeen also goes to **Mo Tat Wan**, one of the oldest villages in Hong Kong, and Sok Kwu Wan. The East Lamma Channel here is one of the main approaches to the inner harbour. Late at night huge container ships come sliding through at high speed, huge black shapes cutting out the lights of Aberdeen. Individual sampans can be hired at Aberdeen pier late at night long after the last ferry has gone; these are emphatically not to be taken in strengthening winds however invulnerable alcohol may make you feel.

Lantau island is bigger than Hong Kong island but has a population numbered in thousands not millions. It's easy to feel solitude here. This peace, however, is being shattered as the construction work for the new airport at Chek Lap Kok gets underway.

The main landmark is **Po Lin Monastery** —'precious lotus'—Hong Kong's most important religious foundation initiated by three reclusive monks 90 years ago and formally recognized in 1917. The main complex was started in 1927, greatly expanded during the 1960s, and most recently has become the site of the world's largest bronze statue of the Buddha. More than a thousand visitors a day take the bus from the ferry pier at Mui Wo, also known as Silvermine Bay, before changing onto a small single-decker for the ride up to the isolated monastery.

Po Lin is unusual for many reasons. The only access used to be the pilgrims' path from Tai O, but it's still an oasis of serenity that somehow coexists with the noise brought by the crowds of visitors, and sometimes conspires with it. Senior monks have been known to use walkie-talkies, a public address system relays messages and prayers, and television is not banned within the precincts. Yet its 40 or more monks live a spartan life, rising at 4.30 am for their first studies and meditations. Visitors can take a vegetarian lunch of huge black mushrooms, noodles and *dofu* by buying a ticket in the office on the right-hand side as you enter the monastery. Prayer time is mid-afternoon, around 3–4 pm. There is also a peaceful garden at the rear. It may be possible to stay the night ($100 per person) if space is available: it usually is. There are two dormitories divided into twin rooms.

The buildings are not especially impressive architecturally. The upper floor of the central temple has three Buddha representations: Sakyamuni in the centre, the Healing Buddha on the right, and the Lord of Western Paradise to the left. The room below is dedicated to the three *bodhisattvas* that aid the spirits of the dead: Kwun Yum, the Goddess of Mercy, Wen Shu, the Goddess of Wisdom, and Pu Hsien, who protects sacred Mt Emei in Sichuan province. Across the way is a temple to Wo Tei, guardian of Buddhist shrines.

More spectacular is the giant Buddha statue outside the gates. Thirty-four metres high, it weighs 160 tonnes and took six years to construct; 202 pieces of bronze, each a centimetre thick and weighing about 800 kg, rest on a steel frame. Several sections of the 250-tonne edifice, especially the neck which is leaning forward, have been reinforced to withstand typhoon-force winds. The whole thing was engineered and built by mainland Chinese consultants at a cost of around $70 million. When the largest cast section—the face—was brought up as a single piece, the main road to the monastery had to be shut for three nights and telephone cables rerouted. The Buddha was designed by the monks themselves and is mounted on a pedestal copied from the Hall of Prayer for Good Harvests in the Temple of Heaven in Peking. Two floors inside the Buddha are set aside for meditation. The figure's features can be read as one might read a book, looking for a deeper symbolic meaning. The spiral curl between the eyes was said to generate light when the Buddha taught true doctrine. The extended right hand offers relief from suffering whilst the left hand symbolizes the bestowing of happiness.

Nearby is the tea garden of Lantau, 160 acres producing Hong Kong's only locally-produced tea, known as *wan mo cha*, 'the tea of cloud and mist'. A small café offers it with local cakes.

At the far western end of the island is Lantau's largest and richest village, **Tai O**, the 'big harbour'. The fishermen's houses sit on stilts above the creek and the salt pans nearby are disused, yet the village is rich because of the smuggling rackets with mainland China that load up nearby with contraband videos, televisions and other electronic goods. Until recently the transport of goods without a manifest was scarcely a crime in Hong Kong, but incursions by mainland Chinese naval patrol boats into Hong Kong waters, including a brazen kidnapping in 1990 of an undercover police group whose 'sting' accidentally netted a People's Liberation Army gunboat engaged in smuggling, have changed that tolerance. Not, however, before Tai O made a fat profit moving electronic goods over the international boundary which lies just a few yards off the pier.

You would hardly guess any of this during the daytime. A rope-drawn sampan laboured by two old women crosses the creek for a mere twenty cents. The village has two major temples. **Kwan Tai** (confusingly also known as *Kwan Kung*) is honoured at the right-hand end of Market St in a temple built originally in 1748 with a bronze bell that is older still. The God of War and Righteousness is flanked left and right by the gods of health and wealth. At the seashore end of the main street is a temple to **Hau Wong**, built in 1699 to commemorate the last emperor of the Song dynasty who fled to this place whilst being pursued by marauding Mongols. Inside, amid the flowers and offerings, are a whale's head and some sharks' bones found nearby, and the dragon boat used in the spring races.

Tung Chung on the northern shore of the island has the most accessible of the three ancient forts in Hong Kong, this one built by the viceroy of Kwangtung province in 1817. His six cannons weren't enough, however, to keep the British out. This whole area as far as the eye can see will be gobbled up by the new airport reclamation. To get here you can catch the *kaido* from Tuen Mun at 10.30 am, dodging container boats and dredger barges, to land on **Chek Lap Kok**, still just a few farms and hidden forests. The village exports shallots and clams, and has a small temple dedicated to Hau Wong. The *kaido* doesn't connect with the bus that runs to Mui Wo. The last *kaido* back to Castle Peak Bay leaves at 4.30 pm.

The best excursion on Lantau is the **Trappists' stone chapel monastery** at the eastern end of the island. This is most conveniently reached by a 25-minute *kaido* ride from Peng Chau. The monks are exiles from Peking who fled China after the 1949 communist takeover. Today there are 18 who keep 80 head of cattle for the milk which is for sale there. Retreats are possible. On the way back, take the path to Silvermine Bay which leads off from the left-hand side of the dock along a rocky, well-marked path that passes through gorges, over a ridge and down through a forest to a farm overlooking a secluded beach.

Lantau's best beach is the 3.5 km-long dark expanse of **Cheung Sha Upper beach**, on the main road along the south of the island past milestone 4.5. You can sit here on weekdays in total peace and watch the Macau-bound jetfoils cruise by. (For walks on Lantau, consult the 'Walks' section, page 196). The southern coast villages are very popular with weekenders; you can find holiday lets in the Chinese press classifieds. You can walk to the Frog & Toad pub set back from the beach on **Tai Long Wan** at the southern end of the Chi Ma Wan peninsula. From here you can page a *sampan* to take you back to the ferry at Cheung Chau.

The distant **Soko islands** can be explored using a *kaido* hired from Cheung Chau; the trouble is most of them are off-limits and close to the international border. **Shek Kwu Chau** is a tiny rock that has long been a drug rehabilitation centre. **Tai Ah Chau** was depopulated a few years back by a scheme to turn it into a luxury marina. Just one old couple hung on there, but even they were driven off when the government turned it into an emergency Vietnamese holding centre which was later temporarily closed after international protests about its poor living conditions. Neolithic artifacts dating back 4,000 years have been found here. Neighbouring **Siu Ah Chau** has a pretty beach, deserted paddy fields long gone wild, and abandoned implements like grinders, chests and tables. It has no electricity and only one couple who still managed to raise eleven children there.

SHOPPING ADVICE

'Born to Shop' the T-shirts read, and in Hong Kong that is no lie. The city prides itself on its free-wheeling attitudes and free-port status, explained to me graphically by one trader as 'no sales tax or any of that bullshit'. HKTA statistics show that 51 per cent of all money spent by tourists in Hong Kong was spent on shopping, so if you researched prices at home before leaving you are now ready to begin shopping in earnest (see 'Pre-planning your shopping' on page 17).

Shopping hours extend into the late evening in many cases, especially at the weekends. Central closes first around 7pm, Tsim Sha Tsui around 8pm, though parts of Causeway Bay remain open until 10pm. Most department stores close around 8pm. Most stores don't open until around 10am, though they are open seven days a week. Some Japanese stores close for one weekday. Almost all are closed during major public holidays. Virtually every shop of any size is shut during the four days of Lunar New Year celebrations.

Payment methods are flexible too, but don't always work in the shopper's favour. Credit cards are accepted almost everywhere, though most traders in small shops will add a 3–6 percent surcharge to the first quoted price which they will then redefine as a 'cash price'. Since no prices are marked you have no comeback. There is no point in arguing, so always assume the price quoted is a cash-only price. Some shops will take foreign currency in cash, though do not rely on this as only the sharpest electronics traders will usually consider this method. They will check the current exchange rate, but you should be aware of it too. Travellers' cheques are also accepted widely.

Deposits of around 50 per cent are often required for custom-made goods or bespoke tailoring. This is also sometimes demanded for items the retailer has to order from outside, even if this only takes a matter of hours. For bulky items the trader will usually deliver the goods free of charge if the hotel is nearby but may demur if it requires crossing the harbour. Deposits are not generally refundable, though this does sometimes happen. Note that goods in general are not returnable nor purchases refundable.

Prices are always arbitrary and a 'fixed price' sign doesn't always mean that you can't ask, especially if you're the first customer of the day. That prices vary from shop to shop doesn't mean traders are necessarily trying to cheat you, they're just giving you a lesson in supply and demand. Your return to their shop merely confirms they were at the wrong point of the trade-off, so don't be surprised, as I once was, to lead a guest through a row of shops to look for the best deal only to find that the cheapest price was unavailable on a second visit. You can try and bargain, especially if you are buying several items, but you will find it easier to accept an offer if you compare it to the price back home. Remember: gleaning the last 10% of any bargain is always the hardest deal to make and Hong Kong's traders practise a lot more than you do.

Guarantees must be checked during price negotiations. Ask to see them. Many will only be local warranties valid for one year even if they have the stamp of the principal agent in Hong Kong. If you are worried about having a guarantee, telephone the main dealer or distributor first. A precious list can be found in the back of the Hong Kong Tourist Association's free shopping guide. International guarantees are pre-printed but require the retailer's chop and date stamp as proof of purchase. Make sure also that your receipt is clearly marked with the model number of the product, its individual production number, the date of purchase and the price.

Customs and shipping regulations should be checked before you leave home, though consulates in Hong Kong will have an enquiries system that can answer routine questions. If you are feeling masochistic, or want to mail goods home yourself, you can try the government's Trade Department in Canton Rd, Tsimshatshui. Import duties can be high so it is important to check before purchasing. When shipping it is advisable to buy an all-risks marine insurance policy to cover against potential damage or loss. Many shops advertize or can arrange to ship or mail goods for you direct.

One or two **caveats** remain. Some shops— particularly in the Tsimshatshui tourist area where rental levels are exorbitant —may attempt to intimidate you to part with your money before you are ready to close a deal. If you find a particular dealer unpleasant, bearing in mind that traders have a high-volume turnover and a low patience threshold—leave the shop. In Tsimshatsui I was once forced to agree to a price for a 'new' camera before the shop owner would take it out of the window for me to inspect. It was quite serviceable but definitely second hand, part of the grey market of almost-new photographic goods imported from Japan. Dollar prices should mean Hong Kong dollars, not American greenbacks, so be suspicious if someone starts asking for US currency.

Getting reliable consumer information (A–Z page 231) can be a problem, especially regarding electronics standards and the technical compatibility of telecommunications systems. You just never know whether you're getting the whole story, which sometimes you aren't simply because the shop assistant is new to the job. Good homework is the best solution, though the HKTA does have a useful leaflet relating to video and television transmission standards.

Infrequent retailers may switch goods once purchased for inferior or faulty ones. This can happen for simple reasons. For example, some people want their own spectacle lenses mounted in brand-name frames, so a shopkeeper would take a designer label pair from stock and separate the frame from the lens. He might then be tempted to sell the surplus designer lens in a local frame, but at the price of a designer package. It's best to check the whole process from agreement to receipt, from selection of goods to packing. Bear in mind that a Hong Kong trader's informality can come across as evasiveness even when they're being straightforward. You can pre-empt the problem by using only shops with the distinctive HKTA logo of the red junk (A–Z page 231).

A more recent problem in Hong Kong is simply the lack of staff training. You may walk into a shop and find the assistant either cannot be bothered to look at you or knows nothing of the product. A diffident manner undercuts any information they may give you. Even places like the main Sony dealer in Central, Chuen Yuen, can be like this. Salesmen may even try to persuade you that the sky is blue when it is obviously grey. Gilman, the leading Apple computer dealer, once tried to palm off an Apple monitor in an old box as brand new when the date of manufacture on the back showed it was actually 46 months old. A new one was sent one week later.

Often the big companies are really only interested in turnover. Shops in the main tourist districts have the same attitude, and there's always a constant flow of customers through the door. Try and find a smaller shop, often hidden away in a back street, that will give you a keen price and better service even if they are tucking into a lunch-box when you walk in. Finally, don't underestimate the language problem, even if someone seems fluent in English. If you are asking a complicated technical question they may simply not understand or will assume they know what you mean and answer a question you have not asked. Sometimes they will be literally accurate—the only television in most shops that can receive French transmissions is a large and expensive model—and just economical with the truth—any inexpensive multisystem TV can be hooked up through a video fitted with a French SECAM tuner to receive a picture, should you move to France.

After the warnings, remind yourself of the advantages of buying in Hong Kong. The same flexibility means that prices are genuinely lower even if the manufacturer is a multinational operating a world-pricing scheme. Apple computer prices are quite similar in London and Hong Kong, yet the Far East dealer can often be persuaded to give a discount much earlier than you'd get it abroad, and you avoid the 15 percent British value added tax. If your conscience allows it, many smaller establishments will under-invoice if you want to try to cheat your own country's customs collectors, and they will also pre-date invoices. Check, however, the date of arrival in Hong Kong of the model you are buying as it is quite likely to be new on the market, something any customs official will know.

TOURIST SHOPPING

Below is a list of information about the most popular purchases made by visitors to Hong Kong. I have not attempted to go into exhaustive detail or make a long list of recommendations of individual shops. The HKTA produces an excellent booklet called simply *Shopping* which lists HKTA member-shops by categories. This is available at any HKTA outlet and often in hotels. Especially useful is the list of *sole agents* of major brand name goods at the back. This includes electronic and audio equipment, crystal and glassware, computers, cosmetics, cigarette lighters, optical goods, photographic equipment, silverware, sports goods, stationery and watches. You can check the main 'Business' telephone directory, the 'Buying Guide to Hong Kong Island' and the 'Buying Guide to Kowloon' yellow pages supplements which list the head offices of international companies and their principal showrooms.

ART AND ANTIQUES (A–Z PAGE 246)

Most dealers have their showrooms in Central or Admiralty. Wyndham St is popular as is the eastern end of **Hollywood Rd,** though many shops have now moved further down the road towards the **Cat St flea market. Lyndhurst Terrace** nearby is also a good place to look. There are around a dozen galleries in the Hong Kong hotels shopping area that are also worth investigating. Top class dealers will label antiques with details of their origin, age and amount of restoration. Certificates of antiquity are normally issued for any item more than a century old.

For **contemporary fine arts** try **Hanart TZ Gallery** run by Johnson TZ Chang in Central (closed Mondays). For Chinese paintings try **Susan Chen & Co, Lattices, Alisan Fine Arts** and **Gallerie du Monde.** For furniture and silverware, **Honeychurch Antiques** or **Ian McLean. Chan Shing Kee** supplies furniture for export and other curios. For porcelain head for **Helene Bennett Antiques** in Hollywood Rd, or the more expensive branches of **P. C. Lu.** For jade go to **the Jade House** in Tsimshatsui. One of the best collections of antique snuff bottles is found at **Y. F. Yang** in Ocean Terminal in Tsimshatsui. The best selection of Korean chests is at **Tong-In Antiques Gallery**, also in Tsimshatsui. If you're looking for inexpensive mainland Chinese figurines or antiques handled by official Chinese channels, go to the **China Resources Artland Centre** in Wanchai or the **Pok Art House** in TST. Some of the nicest modern pottery made by local artists is displayed at the **Pottery Workshop** in Wyndham St just below the Foreign Correspondents' Club, or at **Koto Arts** in the Arts Centre in Wanchai.

CARPETS AND RUGS (A–Z PAGE 250)

Hong Kong is an import centre for carpets from all over the Asia region including Turkey, Afghanistan, Pakistan, Iran, India and China. There is also one major Hong Kong manufacturer, **Tai Ping Carpets**, which makes its own designs using imported New Zealand wool. A series of carpet shops are clustered in Wyndham St in Central. The quality, and hence price, of an Oriental carpet depends on four factors: the quality of the yarn, whether it is wool, cotton, silk or a blend; the quality of the workmanship; the complexity of the design; and the number of knots per square inch which defines the fineness of the weave. Discounts are standard at all shops so take your time to make a selection. Auctions are regularly advertized in the *South China Morning Post* and usually take place in the Hilton Hotel. A select list of reputable shops and dealers is included in the A–Z section on pages 250–1.

CERAMICS

Leading international makes of porcelain are significantly cheaper in Hong Kong's showrooms, though the dangers of transportation back home are an additional risk. Cheap handpainted Chinese porcelain fills the two mainland-stocked chains of **China Arts and Crafts** and **China Products**.

CAMERAS, COMPUTERS, AUDIO AND VIDEO EQUIPMENT (A-Z PAGE 248)

The third floor of Ocean Terminal and Harbour Centre on Canton Rd in Tsimshatsui, and the neighbouring side streets, are the best places to look for audio equipment. On Hong Kong island, try the second and third floors of Prince's Building in Central, but check also the side streets leading towards Western.

Computer shops are congregated most visibly in the basement of the **Silvercord** building on Canton Rd in Tsimshatsui and nearby. The old **Golden Computer Arcade** in Shamshuipo no longer sells pirated software or nameless IBM clones. The trend for several years has been towards name brand models and Silvercord's dealers offer similarly priced deals.

For a run-down on television, video and camcorder transmission standards, look for the HKTA's *Shopping Guide to Video Products.* Check the electrical rating of equipment you buy. Most equipment switches automatically between 110–250 volts, but larger items like laser printers and smaller items like fax machines may not. If you're looking for electronic keyboards head for **Tom Lee** music store in the heart of Tsimshatsui.

The camera shops used by professionals in town are **Photo Scientific** and **Color Six**, both in Stanley St, Central.

CUSTOM TAILORING (A-Z PAGE 290)

This is still one of the prime attractions for Western visitors despite the growth of ready-to-wear clothing. Most tailors will copy men's and women's clothing from a pattern but not from a picture or rough design. Standard patterns for classic items will generally turn out more favourably. Allow time for at least two fittings and expect to pay a 50% non-refundable deposit. In general, you pay a premium for your ease of mind. Tailors located in the main hotels are reliable, aware of Western fashions and tastes, and speak good English. Savings may prove deceptive going elsewhere, except by recommendation. Tailors are adept at delivering items at very short notice to your hotel minutes before you depart. This will probably fray your nerves more than theirs, and should be avoided unless you like living this way! Top-class tailors will keep customers' measurements on file for a few years so you can order further shirts by mail if you wish.

CUSTOM SHOES (A–Z PAGE 288)

There are several reputable cobblers in Hong Kong whose crafted work will more than complement your custom tailoring.

FURNITURE

Chinese pieces in rosewood, camphorwood, teak and other woods are made in Hong Kong. Check that the rosewood is genuine and not just a rosewood finish. Imported furniture from Korea and Japan, both antique and modern, is also easy to find. Rattan is widely available. Made-to-order designs can be undertaken but you should oversee the production process to ensure a faithful reproduction and workmanship standards.

JEWELLERY AND GEMSTONES (A–Z PAGE 284)

Jewellery and loose gemstones are exempt from tax and import duties in Hong Kong, so prices are very keen. Hong Kong is the world's third largest diamond-trading centre and a major trading market for freshwater and saltwater pearls. Prices are often heavily discounted and shops are required by law to disclose and mark the content of gold and platinum. The HKTA issues a specific *Shopping Guide to Jewellery* with further hints and details, and the *Gault-Milleau Guide* has a good section listing stores and outlets. Appraisals can be carried out by a number of insurance companies, or arranged through the Gemnological Association of Hong Kong on 3666006.

OPTICAL GOODS

Spectacle lenses are spectacularly cheap in Hong Kong. Single lenses can be ground and polished within two days, whilst bi-focals take up to five days to make. Special lens finishes are commonplace and frames are cheap. Binoculars are also a very good buy.

WATCHES

Hong Kong has a fetish about time and watches as social accessories are heavily advertized on TV. All the major exclusive brand names are available in Hong Kong. You can check with the HKTA for the name of the local agent or supplier. Several household names, Seiko, for example, have their own shops. There are also medium-priced stores like **City Chain** which offer good prices. Check the serial number of the watch against the number on the guarantee and mark the watch-strap as genuine as this can affect the validity of the guarantee.

Touts offering fake Rolex, Dunhill and other upmarket brands hover around the Hyatt Hotel in Tsimshatsui ready to whisk you down a back alley. The Temple St market is also a good place to look for these bargains which should be priced at around $400–500. Many countries forbid the import of such fakes.

OTHER COMMON PURCHASES

AIRLINE TICKETS AND THE TRANS-SIBERIAN RAILWAY (A–Z PAGES 245, 259 AND 292)

Several courier companies offer cheap tickets for onboard couriers flying to Europe, the United States, Australia and other Asian destinations. Most require several weeks or months' notice, but you can try for last-minute cancellations. Some companies restrict you to hand luggage only. Most will demand a non-refundable deposit. It's wise to check whether the route is non-stop and on a reputable airline as some courier flights take roundabout routes that offer only marginal savings on regular fares. One of the largest companies offering such tickets is **Jupiter Air** on 7351946. Check the classified section of the *South China Morning Post* for the most up-to-date information. Never make an informal 'courier' arrangement at the airport: you don't know what you may be carrying.

Hong Kong is an international airline hub with non-stop flights to three continents. The cheapest flights to Asian destinations like Bangkok, Manila and Singapore are on non-Asian airlines that stop over in Hong Kong en route. Not all of these are daily flights though, and some are only once a week. Conversely, the cheapest flights to Europe are on airlines that stop over elsewhere en route. Check the prices on Lauda Air, Malaysian Airline System, Philippine Airlines, Air Lanka, Emirates and Gulf Air. These routes are often exhausting. Some flights are shared between two carriers but have a price differential. Try to compare the prices of long-haul and round-the-world flights before you leave home. Check with agents or the back page of *Business Traveller* magazine for updates on round-the-world fares. Dozens of airlines operate round-the-world deals via Hong Kong. Even more include Singapore, Bangkok or Manila from where you can make a detour to Hong Kong. Flights within Asia are radically cheaper than similar sectors in America or Europe. It pays to shop around with agents as some will try and push you towards a particular airline or not bother to check all the alternatives. Those listed in the A–Z section on pages 291–2 are reliable, as are all HKTA-registered agents.

Several companies including **Hong Kong Student Travel** will offer you a quote for the trip to Europe on the Trans-Siberian railway. Trips to Tibet are organized by **Mera Travel** in Yau Ma Tei. Trips to China can be found with a wide range of companies, or through the offices of the China Travel Service in Central or Tsimshatsui.

BOOKSTORES (A–Z PAGE 249)

Hong Kong is not the best place to look for books. Prices are marked up to cover freight costs, and selection is limited. The most helpful is the **Professional Bookshop** in Alexandra House. It can order any volume in print but shelves only legal, accountancy, management and other business books.

The **Arts Bookshop** in the Arts Centre is an affiliate and often has discount sales on art books. Mainland Chinese books can be bought in the branches of the **Commercial Press** in Causeway Bay, the **Chung Hwa Book Company** on Nathan Rd and the **Joint Publishing Co** on Queen Victoria St. The **SCMP Family Bookshop** chain sells modern paperbacks, as do **Jumbo Grade Books and Stationary, Kelly & Walsh,**

Hong Kong Book Centre, Harris, Swindon's and **Times** bookshops. **Bookazine** in both Prince's Building and adjacent Alexandra House is the place to look for periodicals and local guidebooks. **Wanderlust,** tucked away on the corner of Hollywood Road and Shelley Street, specializes in travel books.

COMPACT DISCS (A–Z PAGE 253)

The best selection of jazz CDs, filed idiosyncratically by first rather than family name, is held by **United Records** in Causeway Bay. Compilation albums are generally overpriced while specialist labels are good bargains: the standard cash price is $100. This store stays open until 10 pm. For classical CDs, **Delight Music** on the second floor of the Hong Kong Hotel arcade has the best all-round selection, especially for boxed sets. It is open daily until 8 pm, though on Sundays 1–7 pm. The **Art Centre's Track One** offers a 10 percent discount for members (annual membership is $200). It has the most eclectic selection in town, though not very wide, and closes at 8 pm. Late night shopping is possible at **Samson & Co** in Tsimshatsui's Mandarin Plaza until 11 pm.

SOUVENIRS (A–Z PAGE 289)

This has to be a brief and personal selection, but I've been asked this question so many times that I can't leave it out. For **fine teas** go to **Fook Ming Tong** which has shops in Central and Causeway Bay, or the Mandarin Oriental's delicatessen. For rattan goods, try **Hong Kong Rattan Art and Craft Ware** in Central. Expatriates favour the Asian handicrafts and knick-knacks in the **Amazing Grace Elephant Company's** outlets in Central and Tsimshatsui. For all sorts of curios and odds-and-ends try **Mountain Folkcraft.** For Indian cottons and Thai silks try **Design Selection.** My favourite curio shop is the **Art Deco Antique Shop.** All of the above are in Central.

FACTORY OUTLETS

Factory outlets have become a byword in Hong Kong for style- and price-conscious buyers. With so many designer label goods being made here, or in Hong Kong-run factories over the border in China, there are always overruns of clothing, or runs containing minor faults that prevent them being sold at full price, or one-off experiments that were never taken further, all of which can be off-loaded through small shops around the market areas of Tsimshatsui and Central. The practice has become so developed that manufacturers often run their own outlets instead of passing goods on. Some are located in readily accessible areas, but many require dedicated searching and journeys by taxi to otherwise unvisited parts of the colony. A good place for casual browsing is the Pedder Building in Pedder St, Central. For a list of factory outlets that are HKTA members, consult the HKTA's *Factory Outlets in Hong Kong (Ready-to-wear & Jewellery)*. For a more complete guide with tips, Dana Goetz's annually-updated *Factory Bargains* guide is indispensable. If you're looking for cheap clothes you would be better off scouring Tsimshatsui's shopfronts rather than spending time going out to Stanley where the prices are no longer rock bottom.

DEPARTMENT STORES (A–Z PAGE 261)

The Japanese have been steadily upgrading Hong Kong's department stores over the past decade, spreading quality across Causeway Bay to outposts in Taikoo Shing and Shatin. **Daimaru** and **Mitsukoshi, Tokyu, Isetan** and **Matsuzakaya** were the firstcomers. **Sogo** in Causeway Bay was a revelation when it opened in the mid-1980s, though actually it's laid out like a Chinese store, very crowded, fluorescent-lit and full of shoppers. **Yaohan** is now making a mark in Shatin. On an even larger scale is the **Seibu** store in Admiralty's Pacific Place. Their food hall is the best in the colony, though service is slow. Completely the opposite are the mainland Chinese stores like **China Products, Yue Hwa Chinese Products Emporium** and **Chinese Arts & Crafts**, which are full of cheap wares and artistic kitsch. The oldest Hong Kong store of all is **Lane Crawford**. More elusive and locally-oriented are **Wing On, Sincere, Shui Hing** and **Dragon Seed**.

SHOPPING MALLS

The great malls are in Kowloon, the echoing corridors of the combined **Ocean Centre, Ocean Terminal** and **Harbour City** that runs the length of Canton Rd on the western side of

Tsimshatsui. The **New World Centre** under the hotel of the same name on the waterfront is also massive. The best shops are in the basement. The most upscale shopping is the arcade of the Peninsula Hotel in Kowloon. On Hong Kong island, Central is really one large mall connected by a series of overpasses. The main buildings are **The Landmark, Alexandra House** and **Prince's Building**.

The most upmarket boutique chain is **Joyce** which stocks a wide range of designer label clothes. The very young trendy set head for a shopping plaza above the Jordan MTR station in Kowloon where several young Japanese designers have set up outlets. The most typical Hong Kong clothes store for simple ready-to-wears and casuals is the **Giordano** chain.

Street markets are a famous feature of Hong Kong. The back streets of Central have several lanes, crowded back streets selling cheap goods including clothing, leather and luggage. The best are **Li Yuen St East** and **Li Yuen St West** between Queen's Rd East and Des Voeux Rd, west of Pedder St. Nearby, Pottinger St climbs from Queen's Rd Central to Wyndham St and is known as **Button Alley. Cat St**, above Queen's Rd Central, down in Sheung Wan, is good for antiques, and from here you can walk back past the Hollywood Rd galleries. **Egg St** in Wing Sing St next to the bijou jewellery stalls in Wing Wo St and the **Cloth Alley** fabrics market at Wing On St are good too. **Man Wah Lane** is known locally as Chop Alley after the chop carvers set up there.

The most famous street market of all is the **Temple St Night Market** in Yaumatei on Kowloon side. This is most active between 8–10 pm and is really two markets in one. South of Kansu St are the cheap outdoor cooked food vendors and hawkers selling cheap clothes and bootleg tapes and watches. North of Kansu St there are Chinese opera singers and palm readers.

Local produce markets are well worth exploring. Ignore the live market in Central in a white three-storey building just a few minutes' walk west of Pedder St. Go to the Bowrington St market off Morrison Hill Rd in Wanchai, or the North Point Rd market which is lined up either side of the North Point tram loop off King's Rd. The largest produce markets are in Mongkok and Yaumatei, like the Kwun Chung market at the lower end of Shanghai St. Many streetside vendors stay open until midnight selling fruit, though the wet goods and vegetables usually close up by eight in the evening. The best time is first thing in the morning, but you may not be ready then for the sight of frogs being skinned alive and steaming cattle heads dumped in wicker baskets.

Flower markets in Hong Kong are especially lovely. The best one is behind Jardine's Bazaar in Causeway Bay, which closes around 10 pm. There are several attractive flower stalls at the lower end of Wyndham St and Lan Kwai Fong in Central, which demand higher prices. Favourite sprays are *ngan lau* silver buttons, or baby's breath surrounding a spray of *geen lau* gladioli, *moi gwai* roses, *guk fa* spikey chrysanthemums, *lam fa* orchids, or *heung ngai hing* carnations.

Flowers play a special part during Chinese New Year celebrations, along with ornamental kumquats which are supposed to ensure good fortune for the coming year.

DINING OUT

Hong Kong has always been famous for its food. The good news is that the growth of a wealthy middle class during the 1980s has sparked a renaissance in Chinese cooking. Many famous restaurants lived for long on their reputation. The arrival of new venues, often with young chefs, proved that Cantonese cuisine was ripe for change and experimentation. Old dishes have been revitalized, previously unthinkable creations have started appearing on menus, and a Western health consciousness and suspicion of everyday food additives and enhancers has taken root.

Hong Kong's trend-conscious public ensures that the movement is always up-market, though that doesn't mean prices have to go through the roof. In 1990 a spread of excellent restaurants opened where it's possible to eat for around $200–300 per head, a modest price by Western standards for excellent food in a capital city. Of course, the most expensive restaurants still have their reputations, their often prestigious locations and clientele. Since they're so easy to find I've concentrated on mid-price restaurants that are within the reach of those with little money who want an unforgettable night out, as much as those for whom money is no object but quality vital. This choice is idiosyncratic and incomplete, but since most visitors spend on average only four or five nights in Hong Kong I see little point in suggesting too many to choose from. Reservations are essential for the top-flight restaurants, though it can be quite serendipitously amusing to cast yourself out upon the streets without one in search of a great meal. As with the expensive restaurants, lists of places to eat out are easy to find in the tourist brochures and from the HKTA. All the restaurants listed in the A–Z database are of good quality, but see the text below for special recommendations, and a summary of dos and don'ts. Practically all restaurants in Hong Kong take the major credit cards, though everyone prefers cash.

ETIQUETTE

At its best a Chinese meal is a group affair with a round table and a stream of communal dishes, hot towels and continuous pots of Chinese tea. If you don't monopolize the whole table some total strangers will likely be shown to the spare seats within minutes if the restaurant is crowded. No one minds about this in Hong Kong and it would be discourteous to demur.

Charges are made for the small nuts, pickles, hot sauce, mustard, pineapple and tea placed on the table. Receipts are not always itemized and over-charging common. Ask the waiter to give you an estimate, or at least check the prices whilst you're ordering. Most menus will be written out in English, often in colourfully undescriptive language. The most interesting dishes are often on lists of specials printed on little cards on the table or on the wall. Don't order dishes marked 'seasonal prices' without asking the price first, and ask for small or medium-sized dishes rather than large ones if you're in a group and want a cheaper, wider selection. Aim for one dish per person around the table even though all the dishes will be shared from the lazy Susan.

The larger of the pair of bowls by each place is for rice. This is often served at the end of the meal, though waiters are tolerant when foreigners disrupt this pattern. The accepted practice is to bring the bowl towards the mouth when eating rice, the opposite of the way mother taught you to behave.

CHOPSTICKS

Every restaurant from the highest to the lowest will set the table with chopsticks, though you can ask for knives and forks in all but the smallest restaurants. Chopsticks are easy to use: hundreds of millions of people use them at every meal. Rest the bottom stick on your third finger and hold it in place in the gap between your first finger and your thumb. Now grasp the upper one between your first and second finger and hold that in place with the ball of your thumb. Keep the lower one fixed and use the upper one as a moveable mandible to grasp pieces of food.

Some dishes will have large ornamental spoons while others will have serving chopsticks, in which case you shouldn't use your own. Tea is poured by one person for as many people as can be reached. You can say 'thank you' for this without words by tapping two fingers twice on the table, a practice which imitates in miniature a mandarin's kowtow, and supposedly originated when a 12th-century emperor was travelling clan-destinely to flee the Mongols. Draw the waiter's attention to your need for a refill of water by leaving the lid askew on the pot.

COOKING METHODS

The best modern Hong Kong cooking is very pure, a throwback to the traditional virtues of the Cantonese style with fresh ingredients and simple preparation by steaming or stir-frying. Conversely a lot of run-of-the-mill restaurants serve up salty food that is very heavy-handed. There are eight main cooking methods used in Chinese cooking: stir-frying, pan-frying, deep-frying, long and short steaming, boiling, simmer-ing and roasting. Cognoscenti will tell you that meals are supposed to be balanced, taking into consideration different methods of cooking and the internal qualities of the food, but I have yet to sit down with Chinese friends who give a thought to this in reality. Waiters generally know the best dishes and seasonal specials. Sizzling dishes and hotpot stews are popular in winter.

SEASONAL DISHES

Summer marks the time paradoxically when the winter melon arrives for excellent soups. There are many summer vegetables, including sweet pea shoots called *dai miu,* and bitter melon. In **autumn** the prime delicacy is Shanghai fresh-water hairy crab, trussed in green straw and flown down the coast in their thousands with casual disregard of hepatitis fears. The females arrive in September, fat with golden roe that is thought to enhance complexions, whilst the males arrive in October. **Winter** is the season for game dishes, often served as kebabs. Snake meat shredded into soup with a variety of ingre-dients is especially popular, garnished with chrysanthemum petals and lemon leaves. The petals are supposedly good for the eyes whilst snake juice, in particular the gall bladder, is positive proof against rheumatism and winter chills. Snow frogs from Manchuria are also a skin tonic and the female frog's fatty innards served in double-boiled soup are held to be good for asthma.

SAUCES

The different Chinese cuisines are particular about their accompanying sauces which will always be brought with the dishes as they're ordered. Tables are likely to be set with small mustard, soy sauce and chilli sauce dishes. Roasted meats like duck, quail and goose are accompanied by a thick *hoi sin* plum sauce, more tart than sweet in the case of goose dishes. In Peking restaurants the roasted duck comes with a sweet soya paste, as does roasted pig elsewhere. Shanghainese dumplings called *xiaolong bao* come with shredded ginger to which you add vinegar and/or soy sauce. Steamed or poached shrimps are best with a soy and chilli sauce. Steamed crab and steamed dumplings go with a salty combination of minced ginger in vinegar; and shellfish and some beef dishes are often cooked with oyster sauce. Cuttlefish are accompanied by a fishy shrimp roe sauce. Steamed chicken comes with minced ginger, scallion and peanut oil, and roast chicken with a stronger mix of flavoured pepper and salt. Some sauces are made locally: purple fermented shrimp paste on Lamma and fermented bean curd on Lantau.

RICE AND NOODLES

Rice is one of the daily necessities and comes in many forms. The most satisfying is simply white steamed rice *bak faan,* though served with chopped meat and vegetables and then fried it becomes *chow faan.* Noodles *meen* come in a huge number of varieties: fried and crispy, flat and braised, plain ones, fat ones and stringy thin ones, and served with meat, crabmeat or vegetables. Rice vermicelli *mai fun* is often mixed into soups or fried à la Singapore or Amoy (Xiamen).

MEALS

Breakfast Hong-Kong-style is a quick stop on the way to work at a fast food shop like Maxim's or the Café de Coral, or to the neighbourhood *daipaidong* for a bowl of noodles, fried dough-sticks or rice-flour stretched dumplings. Congee or *juk* rice porridge is also popular. Cafés offer rare delights like condensed milk on toast. *Dim sum* snacks are taken in the late morning, usually as lunch or in addition to a main dish. These bite-sized morsels are hidden away in small bamboo baskets wielded by squawking old ladies, usually in massive restaurants with insistent noise levels well above industrial safety levels. The crush starts around 12 am and they'll be rushing orders to move satisfied tables out again to pack more people in before 2.30 pm. *Dim sum* is literally something that touches the heart, through the stomach rather than the wallet, and is a vital part of *yum cha*, drinking tea, the morning gossip and nibbles session. The best hotel *dim sum* is at the Marriott in Pacific Place, Admiralty.

Lunch boxes are *de rigueur* for the masses, usually a few slabs of *cha siu* pork, roast duck or chicken on a bed of rice. You can often see old men and women staggering under a stack of metal boxes wrapped in a cloth and slung from a bamboo pole. These are Hong Kong's equivalent of Bombay's *dabba-wallah* lunch delivery men. In the sleek office blocks, of course, it's sandwiches for the yuppies and lunch out for the managers.

Tea in a traditional Chinese-style tea shop is a hallowed custom, especially at weekends, complete with sweetmeats and cakes. Modern settings in hotels don't quite match up, though the buffet in the Hilton in Central is huge and the Peninsula's set tea calm and reverential. The China Tee Club in Central's Pedder Building is one of the few places where you can simply drop in, despite its 'members only' warning.

Dinner is taken any time between 7 pm and close to midnight as many workers keep irregular hours. The amazing thing about Hong Kong restaurants is that they always seem to be full. People eat well in this city. Even at home a four- or five-dish meal is the norm. There is less post-work drinking with office partners than in Japan, though the custom of singing songs to a back-up tape, known as *karaoke,* is popular after dinner.

Daipaidongs are raucous communal settings for dinner, featuring outdoor cooking Cantonese-style. They used to be widespread in Wanchai but have almost all been cleared away. The best ones are further afield, in North Point Rd in North Point and the back streets of Mongkok and Yaumatei around Shanghai St. These can stay open to 1.30 am or thereabouts in summer and to around midnight in winter. The sanitation is not good but they score high on atmosphere.

Outdoor dining is popular on the islands of Lantau, Lamma and Cheung Chau, where there are some good restaurants well worth making a ferry trip to sample. The floating restaurants in Aberdeen harbour and Causeway Bay typhoon shelter are touristy rip-offs of dubious value. **Specialist food shops** mark the passing seasons, particularly the snake meat and soup restaurants that flourish in the winter. Some restaurants offer game and fowl, whilst the New Territories is famous for its seafood, *tofu* bean curd and pigeon dishes. Some will offer unusual animals like pangolin, bears' paws or even monkey brains. These are forbidden by law and should not be encouraged.

DRINKS

Chinese teas come in three main types: unfermented green teas, black or red fermented teas, and partially fermented teas like *oolong.* Tea is drunk hot and unadulterated with sugar or milk, the pot being regularly replenished with hot water throughout the meal. The standard is *heung peen* jasmine tea, though you can ask for Dragon Well or Cloud Mist varieties too. For a stronger taste ask for *bo lei,* a dark rich fermented red tea that thickens in the pot, or even *bo lei fa* which is dark tea lightened with chrysanthemum flowers. Chiu Chow restaurants also serve thimble-sized tumblers of *tit kwun yum* before and after the food. An acrid-tasting digestive, it translates colourfully as 'Iron Goddess of Mercy.'

Chinese wines are generally to be avoided. They are spirits distilled from rice, millet and other grains, terrible to confront and even worse to remember in tranquillity. They aren't as pure as Japanese *sake* and are often infused with herbs, flowers, snakes, lizards and other gecko-like creatures. They're none-theless popular with local people, usually the older generation, most of whom don't bat an eyelid at mixing fine French cognac with Coca-Cola, which gives you an idea of what the local stuff has done to their taste buds! If you absolutely must, try *siu hing* which is rice-based and fairly mild, rather than *Maotai* or *go leung,* the 70 percent proof sorghum-derived shockers. Some expats swear *Maotai* is fine with food and that 14-per cent Shaoxing tastes like a dry sherry, but proceed carefully.

The prime local choice for **beer** is split between *Ka see ba,* or Carlsberg, and a Filipino beer called San Miguel, both locally brewed. Expats often plump for *Tsingtao,* a sweet Chinese-brewed beer from the old German port of Qingdao, a remnant of colonial days. The only draft German beers are to be found in two bars, Schnurrbart's and Finealley's, both in Central. Supermarkets offer a wide range of international beers at low prices, while drinkers of fine wine from abroad are penalized with a high tax.

DIM SUM

The variety of *dim sum* available is simply exhausting. Many are old favourites found everywhere all year round, others are seasonal, and some are particular to individual restaurants. The old ladies with their trolleys bring around the most common kind, including most of those listed below. A menu will supplement them with other dishes and a smaller set of cards placed on every table will add daily and seasonal specialities. The only answer is to go with a Cantonese-speaking friend. When you select dishes the old lady will stamp your table's card which the waiter will tot up when you pay the bill.

The most easily recognizable is *har gau,* a whole shrimp encased in a rice flour dumpling, closely followed by *shiu mai,* a mixed pork and shrimp dumpling in a green flour casing. *Cha siu bau,* are steamed buns filled with barbequed pork, while *dou sha bau* and *lien yong bau* are filled with sweet red beans and creamy crushed lotus seeds respectively. *Chun kuen* are fried spring rolls filled with bamboo shoots, bean sprouts, mushrooms and shredded meat. Deep-fried taro rolls are called *woo kok,* and steamed rice-flour rolls filled with meat or shrimps are *cheung fun.* Steamed dumplings with pork, shrimp and bamboo shoots are *fun gwor,* and *jin fun gwor* are pan-fried *fun gwor* served with consommé. *Ho yip fan* is steamed fried rice in a wrapping of lotus leaf and *nor mai gai* (sounds like 'Oh my God!') is a similar concoction made of steamed glutinous rice. There is a variety of desserts including *daan ta,* a sweet egg custard tart, *hung dao sa,* red bean soup, and *nor mai chi,* a coconut snowball.

CHINESE CUISINES

Modern **Cantonese** cuisine (A–Z page 264) is characterized by its fresh ingredients and light styles of cooking, mainly stir-frying and steaming with a heavy accent on seafood. Meat dishes include barbeque pork, deep-fried spareribs, roasted goose and suckling pig. Stir-fried beef fillets with oyster sauce is a favourite, as are pan-fried chicken with lemon, diced chicken with walnuts and diced roast pigeon wrapped in whole lettuce leaves.

Seafood exists in profusion: abalone, urchins, shark's fin, eels, crabs, lobsters, scallops, mussels, whelks, oysters, prawns, shrimps and huge fresh-water and ocean fish. A popular dish is drunken prawns where the live produce is marinated in rice wine before being sautéed. Another favourite is deep-fried crab claws, though for the money the best treat of all is a simple *jin yu* steamed fish in soya juice and garnished with spring onions and ginger.

Soups can be clear or double-boiled into a thick mélange. Fried milk, which looks like scrambled eggs, and deep-fried milk are delicacies. Vegetables, or *choi,* are many and various. The most succulent are *dau miu* sweet pea shoots, *tung choi* water spinach, and *bak choi,* a dark-leaved spinach with a thick white stem. Chinese mustard plant is very tasty, though a winter dish. Vegetarian restaurants are very inventive with *tofu* beancurd, including cooking, cutting and marinating it to look like meat. Desserts are often sweet soups like red bean or almond, or bird's nest as a delicacy.

Chiu Chow (in Mandarin, Chaozhou) cooking is renowned for its subtlety and tastiness. (A–Z page 266) Chiu

Chow restaurants customarily stay open a while later than other restaurants. The name comes from the Shantou coastal area in eastern Guangdong province. It is noted for its seafood dishes, pickled cabbage and peanut starters, and pungent *tit kwun yum* oolong tea served in tiny thumbnail cups before and after meals as an aid to digestion. It also prides itself on giant vegetable carvings of flowers, dragons and phoenixes made from carrots and stems of ginger.

The most famous Chiu Chow dish is a starter of cold-cut sliced goose with beancurd. Another starter is the 'four combination meats' of goose, pork, jellyfish and prawn balls. Deep-fried pearl leaf vegetables in *chuenjew* sauce is a favourite, as are shellfish dishes, pumpkin, prawn and crab balls. Duck with lemon sauce, deep-fried spiced duck, beef and fish balls with seaweed soup, sliced pigeon in plum sauce, pork with pickled cabbage, fried chicken pieces with crispy *chuenjew* leaves, stewed Tientsin cabbage with minced chicken, bird's nest in watermelon soup, and fried kale with dried fish are all popular. For dessert, try sweet mashed taro with ginko nuts or crystallized taro root.

Hakka food shows traces of its northern origins, derived from clans of nomads who moved south centuries ago. Two salty dishes are highly prized: the salt-baked chicken, with a salty crust over the soft sweet meat, and salt-baked shrimps. Stuffed beancurd dishes are popular, as is duck stuffed with a mixture of glutinous rice, diced meat and lotus seeds. Pickled cabbage for starters.

Taiwanese cooking (A–Z page 269) is another amalgam, heavily influenced by Fukienese, Chiu Chow, Okinawan and modern Japanese styles. It favours soy sauce used in slow stewed or braised dishes and seafood cooked in contrasting ways. Thus you can find fried dishes served with nuts, spiced and herbed prawns, cuttlefish cooked with egg yolk and black mushrooms, and omelettes with tiny rock oysters or finely shredded turnip. Seafood specialities include fried clams in garlic and chilli, a fish soup seasoned with preserved vegetables, a warming seaweed soup mixed with seafood, fried squid with pig's kidneys and chillies, and sizzling chillied veal steak. The Okinawan link adds Japanese mushrooms, and sweet potatoes in the *congee* rice porridge. The noodle soup has a sweet stock as its base, very different from, say, its Sichuan counterpart.

Shanghai style food, as one might expect from a major seaport, is a blend of others' creations (A–Z page 268). It is the heaviest and oiliest Chinese food, rich and sweet and served in large portions. It is the first cuisine north of Hong Kong where you can feel the strong breath of winter in the dishes. It favours preserved vegetables, pickles and salted meats. Dumplings, bread and noodles are preferred to rice. *Dim sum* favourites are the fried thick-skinned dumplings called *war tiu* in Hong Kong, and *jiaozi*—steamed mashed-pork dumplings, great in winter.

Delicacies include the autumnal hairy crab, ginger flavoured 'hundred-year-old' eggs and 'eight treasure' duck—the fanciful name refers to the number of ingredients. Drunken chicken, braised eel and yellow fish are also popular. Hot and sour soup is a winter favourite. Others are sautéed shrimps with crispy rice, sautéed pea tendrils, Shanghai cabbage with slices of ham, and baked sesame cakes. Steamed, dried and preserved vegetables figure prominently with egg dumplings. Unusual dishes include the often expensive steamed chicken in lotus leaves, and sliced ham with lotus seeds in a honey sauce, a dish from nearby Nanjing. Desserts include a sweet black sesame dumpling, banana fritters or crispy shredded coconut cake.

The **Hangzhou**-style variation (A–Z page 267) stems from the former imperial capital that captivated the Venetian traveller, Marco Polo. It emphasizes fresh-water fish, watercress, and a fish dish called fried croaker with pineseeds. The local *lung ching* tea delicately favours seafood dishes, particularly abalone and shrimps. Popular dishes are 'beggar's chicken' and steamed fish in vinegar sauce. The beggar's chicken *is* usually ordered a day in advance as the whole chicken is stuffed with mushrooms, pickled cabbage, onions and herbs, wrapped in lotus leaves, sealed in clay, and cooked slowly.

Sichuan food is heavy and spicy, a product of its isolation in central-western China, and its proximity to Yunnan Province and India, as well as its humid and clammy winters

(A–Z page 269). It was also Chairman Mao's favourite. Popular spices are star-anise, fennel seeds, black peppercorns, chillies and coriander. A large proportion of dishes are heavy on garlic and coated in thick sauces, and the food is often simmered or smoked rather than stir-fried or steamed. Like Shanghai and Beijing cuisine, breads, onion cakes and dumplings are favoured and noodles chosen over rice, except for the crispy rice *guoba* that is served along with rich sauces.

A popular starter is thin-sliced crispy beef flavoured with kumquat. The smoked duck takes a day to prepare, first marinated overnight in Chinese wine, cinnamon and coriander, then cooked over a fire of camphorwood chips and tea leaves. Foreigners like the braised spiced eggplant and the *mapo* chillied *tofu*.

Hunan food resembles Sichuanese and is often modified for more sensitive southern palates in Hong Kong (A–Z page 267). Hunan is the cuisine that features fried chillies as a side dish! It has a tasty mustard sauce to go with ducks' tongues, minced bean paste to go with fish and scallops, and a honey sauce for water chestnut dessert with cassia-flower cakes. Hunanese ham, served like Peking duck in thin pancakes, also has a distinctive honey glazing. There are many soup noodle combinations. Rice is the staple, as well as beancurd rolls, dumplings and savoury buns. Popular dishes include spicy vegetable rolls, cuttlefish with a dried pepper and spring onion sauce, mashed chicken soup with bamboo shoots, shredded eel with garlic, a beancurd dish of meat and chillies similar to Sichuanese *mapo tofu,* and bamboo shoots with preserved bean paste. Desserts include shredded yam and turnip cake, and a colourful 'lily and lotus' sweet.

Beijing cuisine combines influences from Sichuan, Shandong to the east and the far northeast regions of China (A–Z page 263). It makes good use of strong-flavoured roots and vegetables. It is generally thick and more sustaining, being designed to combat cold winters, and favours noodles, dumplings and baked breads over rice. Sizzling dishes are popular as are hotpot stews in winter. Common spices include peppers, garlic, fresh coriander—known as Chinese parsley—and ginger.

Peking duck is the eponymous favourite and takes a day to prepare when done properly, though some Hong Kong restaurants skimp on it and deep-fry rather than roast the bird. The duck should be coated with a syrup, air-dried and then roasted. When unveiled at the table, the crispy skin is carved and served with thin pancakes. These you make into a roll by adding raw spring onions or leeks, or sometimes cucumber, and fermented bean sauce. Later the meat can be sautéed with beansprouts and the bones turned into a soup mixed with Tientsin cabbage and sometimes milk.

Other favourites are cold meat starters, smoked fish, and chicken in rice-wine sauce. Fried onion cakes are a speciality, as are clear soups, steamed or grilled herring, and deep-fried sweet and sour fish. Meat dishes include shredded beef with chilli sauce, sizzling beef with spring onions, stir-fried pork with scrambled eggs, sautéed mutton with leeks, Tientsin cabbage with black mushrooms, casseroled beancurd, and shredded scallops with bamboo shoots, salted cabbage and walnuts. Favourite desserts are apple and banana fritters or mashed date pancakes.

OTHER ASIAN CUISINES

Other Asian cuisines, different in style and content from Chinese cooking, are easy to find in Hong Kong. Often the spicier dishes are subtly toned down for local and Western palates, and slowly but surely they show signs of adapting dishes to local tastes. Japanese fast food in Hong Kong bears an unmistakable Cantonese flavour to it. A Tokyo resident would barely recognize it.

Thai cuisine (A–Z page 273) is delicately spicy food characterized by coconut milk curries and chillied steamed fish. **Burmese** food (A–Z page 270) is equally strong but heavier. **Vietnamese** food (A–Z page 274) is also spicy, with shades of the French colonial influence. Spring rolls come wrapped in lettuce and mint, and are dipped in a clear chillied vinegar. **Filipino** food (A–Z page 270) has Spanish echoes, though it doesn't leave as strong an impression as other Asian food. It's not an upmarket cuisine in Hong Kong at all. **Indonesian** food (A–Z page 271) is a hybrid Southeast Asian cuisine influenced by Dutch settlers who introduced the multi-course *rijstaffel*. Malaysian and Singaporean food is basically a mix of Chinese and Indonesian.

The **Japanese** food in Hong Kong serves two communities (A–Z page 272). Authentic *sushi* and *sashimi* bars look after the growing Japanese expatriate population in Hong Kong while pseudo-Cantonese clones cater to the local desire for the delicate upmarket cuisine. The popular places often sound like any other local restaurant, compared to the quiet and intimacy of a typical Tokyo eating place. *Teppanyaki* bars have become popular recently, as have take-away *sushi* shops. **Korean** food (A–Z page 273) is very hot and spicy. A favourite is the hot-pot, as it is in **Mongolian** restaurants. **Indian** food (A–Z page 270) is popular as there is a large Indian community in Hong Kong. Most of the large restaurants serve a range of Indian regional dishes. Dotted around Central and Tsimshatsui are dozens of 'curry clubs' serving halal, Pakistani, Bengali, Sri Lankan and other regional specialities. These are cheap and cheerful places, usually charging around $50 for a set lunch and not much more for dinner.

VEGETARIAN (A–Z PAGE 270)

Vegetarian food has become voguish in recent years, the old places have spruced themselves up a lot and menus have become broader and a little more imaginative, while they were already good to start with. The staples are *tofu* beancurd and smashed taro. The beancurd is often shaped into replicas of different meats, but is a great source of protein in its own right and easily digestible. Vegetarian restaurants are good places to taste the wide variety of vegetables that Asia has to offer. A good place will use dozens of types of mushrooms, for example, from giant Japanese black mushrooms to Taiwanese baby button ones and local dried mushrooms. Salads are paradoxically very rare. Most dishes are cooked and starchy, usually stir-fried in the Cantonese style to retain the flavour or nutrients. Ordering can be a problem as English translations are often flowery and ornate, hiding rather than revealing the nature and ingredients of the dish. It's good to go with an aficionado, scrutinize the list of specials and consult the waiter.

RECOMMENDATIONS FOR A SHORT STAY ON A LIMITED BUDGET

Best Cantonese:	Some Like it Hot, Steam and Stew Inn, One Harbour Road Restaurant in the Grand Hyatt Hotel
Best Sichuan:	Fung Lam Szechuan
Best Shanghai:	Lao Ching Hing
Best *dim sum:*	Marriott Hotel
Best seafood:	Chuk Yuen
Best vegetarian:	Vegi Food Kitchen
Best Japanese:	Paper Moon
Best Indian:	Bombay Palace
Best Thai:	Thai Delicacy
Best Italian:	Grissini, Niccholini's, Capriccio
Best value lunch:	Pizzeria in the Kowloon Hotel
Most stylish hotel bar:	Champagne Bar in the Grand Hyatt
Most relaxing hotel bar:	Chinnery Bar in the Mandarin Oriental
Worst hotel bar atmosphere:	Dragon Bar in the Hilton
Best small bar in Central:	Le Jardin
Most pretentious bar in Central:	Post 97
Best beer in Central:	Finealley's, Schnurrbart
Best coffee shop:	Hilton Coffee Shop
Most relaxing coffee shop:	Mandarin Coffee Shop
Most exclusive lounge:	Clipper Lounge in the Mandarin Oriental
Best hotel view for cocktails:	Lobby lounge bar in the Regent
Best take-out pizza:	Marco Polo Pizza Gourmet
Best French bakery:	Point Chaud

RECOMMENDED RESTAURANTS
(A-Z PAGES 263-78)

Restaurants in Hong Kong can go in and out of fashion very quickly. Some are fêted because they are known to be exclusive and expensive, not because the food is radically better. Some very expensive restaurants provide quite mediocre service. Others remain consistently popular with foreigners because their cuisine is adapted to their tastes even if the food is less authentic. With price ranges and levels of opulence ranging so widely, recommendations will be restricted to a handful of places that have proven over the years to be consistently enjoyable, and to restaurants that have opened since 1990. Remember: you don't have to be rich or famous to eat like a king if you're searching for food rather than status points. Expect to pay around $200 per head without drinks as a rough average.

Hotel restaurants will offer a consistently high standard, but at higher prices. It's hard to be specific, but expect to pay at least US$100 per head in the finer spots. Smaller restaurants have a more authentic ambience. Generally, if you want something quiet, discreet and relaxed you will have to look for it. The *Gault Millau* guide to Hong Kong has an exhaustive section on restaurants and is highly recommended.

For **Cantonese** food the **Flower Lounge** restaurants in Mongkok and Wanchai and the two **Fook Lam Moon** branches in Causeway Bay and Tsimshatsui are highly praised up-market restaurants. **Lai Ching Heen** in the Regent is considered by Gault Millau to be the best restaurant in the colony, but the Cantonese restaurants in the Shangri-La, the Peninsula and the Mandarin Oriental are all rivals. For my money, better value by far is the **One Harbour Road Restaurant** in the Grand Hyatt Hotel. For a typical Chinese evening you can experiment with the **Ocean Palace Restaurant and Nightclub** which has three floorshows and cabaret every night or the similar **Ocean City Restaurant and Nightclub** (not to be confused with the seafood restaurant in the same building.)

If you want to try **nouvelle Cantonaise cuisine** in its up-market incarnation you should try **Zen** in Pacific Place, which is a popular yuppie hang out, or **Heichinrou** in Tsimshatsui.

The best simple but modern Cantonese food I have ever tasted is in the **Steam and Stew Inn** in Wanchai. On a par with this is **Some Like It Hot**, which actually bills itself as a Chinese restaurant and merges several styles and cuisines. A meal here should be around $250 per head, a third of the price or less than in the most expensive upmarket restaurants. The best Chinese vegetarian food is served at the **Vegi Food Kitchen** in Causeway Bay.

The other Cantonese restaurants listed in the A–Z section are generally priced at the lower end of this scale, a minimum of $200 per head. **Jade Garden** is part of a chain of regional Chinese cuisine restaurants offering consistency if not adventure. **North Park** is a good large restaurant in Tsimshatsui much favoured by a Japanese gourmand friend. The three **Flourishing** outlets in Tsimshatsui can also be recommended, as can the **Sunning Unicorn** and the delightfully-named **Boil and Boil Wonderful** in Causeway Bay, and **Tao Yuan** in Wanchai.

Chiu Chow food is served in the **Carriana** and **City Chiu Chow** chains throughout the main tourist districts. For a typical Hong Kong experience amid glowing pink tablecloths and pastel blue walls, try the **Harbour City Chiu Chow** in Causeway Bay. (A–Z page 266)

For **Beijing** food (A–Z page 263) the **American Restaurant** in Wanchai is an old expatriate favourite, as is the **Spring Deer** in Tsimshatsui. You can always fall back on the two **Peking Garden** outlets in Central and Causeway Bay. **Pine and Bamboo** in Causeway Bay makes a good Peking duck. **Hunan** food is only easily available at the **Hunan Garden** in Central (A–Z page 267). For **Sichuan** food, the **Cleveland** is very popular with expatriates, mainly because the food is sweeter here than elsewhere (A–Z page 269). **Pep 'N'Chilli**, **Sichuan Lau** and **The Red Pepper** are recommended on the island, **Fung Lam Szechuan** and **Prince Court Szechuan** in Tsimshatsui. **Shanghai** food (A–Z page 268) can be sampled at the **Great Shanghai** in Tsimshatsui or the **Shanghai Garden** in Central. **Lao Ching Hing** in Causeway Bay is very highly thought of. **Fung Lum** in Tsimshatsui is downmarket but serves excellent food, as does the nearby dumpling restaurant on Prat Avenue. Two popular **Taiwanese** restaurants (A–Z page 269) are the **Tin Tin Hot Pot** in Tsimshatsui and the **Ching Yip** and **Forever Green** in Causeway Bay.

Seafood can be taken at any of the places listed in the A–Z section (A–Z page 267), though the **Ocean City Seafood Restaurant** in the New World Centre in Tsimashatsui is well known. **Fat Siu Lau** and **Tin Tin Seafood Harbour** in Causeway Bay are personal favourites. If you have time to travel out of the city centre a bit it's well worth taking a ferry to **Sok Kwu Wan** village on Lamma island where there are half a dozen good seafood restaurants. Further afield in the New Territories you can try **Tap Mun** island, **Lau Fau Shan** and **Lei Yue Mun**, though there are good small restaurants by the wayside on **Cheung Chau** and **Lantau** also. Vegetarian food is served at my all-time favourite, the **Vegi Food Kitchen** in Causeway Bay. In Tsimshatsui the best place for Chinese vegetarian is the **Bodhi Vegetarian**, or the south Indian cooking of **Woodlands** (A–Z page 270).

The best **Indian** food in town (A–Z page 270) is served at the **Bombay Palace** in Admiralty. The **Tandoor** in Central also has a nice ambience. There are lots of cheap 'curry clubs' in the back streets of Tsimshatsui, Central and Wanchai, some of which are listed in the A–Z section. **Japanese** places (A–Z page 272) are more expensive than Chinese restaurants, especially those in the big hotels like Ginza, Sagano and Nadaman. The best food is to be had at the tiny **Paper Moon** in Causeway Bay. Also good is the **teppanyaki bar Hanagushi** in Central, a good lunch place. There was a big explosion of the locally-oriented outlets during the boom years of the 1980s, explained succinctly for me by one manager as 'small food, big profits'. It's well worth looking at one of these Cantonese-style places, and nowhere better than the **Sui Sha Ya** outlets in Causeway Bay and Tsimshatsui. Japanese fast food places are also now very common. Favourites are **Gomenbo** in Central, **Ganruku** in Wanchai, and **Ueno** and **Ah-So** in Tsimshatsui.

Everyone has their favourite **Thai** restaurant (A–Z page 273). Mine is the **Thai Kitchen** right in the heart of Causeway Bay, not least for the fact that they held a table for eight vacant for half an hour on a busy Friday night; the food is also excellent. There is a range of places in Central, like **Supatras** and **Silks**, favoured by expats, as are the **New Chili Club** and **Golden Poppy** in Wanchai. **Heng Thai** is authentic and downmarket—you can check your bags in at the airport and walk over the road for a last bite at one of several Thai eateries tucked behind the Regal Meridien Hotel. **Thai Delicacy** in Wanchai is also cheap. On the Kowloon side, try the **Golden Elephant** or **Sawadee**.

There are few places to find **Burmese** cuisine in Hong Kong any more. Try **Rangoon** in Causeway Bay (A–Z page 270). For **Indonesian**, go to the **Java Rijsttafel** in Tsimshatsui and in Causeway Bay (A–Z page 271). If you wish to eat **Malaysian** food make the exodus to **Cosmo** in Tai Po; reservations essential. **Vietnamese** (A–Z page 274) is best served at the expensive **Golden Bull** in Tsimshatsui, the equally expensive and busy **Paterson's**, the mid-priced **Perfume River** in Causeway Bay, or the cheap and adventurous **Professional Musicians Club** in Yaumatei. For **Korean**, try the **Arirang** in Tsimshatsui or Happy Valley, or the **Silla Won** in Central (A–Z page 273).

Hong Kong now has a good selection of **French** restaurants (A–Z page 275). My favourite's are **Le Tire Bouchon**, only seven tables but family-style cooking and very romantic, and **La Rose Noire**, both in Central. **Le Restaurant de France** is rated the best by Gault Millau, with prices to match, and **La Plume, Margaux, Pierrot** and **Gaddi's** come a close second. The **Verandah** in Repulse Bay is very pleasant for an evening out, or **Stanley's** a bit further afield.

Both **Grissini** in the Grand Hyatt and **Niccholini's** in the Conrad offer excellent **Italian** food (A–Z page 276). Italian restaurants outside of the hotels don't have any Italian speaking staff, from which you can draw your own conclusions. The latest high-class addition is **Capriccio** in the Ramada Renaissance in Tsimshatsui. **Grappa's** in Pacific Place, Admiralty, is a great lunch spot.

Of the **Western** and **Continental** restaurants **Michelle's** in Central has the nicest ambience, the **Mandarin Grill** has the prestige. **Mozart Stub'n** in Central has been popular for years and is a difficult place to get a table. Many people favour **Chesa**, featuring Swiss cuisine, in the Peninsula. Central is well favoured—many of these places fill up quickly after working hours—with **Dan Ryan's Chicago Grill**, **Duddell's** and **Landau's**. For an after-work drink, try **Brown's** in the heart of the financial district, the quickly popular **Asahi Super Dry**, or the discreet **Le Jardin** in Central (A–Z pages 277–8).

The best **late night food** is found at the **Shanghai Restaurant** on Prat Avenue in Tsimshatsui, which stays open until 3 am, **Tai Fat Hau** in Wanchai until 5 am, and the **Sui Sha Ya Japanese** restaurants in Causeway Bay and Tsimshatsui which are open until around 5.30 am.

Authentic **Chinese** cafés are many, but a favourite in Kowloon is the **Dumpling Shop** on Granville Rd in Tsimshatsui. A cheaper one nearby is the **Can Do Café** on Cameron Rd, also in Tsimshatsui. The most upmarket Chinese tea house is the **Luk Yu** in Stanley St which is almost impossible to get into around *dim sum* time without a personal recommendation from a family friend of the owner.

For **take-out pizza** rely on **Marco Polo Pizza Gourmet,** based in Central, and its delivery service. If you're dying for a take-out cup of coffee in Central, head for the **Point Chaud deli** in Chiu Lun St. If you have a craving for fine food, try **Oliver's** delicatessens in the Harbour Centre in Tsimshatsui or Prince's Building in Central. Oliver's also make sandwiches in special sandwich bars, one of which is in the bottom of Exchange Square at podium level facing the seafront, or there's **Birley's** in the Bond Centre in Admiralty. The Japanese department stores, particularly **Seibu** in Admiralty, have excellent food halls that serve take-away sushi. Fast food in **Gomenbo** in Central and **Ah-So** in Tsimshatsui can also be recommended (A–Z pages 281 and 272).

When in **Macau, A Lorcha** and **Riqueixo** are most authentic and pleasant experiences.

NIGHTLIFE

SIGHTS AND PROMENADES

There are several places around the harbour for unstrenuous but breathtaking evening walks. **Lugard Rd** around the Peak is an obvious choice. This walk overlooks the western harbour approaches and Lamma as well as the Kowloon peninsula and Tsimshatsui. **Bowen Rd** lower down the hill also offers good views of the harbour. Take a taxi to Stubb's Rd and walk back towards the Mid-Levels. From the western end you can walk down into Central via Cotton Tree Drive. The best waterfront promenade is outside the **Regent Hotel** in Tsimshatsui East which gives you a sparkling view of the advertising signs and skyscraper skyline of Hong Kong island.

WINE BARS AND PUBS (A–Z PAGE 278)

Contrary to its reputation, Hong Kong is not an exciting place for nightlife. Somehow, though it tries hard, Hong Kong is a big city on the south coast of China that just isn't as quirky as Tokyo, as vibrant as London, or as outrageous as New York. There is a dearth of upmarket exclusive winebars outside of the top-flight 'members only' clubs patronized by the colony's business leaders and society queens. The best is **Brown's** in the west wing of Exchange Square.

The best selection of draught beer in town is served in two German bars named **Schnurrbart** in D'Aguilar St, Central, and Hart St in Tsimshatsui. They serve three beers—a tart-tasting Jever, the fruitier Warsteiner and sweeter Konig—which can take ten minutes to arrive but are worth the wait. The menu offers appropriate North-European food like rollmops in sour cream with fried potatoes. **Finealley** on Glenealy above Central also serves excellent Munich-brewed Erdinger weissbier and good home-made food. In Tsimshatsui try the **Biergarten**.

The trendiest place to be seen in Central is still the back street of Lan Kwai Fong. This has been popular for over a decade and in any normal city would have died a slow death by now, but Hong Kong is a small place and Lan Kwai Fong seems to go from strength to strength, recycling old ideas and hosting new ones, usually only briefly. **Café 97** takes on a kind of bohemian air after dark serving cocktails as readily as cappuccinos. It has the worst service in the colony. **California** just around the corner has a long bar and a salad bench. Outside of Lan Kwai Fong the latest fad is the **Asahi Super Dry** bar in Admiralty.

The best new bar in Central is **Le Jardin**, tucked away on a terrace a stone's throw from Lan Kwai Fong. Unpretentious and not so packed, it really is a pleasant surprise. Also good is **The Jazz Club,** which is excellent value during happy hour before the band begins.

Other bars attempt national themes with a variety of success. The **Cactus Club** in Lan Kwai Fong serves Mexican beers like Sol and Dos Equis with a good range of snacks. **La Bodega** in Wyndham St is a Spanish-style tapas bar and aims at the salaried market wearing ties. **Mad Dogs**, now re-located futher down the hill on Wyndham St, is less pretentious and very popular with the Scots and Brits. It serves gassy British Bass as well as the ubiquitous Carlsberg, and pub grub like steak and kidney pie. **Joe Bananas** in Wanchai is a sister to Mad Dogs and has slightly more upmarket decor and prices. Other English pub clones include the **Bull & Bear** in Hutchison House, Admiralty, and the **Friar Tuck** in Ice House St in Central, both drearily tasteless and packed with office workers drinking yet more Carlsberg. The grottiest bar in Central is a teenage haunt called **Thingummy's** which has an anarchic jukebox, a smashed urinal and a price list that rates a scotch plus a Carlsberg a mere $30. The back streets of Tsimshatsui and Lockhart Rd in Wanchai host many other seedier joints that are easy to find and quite dull.

Happy hour runs in most bars between 5 pm and 7 pm, though a few places start earlier and even end later. Most offer two drinks for the price of one, but a few like **Café 97** offer reduced prices instead. Here a glass of rather insipid champagne comes down to $17 and a cappuccino to $11.

Hotel bars can be, at best, anonymous, though heaven help anyone seeking to keep a liaison clandestine for very long in one of Hong Kong's major hotels. They score for convenience and decor, which is not the same as atmosphere. The **Captain's Bar** in the Mandarin serves the best margaritas, insists on jackets and ties for men and will even offer you one if you're bereft on arrival. It's open until 2 am, unlike **The Chinnery** on the first floor which closes by 9 pm but which is probably the most relaxing bar in town, furnished with plush red leather seats carefully partitioned off into booths. It also has what must be the largest collection of malt whiskys of any bar in Hong Kong. The **Dragon Boat Bar** on the reception level in the Hilton is a businessman's rendezvous favourite but a bit of a bear garden until early evening when it goes completely dead. The **Dicken's Bar** in the Excelsior is downmarket as well as subterranean. The most upmarket is without doubt the **Champagne Bar** in the Grand Hyatt Hotel in Wanchai. There are two rooftop bars worth investigating, the **Sky Lounge** in the Sheraton in Tsimshatsui and The **Talk of the Town** in the Excelsior in Causeway Bay. The view from the Victoria Hotel in Sheung Wan is also fabulous when the weather's good. **Revolving 66** on top of the Hopewell Centre in Wanchai is the highest, but it's not a nice place. Actually it's on the 62nd floor. It's called 'Revolving 66' because it takes 66 minutes to complete one revolution.

On the Kowloon side the classiest place for a drink is the **Lobby Bar** in the Regent Hotel. Perhaps the quietest is the **Sky Lounge** in the Nikko Hotel in Tsimshatsui East, the most discreet the first floor bar in the west wing of the Peninsula Hotel. The noisiest is the packed and Westerner-favoured **Someplace Else** in the basement of the Sheraton Hotel on Nathan Rd. The most tasteless by a long chalk is **Bottom's Up**, where tired bar girls bare their air-chilled breasts for jaded businessmen. The maddest is **Ned Kelly's Last Stand** which has a live and eccentric band of traditional jazz stompers playing nightly.

Bars with girls are one of Hong Kong's biggest rip-offs, unless you are a student of the Asian female underclass that works the few tired joints left in the former red light district of Wanchai. Those left over from the 1960s are situated on Lockhart Rd or its side streets. The most famous is the **An-An Bar**. These places are full of tricks, especially when your eyes are not at their best at focussing; extra drinks chits appear on the tally and the girl's champagne tastes suspiciously like fizzy sugar-water. **Bottom's Up** in Tsimshatsui claims its fame from a long-ago James Bond movie when the ace spy was still the debonair Sean Connery and had a First Class degree in Oriental languages from Cambridge. How times change.

Karaoke took off in Hong Kong around 1988 but it isn't the wildly drunken and uninhibited riot it is in Japan. **Canton East** in Tsimshatsui East is by far the biggest and most access-ible, though others have been springing up everywhere, includ-ing one in Wanchai that grandly styles itself the **Karaoke de St. Encore**. They are generally interesting in inverse propor-tion to the gaucheness of their names and are very popular with large groups of Chinese office workers. **Video parlours** haven't caught on here, unlike Taiwan where unlicensed video rooms serve as cosy love nests for forlorn teenagers. **Canton** disco shows some videos but the best bar with videos is the mezzanine bar in **Hot Gossip**. Both are on Canton Rd in Tsimshatsui.

Hong Kong has only one international-class casual live music venue: **The Jazz Club** in D'Aguilar St, Central. Since it opened in 1989, the Jazz Club has hosted tenor sax legends Johnny Griffin and Archie Shepp, the great blues artist Jimmy Witherspoon, Australian trumpeter James Anderson and a host of other big names. This is one of the few places in the world where you're ever going to have a chance to listen to these names in a small club atmosphere and get to buy them a drink at the bar afterwards. Prices for guest artist shows range from $150 to $300, though both the house band and the adjacent bar demand no entry fee. Live jazz is also played by a large, raucous ensemble on the first Sunday of every month in the **Dicken's Bar** in the basement of the Excelsior Hotel in Causeway Bay, and nightly in the crowded atmosphere of **Ned Kelly's Last Stand** in Tsimshatsui by a small energetic ensemble. Folk music is played nightly at **Hardy's** on D'Aguilar St in Central.

Hong Kong is edging slowly into the international mega-concert circuit with big-name stars like David Bowie, Elton John and Kenny G playing sell-out performances in the huge

and soulless **Hong Kong Coliseum** during Asian tours. Check
with the HKTA for details when you arrive.

CLUBS (A-Z PAGE 287)

Hong Kong's wealthy businessmen often spend their expense account time in a variety of **Chinese hostess clubs**.
Wanchai and Tsimshatsui East are the two main areas for this
style of nightclub, characterized by crassly ornate interiors and
cute girls with walkie-talkies who will charge their time to your
credit card at the table whilst you sit and chat. In a sense, these
places are just glorified taxi-dance halls, gone upmarket and
offering XO cognac rather than VSOP. Some have cabaret
floorshows, but most don't.

The most famous is **Club Boss** in Tsimshatsui East. This
was known as the 'Club Volvo' for many years until it changed
its name following a rumoured out-of-court settlement with
the tough Swedish car manufacturer. When it opened in 1984,
within days of the signing of the Sino-British Joint Declaration
that supposedly guarantees Hong Kong's future after it is handed over to the Chinese communists in 1997, a leading cadre
from the north proposed a toast to its success, thus firmly
cementing in people's minds the link between power and the
enjoyment of wealth irrespective of ideology.

Next door is the **China City Nightclub** which is much
the same thing, alcohol-induced hilarity and sequinned girls in
fake ball gowns propping up drunken Korean businessmen at
two in the morning who have just paid to take them out. A
friend who worked the rounds of the clubs—the girls usually
circulate every few months to stop appearing too familiar—
told me the record earnings for a girl in a single month was
$300,000, so obviously they're quite busy at all hours. There
seems to be no end to the growth of these luxury clubs. Newer
ones like **Club Metropolitan** in the Chinachem Plaza will continue to try to outdo all the others in opulence.

In Wanchai, try the **New Tonnochy Nightclub** for a
similar atmosphere. There's a slightly more old-fashioned
'taxi-dance' feel about the Wanchai establishments, but for
an outsider there isn't much to shake between them. Expect to
part with at least $1,000 for a casual investigation of this side

of Cantonese culture. The **Ocean City Restaurant & Night-club** and the **Ocean Palace Restaurant & Nightclub** in Tsimshatsui both have cabaret shows.

Discos come and go like fashions (A–Z page 263). In early 1992 the hippest place in town was **JJ's**, a labyrinthine multi-level disco-bar in the Grand Hyatt hotel in Wanchai that once refused admission to guitarist Eric Clapton because he was wearing trainers. Despite this ferocious policy it can be difficult to get inside as midnight nears on a Saturday night. A few years ago **Canton** was all the rage when singer Maria Cordeiro held court waiting for her break to stardom. Now she's gone, and the crowds have gone with her. The place feels like a deserted aircraft hanger in mid-week, attended only by a few Chinese teenagers. In Admiralty, try the recently-opened **LA Café** in the Lippo Centre. Hong Kong's own version of acidhouse, the Depot, also closed after a brief but exciting life in Western.

Most of the other discos are clumped around Lan Kwai Fong, Wyndham St and D'Aguilar St in Central. **Club 97**, the latest incarnation of the downstairs section of the ironically-named 1997, looks like a torture den for would-be sub mariners and probably won't last long in this guise. **California** has a small dance floor and is more of a restaurant than a disco. **Disco Disco** used to be Hong Kong's premier gay haunt but has recently been refurbished and may have taken on a new lifestyle with it. Try the **Yin Yang Club** in Ice House St in Central instead, or **Club Berlin** in Lan Kwai Fong.

The hotels have their own discos which tend to be less raucous and less exciting. The pick are **Faces** in the New World, the **Falcon** in the Royal Garden, **Hollywood East** in the Regal Meridien, all of which are in Tsimshatsui East. The **Starlight** in the Park Lane Radisson and **Talk of the Town** in the Excelsior are the best on Hong Kong island.

Saunas and massage parlours both clean and dubious can be found easily in the tourist areas (A–Z page 288). These are all single-sex, not mixed. There's been an explosion of saunas in the past three years mainly on the Lockhart Rd strip in Wanchai. One of the best is the **New Paradise Health Club** where the very few gweilos are assumed to be policemen and where you can lounge in the hot pool alongside tattooed triads temporarily without their portable phones. Mongkok has many yellow and purple signs advertising massage-related services, but the glitzier ones are quite straightforward. One might question the tenderness of the process, which is not one of the great Chinese arts or a Bangkok-style performance, but a genuine back massage performed by a diminutive Chinese lady walking up and down your vertebrae in semi-darkness whilst supporting most of her weight from a pair of poles is an experience worth relating. The noise (and sensation) of popping bones as she digs her toes into your back to crack your vertebrae or rearrange you neck is unforgettable.

Massage usually means just that. The **New Paradise** mentioned above gave me a male masseur when the US Seventh fleet was in port just in case I got confused where I was and what services I was buying. An hour's massage with a sauna and dips in the hot and cold plunge pools will run to $250–500, depending on the elaborateness of the interior decoration. An untimed dip in the pools and sauna is around $100. Most places stay open until the early hours, around 4–5 am. The **Sunny Paradise Club** on Lockhart Rd is a good place to start.

Short-time hotels can be found in many places in the colony, though they in no way match Japanese love hotels in comfort, decor, fantasy or imagination. Up-market are the **San Diego Hotel** in Morrison Hill Rd in Wanchai, and its other branch in Canton Rd, Tsimshatsui. Waterloo Rd and the back streets near Kowloon Tong also have several rows of love hotels which will even discreetly cover your car number plate whilst you're inside. The down market short-stay places are always found closer to the bars and are usually, like **The White House** in Wanchai Rd, tucked away on the upper storey of a residential tenement block.

Early-morning food can be hard to find after the hotel coffee shops close at midnight. Late openers until 2 am are the **Hilton** and the **Victoria Hotel**. The China City night club chain has partially solved the problem by opening a two branches of a Japanese restaurant called **Sui Sha Ya**, strictly laid out in Cantonese style, in Wanchai and Tsimshatsui.

These stay open until 6 am. Fast food places like the **American Café** stay open all night, as do the 7-**Eleven** stores which usually have micro-waveable *dim sum* on the premises.

Finally, as an antidote to all this high living, the best of the **hotel health clubs** is in the **Island Shangri-La** which has a great outdoor pool and jacuzzi overlooking the Citibank Plaza, a magnificent spectacle at night. The **Hilton** is also convenient on the Hong Kong side, whilst the **New World** in Tsimshatsui and the **Victoria** in Sheung Wan have great poolside views of the harbour.

WALKS

Leave the urban shopping malls behind for a while. Hong Kong's best-kept secret is its hilly countryside, the furthest ripples of the great Asian mountain chain that stretches from southern China up into the mighty Himalaya. Though they never rise above 1,000 metres —around 3,000 feet— the hills here offer some excellent limb-stretching walks that are challenging all year round and even a bit dangerous in the height of summer when the unprepared risk dehydration and sunburn. Hong Kong has 21 designated Country Parks, so there's plenty of choice, and despite the urban sprawl there are almost two plant species growing here for every square kilometre of land. It would take a dedicated walker more than a year of weekends to traverse all of the colony's major walks. Many parks are readily accessible by public transport.

As anywhere in the world, it pays to be prepared and exercise common sense when venturing into the hills, however slight they seem and however blue the skies. A checklist should include the relevant **map** in the government's Countryside Series, available at government bookshops; a pair of stout shoes; several litres of **water** for each hiker, especially during the hot months of July and August; suntan lotion; adequate sun protection for the neck and the knees; a sun hat; and small change for bus fares or a taxi home.

Try and start as early as possible in the morning to avoid the hordes and the heat. Plan your walk so the sun isn't on your back all day and be prepared to rest for an hour or two in the middle of a hike at the height of summer. The best time of year is the autumn, from September through November. Clear days during the winter are fine, but the peak of summer from June through August is strictly for the hardy. The sun can be very fierce in Hong Kong. I have tried to indicate the degree of difficulty and time required for most of the following walks. These are only estimates: check the map before you go. Water catchment paths are handy to walk on but watch out for the snakes sunning themselves in the early morning. Paths marked as indistinct on the maps are in many cases indistinguishable from the surrounding scrub. Rely only on the major ones which are usually easily traceable, though rarely marked with paint, stones or cairns.

Hong Kong has two major trails. The **Hong Kong Trail** traverses Hong Kong Island and is marked with yellow signposts throughout its length. The New Territories has a much longer trail, the 100km **MacLehose Trail**, named after a former governor. This is about forty hours of hard walking in conditions ranging from easy to strenuous. As the trail is divided into ten stages you can do them at different times. It is possible to do the trail from start to finish in three days, but five is more realistic.

HONG KONG ISLAND

LUGARD RD–HARLECH RD:
MAP 1 IN THE 'COUNTRYSIDE SERIES'

This is the standard stroll around **the Peak**. From the Peak Tram terminus this light walk on a level path provides magnificent views overlooking both sides of the island. It can be taken either east–west from Central towards Pokfulam, or vice versa. At around three kilometres, it is a 45-minute stroll. It has several variations. Coming around on the Lugard Rd side you'll pass a sitting-out area in the saddle between Victoria Peak and High West, the hill on the right-hand side. Look on the left for a path known as **Governor's Walk**; this edges up the hillside where it divides and rejoins Mt. Austin Rd. It is possible at the beginning of Governor's Walk to divert down the hill along **Hatton Rd**, past an old battery point and a stone boundary pole marked 'City Boundary 1903' before joining Conduit Rd in the Mid-Levels above Hong Kong University. This is a steep two-kilometre walk on concrete. More exciting is **Harlech Rd** that veers left and downhill at the point where Hatton Rd veers right. This skirts High West leading to a lookout point next to some electricity pylons. From there follow the **Hong Kong Trail** signs left along the hillside. Above the reservoir the trail turns left hugging the contour. An alternative cuts down towards the reservoir itself leaving either a stiff uphill walk back up to Peak Rd or a short one down to Pokfulam Rd. A detour up the steep incline of **High West** is also possible. You can also walk up **Mt Austin Rd** to the very top of the hill and then down towards Central from the Peak by following **Findley Rd** to **Barker Rd** and then left down **Chatham Path** opposite house #15. An interesting walk around **Severn Rd** leads to a path just east of house #20 that cuts down through the underbrush to the petrol station on Peak Rd. Buses run up to the Peak from Causeway Bay (#15B) and HMS Tamar (#15), and to Conduit Rd (#13) from Central. Green minibus #1 runs from Tamar up the Peak.

BOWEN RD:
MAP 1 IN THE COUNTRYSIDE SERIES

This level walk above Wanchai is about 4km from Magazine Gap Rd to Stubbs Rd overlooking Happy Valley; around 1.5 hours for an out-and-back walk past Lover's Rock. It is a good access point for Wanchai Gap from which several good walks lead in different directions.

WANCHAI–ABERDEEN:
MAP 1 IN THE COUNTRYSIDE SERIES

Follow **Wanchai Gap Rd** from a point on Queen's Rd East opposite Tai Yuen St. This crosses Bowen Rd and climbs to Wanchai Gap before leading in half a dozen directions. Looking directly opposite, that is south towards Aberdeen, you have the following choices: (I) the left lane leading up **Black's Link** towards Wong Nei Chong Gap Rd; (II) the second left-hand road, and then bearing left, which rises along **Middle Gap Rd** to **Lady Clementi's Ride** and then forks either left to Wong Nei Chong Gap or right to Aberdeen Reservoir Rd and on to Aberdeen or the Peak; or (III) bearing left on the level road directly in front of you that brings you directly onto **Aberdeen Reservoir Rd** with the option of a left turn onto Lady Clementi's Ride.

WANCHAI GAP–PEEL RISE–THE PEAK:
MAP 1 IN THE COUNTRYSIDE SERIES

This is a fine circular walk that takes a few hours. Enter Aberdeen Reservoir Rd from Wanchai Gap and turn right onto the **Hong Kong Trail** by the information point pavilion. The route follows the contour for about three kilometres until it hits **Peel Rise** where a right turn brings you uphill beneath Mt Kellett and onto Peak Rd. Instead, take a left turn and go down Peel Rise for half a kilometre before taking a signposted right-hand path back on to the Hong Kong Trail. This is a footpath for about one-and-a-half kilometres before it veers right to follow the contour along a tarmacked section. Here you can follow the road, or turn left just before a stream after about 200 meters onto a footpath called the **Hacking Trail**. This shadows the road, recrosses it, climbs a small hillside and redoubles back to join the Hong Kong Trail. From this point you have the option of turning right towards Pokfulam Reservoir Rd and the Peak, or left towards Pokfulam Rd.

WANCHAI GAP–WONGNEICHONG GAP:
MAP 1 IN THE 'COUNTRYSIDE SERIES'

The way past two peaks in the centre of the island—Mount Cameron and Mount Nicholson—has many routes. **Black's Link** is the most direct route. More scenic is **Middle Gap Rd** to the south which cuts left to pick up the **Hong Kong Trail**. You can make a similar traverse lower down the hill and then follow **Lady Clementi's Ride** until it hits the top of Nam Fung Rd above Deepwater Bay or doubles back to Black's Link ending by a brace of expensive apartment blocks.

WONGNEICHONG GAP–TAI TAM PARK:
MAP 1 IN THE 'COUNTRYSIDE SERIES'

This pass which cuts across the centre of Hong Kong island is the starting point for a series of great walks in and around Tai Tam Reservoir. Though 1.6 million people live within a few minutes' ride, summer afternoons can be spent here without meeting more than a handful of them on the path. Most locals seem content to reach the ridge without descending into the park and the reservoir. Start by the Shell petrol station at the top of **Wong Nei Chong Gap Rd** by taking any one of the buses # 6, 61, 64, 262 or 15 going to Stanley, or minibus #5 from Causeway Bay MTR station. The big house opposite, #1 Repulse Bay Rd is owned by Macau casino magnate, Stanley Ho.

Route (I) rises past the hideous-pink Parkview estate and descends towards the reservoir down the concrete road. Turn left over the bridge at the slender end of the reservoir, and left again onto Mount Parker Road. This leads around the knoll on the right-hand side, left over the dam, and left again to rise up from the base of Mount Parker to crest the ridge at **Quarry Gap**. From here you can take a 30-minute walk into Quarry Bay, or turn left along a well-marked path which climbs the steep side of **Mount Butler** before following the ridge past a quarry to **Jardine's Lookout** and back to Wong Nei Chong Gap. This path is exceptionally beautiful in the late afternoon as the sun dips behind Central.

Route (II) to **Stanley** leads off to the right from the bottom of Wong Nei Chong Reservoir, the little catchment area on the way up the hill towards Parkview, and then alongside a catch-water on a track called **Tsz Lo Lan Path** in the direction of Repulse Bay. This path gives some good views of Repulse Bay before hugging the contour to drop down after 3 kilometres towards Tai Tam Intermediate Reservoir. (You can also get to this point by turning right just before the bridge over Tai Tam Reservoir, instead of crossing and turning left up Mount Parker Rd, and then following the water catchment. Alternatively, take a pretty wooded climb up **Violet Hill** starting just below Parkview.) From this point, marked **Tsin Shui Wan Au**, you can cut down to Repulse Bay, continue on to Stanley via another catchment path, or make a 300-metre climb over the top of **the Twins**, or carry on all the way around the series of peaks to the southern end of Tai Tam Tuk Reservoir and Tai Tam Rd. This walk takes about an hour and a half.

Route (III) towards **Shek O** heads right at the point where the path joins Mount Parker Rd. Alternatively you can take a detour to cross the high dam, then double back to cross Tai Tam Reservoir Rd which is simply an extension of Mt Parker Rd within the country park. From this point there is an easy walk down to the main Tai Tam Rd. A much more enjoyable walk is to pick up the Hong Kong Trail again. This crosses the main road a bit further north and goes directly onto another water catchment path that snakes south above a series of villages until it reaches the 'Hobie Cat' club at **To Tei beach** where you can get a drink and some noodles. A walk from the starting point at the Parkview to To Tei beach takes about three hours of dawdling on a hot day. From here it's just 15 minutes back to a bus-stop on Shek O Rd where bus #9 runs back to Shaukeiwan MTR. The adventurous should nonetheless continue up onto the ridge. From here you can bear right and follow a path that recrosses Shek O Rd near a quarry before leading down to **Shek O beach** which you can see in the distance. Even better is to turn north up the **Dragon's Back** for a walk that offers excellent views of the islands on the Pacific Ocean side, including Big Wave Bay which marks the end of the Hong Kong Trail. Deer sometimes scamper on the skyline on the route from Tai Long Wan to Siu Sai Wan. After about one-and-a-half kilometres the path veers left down another clearly marked path before meandering back through woodland towards **Tai Tam Gap**. A more overgrown path suitable only for the hardy walker follows the rise up to **Mount Collinson** and then down again to **Pottinger Gap**. This last section takes about one hour in the late afternoon.

NORTH POINT–QUARRY BAY–ALDRICH BAY: MAP 1 IN THE 'COUNTRYSIDE SERIES'

For a fine set of walks overlooking North Point with splendid views of the airport, take the green minibus #24M from Admiralty MTR, or bus #11 from Central, to Jardine's Lookout. From the top of **Mount Butler Rd**, bear left past the quarry until the road snakes between two large aerials. Turn left onto **Sir Cecil's Ride** a walk of about 5.5 kilometres until it rejoins the tarmacked path leading down from the saddle at Quarry Gap. You can get off this path a bit earlier by dropping down to **Braemar Hill** near the information point. You can extend Sir Cecil's Ride by skirting **Mount Parker** to the north, ending up eventually on Tai Tam Rd. The route here is not very easy. It is slightly easier to cut up above Shaukeiwan to the road leading to the top of Mount Parker, past General Rock, and after reaching the summit to head down towards Tai Tam Rd, either via the road that begins next to the electricity pylon above the main road, or by turning right onto the longer path a few metres before it.

NEW TERRITORIES

THE LION ROCK:
MAP 6 IN THE 'COUNTRYSIDE SERIES'

The obvious place to start in the New Territories is the Lion Rock ridge that overlooks the whole of Kowloon, the airport and Hong Kong island. Access is poor if you're using public transport so it's best to take a taxi. Path (I) is very steep. It leads up from east of the Lion Rock Tunnel entrance and is best reached either by getting out at the Lok Fu MTR station, walking north to Lung Cheung Rd, then heading right towards Lion Rock Upper Village, or by taking KMB bus #11C to the Chuk Yuen Estate from close to the Choi Hung MTR. Path (II) curves up leftwards from the first bend on Shatin Pass Rd underneath several electricity pylons and then directly onto the ridge. Path (III) is actually **Shatin Pass Rd** which climbs steeply to reach Shatin Pass. You can take a detour off to the right near the top to visit a Kwun Yam temple.

At the top the route west follows the signposts of the MacLehose Trail on the northern side of the mountain, re-joining the ridge only on the western side of **Lion Rock.** A secondary path leads to the summit, back to the trail and on to **Beacon Hill.** You can come off the ridge at this point down a winding road, but the transport access at the bottom isn't very good. It's better to continue on the trail which forks north and south of the **Eagle's Nest** before crossing the old Tai Po Rd. If you go east from the top of Shatin Pass Rd the route follows the road beneath **Tate's Ridge.** An exit right comes down Jat's Incline into the Choi Wan Estate area from where you can catch the MTR at Choi Hung. Buses #90, 91, 92 & 93R from Choi Hung stop near Fei Ngo Shan.

KAM SHAN COUNTRY PARK:
MAP 6 IN THE 'COUNTRYSIDE SERIES'

There are literally dozens of walks around this park which lies at the Kwai Chung end of Lion Rock ridge. It is very popular in good weather with several easy family strolls and a host of noisy barbeque pits. The central valley holds four reservoirs and looks eastwards down towards Shatin. The ridge walk from Lion Rock, which follows the MacLehose Trail signs, rises along a concrete roadway from the old Tai Po Rd through some woods until it tucks itself in on the western side of **Smugglers' Ridge**. A secondary path follows this to Smugglers' Pass before dipping to the other side of the watershed beneath the Jubilee Reservoir dam. There are dozens of paths criss-crossing this park, so make your own choices here. The main path on the MacLehose Trail comes down above the dam over the **Shing Mun Redoubt** where Hong Kong's volunteer army was cut down in December 1941 vainly trying to prevent the advance of Japanese troops. Access is a problem again here so continue left on the road circling the reservoir for about 1.5 kilometres until you reach the top of Shing Mun Rd and the Visitor Park where buses and minibuses call at weekends. If you want to start from the old Tai Po Rd, take bus #71 northbound from Jordan Rd (or southbound from Shatin) and get off between milestones 51 and 52. Bus #72 also goes along this road from Tai Kok Tsui in west Kowloon.

SHING MUN COUNTRY PARK:
MAP 6 IN THE 'COUNTRYSIDE SERIES'

The top of Shing Mun Rd by Pineapple Dam can be reached by bus #32 from Tsuen Wan pier or by taxi. This is the best jumping off point for a series of short and long walks in the Shing Mun Country Park to the north of Kam Shan Country Park. These are some of the best in the New Territories, and include several circular routes. A simple reservoir walk is about five kilometres. On the west side it follows a path before joining a small road that crosses a stream. Take the right-hand fork to cross a second stream before dropping right again about one kilometre further on onto a marked path that hugs the shoreline of the reservoir before rejoining the road just above the main dam. More energetic is the six-kilometre hike from the dam to **Needle Hill** which includes a climb of over 300 metres. This passes along the ridge and gives fine views on both sides, east to Shatin and west over the reservoir. This path dips and rises maybe another 350 metres in all until it reaches **Grassy Hill**. From here you can go east towards Shatin by following your nose, remembering to bear right as you go downhill, which will bring you out above Fo Tan KCR station after about 4.5 kilometres. If you continue on the trail from Grassy Hill it veers west and drops down about 250 metres to **Leadmine Pass** less than one kilometre away. If you follow the road downhill, and take a right turn at the first fork, you'll pass an information map. Here the MacLehose Trail turns right towards **Tai Mo Shan**. However, a few metres further on a road to the left leads back down to the reservoir while the right-hand road leads back uphill and into the woods. Alternatively, visit the **Shing Mun Arboretum** by heading towards the reservoir and taking a left turn about one kilometre down the way; look out for the information signs. There is another route running north from Leadmine Pass down to the Tolo Highway and an occasional minibus calling at San Uk Ka. The adventurous can make their way across this section with the map into the **Tai Po Kau Nature Reserve.**

The easiest way into the nature reserve is to alight at the parking area at milestone 49 on the old Tai Po Rd after taking any one of the buses #70, 70K, 72, 72A, or 72B; there are also minibuses passing along this way. The reserve is well laid out with maps by the entrance. It has four walks ranging in length from three to ten kilometres , plus a short nature trail.

TAI MO SHAN:
MAP 6 IN THE 'COUNTRYSIDE SERIES'
The ascent of **Tai Mo Shan** (957 m) can be made from Shing Mun Rd via Leadmine Pass on a 14-kilometre hike which includes a 550-metre climb between six and ten kilometres, and then an easy drop down to Route Twisk onto a tarmacked road from the wireless station on the summit. Going in this direction, westwards, the sun will be dropping during the latter part of the climb to the peak and you can watch it going

down as you descend. To go the other direction, get off bus #51M from Tsuen Wan MTR at the recreation and information area after milestone 12 on Route Twisk. The summit is 450 metres above you. This west–east route is easier to walk. Once you've reached the summit there is only the small climb from Leadmine Pass to Grassy Hill. However, walking in the opposite direction is more spectacular as the sun often sets spectacularly across Tsuen Wan's container terminals with Lantau island in the distance. Going west–east you could continue from Grassy Hill to Fo Tan KCR station for a truly heroic cross-colony hike with only a 700-metre climb. If you do it the other way the sun will be on your back all day and you'll climb more than 1,100 metres.

TAI LAM COUNTRY PARK:
MAP 2 IN THE 'COUNTRYSIDE SERIES'

This is isolated countryside. As the MacLehose Trail moves west, it gently drops another 22.5 kilometres to its finishing point in Tuen Mun. During this leg you can cut off the path to either side, south to Castle Peak Rd or north across the fields towards Kam Sheung Rd and the Vietnamese refugee camp on Shek Kong airfield. These are all long walks and not very accessible for most people to get to in the first place, though the march down to **Tai Lam Chung reservoir** is very impressive and isolated. The well-marked **Kap Lung Forest Trail** leads west from the information point on Route Twisk down to Shek Kong village. **Ho Pui reservoir**, which can be reached from the same starting point and then by turning left off the trail near an isolated information point, is wonderfully peaceful. The walk around the reservoir and back to Shek Kong can take four or five hours as the route is not direct.

MA ON SHAN COUNTRY PARK:
MAP 4 IN THE 'COUNTRYSIDE SERIES'

The massive ridge that dominates this park divides Shatin from Sai Kung and is the most inspiring ridge walk in the colony. You can make the journey all the way on the MacLehose Trail. There are several points of access, though it's best to approach them by taxi rather than by public transport. If you've already climbed onto the Lion Rock ridge from Shatin Pass Rd, take a left turn here and follow the trail's signs to the road where Jat's Incline turns right. The road cuts under Tate's Cairn towards Tung Shan allowing you to walk on to **Kowloon Peak**, or to follow the road which becomes Fei Ngo Shan Rd leading down to Clearwater Bay Rd. The latter isn't a very appealing walk. The MacLehose Trail actually cuts north a bit earlier by the Jat's Incline turning, dropping down to follow the contour under Tate's Pass to the north, and rising over the saddle to cut past **Buffalo Hill** before rising to the reach pass at around 450 metres. This is about a six-kilometre walk from Shatin Pass Rd. From here you can cut south towards Hiram's Highway four kilometres away or continue on the ridge. The trail meanders along barely rising to **Pyramid Hill** another three kilometres further on, finally cresting the ridge again to the north and rising about 200 metres in all before turning sharply right and heading for **Shui Long Wo**. From here it is steep downhill walking for one kilometre and then a gentle walk for another four kilometres.

Thus far is 16 kilometres, but it's worth taking the detour to the top of **Ma On Shan**, the fourth highest in the colony at 702 metres, though the last 150 metres up is a stiff climb for tired limbs. The view to the north is marred by new housing developments stretching around the coast from Shatin and the huge camp for 40,000 would-be Vietnamese refugees at Whitehead that looks positively menacing. The trouble with Ma On Shan is there is no quick way off the mountain if the weather deteriorates or if you're tired. If you need to exit quickly, continue north and follow the ridge as it curves left, which will eventually bring you down. If you want to walk east-west along the MacLehose Trail, take the #99 bus from Sai Kung and get off at a campsite about one kilometre after the road takes a lefthand turn at a roundabout.

SAI KUNG EAST COUNTRY PARK: MAP 4 IN THE 'COUNTRYSIDE SERIES'

This area is also remote but well served by bus #93R from Choi Hung (Sundays and holidays only, last bus 7.30 pm) and #94 which runs hourly on the hour from Sai Kung, which both disgorge their load of trippers at **Pak Tam Chung**. This is the beginning of the MacLehose Trail. A circular route back to the bus stop is roughly 23 kilometres long, a six- or seven-hour walk in hot weather. It follows the access road for almost one third of its route round to the two main dams of High Island reservoir, dropping to Long Ke Wan beach, then climbing steadily to a 300-metre ridge. It calls in at two more beaches, then cuts across the Tai Long peninsula before regaining Pak Tam Rd. This is exhausting in hot weather. Two opportunities to drop out exist about halfway around which cut the total length of the walk by about a third. However, this means taking Sai Kung Sai Wan Rd, a hot walk on concrete, not on natural paths. Other walks extend to the furthermost extremities of **General Rock** and **Fung Head** but add about another five to eight kilometres. The waves here are magnificent as they come rolling in unimpeded from across the Pacific. Some expats and locals surf here in the summer, renting the tiny cottages in these deserted hamlets for around $2,000 a year.

The **Tap Mun ferry** calls in at several deserted piers along this wild coastline, at **Kau Lau Wan, Sha Tau** (also known as Chek Keng) and at **Wong Shek** twice a day. The morning boat leaves the pier at Ma Liu Shui (a short walk from the Chinese University KCR station) at 7.25 am and calls in at these small piers on the way back from Tap Mun island about an hour and a half later. The afternoon boat calls back between 4–5 pm, heading then for Tap Mun before returning direct to Ma Liu Shui. There is also a *kaido* service linking Wong Shek, Kau Lau Wan and Tap Mun Chau. A special holiday bus #95R runs from Pak Tam Chung to Wong Shek between 8.35 am and 6.35 pm. The well-prepared walker can retrace steps along the road from Wong Shek, take the coast path north and follow his nose to Hoi Ha and back on to Hoi Ha Rd. These villages are very sleepy; almost everyone has long emigrated overseas and many places are abandoned. None of the hills are above 400 metres so you can pick your own way around, rejoining the MacLehose Trail at a peak called Lui Ta Shek which is actually in Sai Kung West Country Park.

PLOVER COVE COUNTRY PARK:
MAP 5 IN THE 'COUNTRYSIDE SERIES'

Another massive country park in the colony's isolated north–east quadrant, this one has been radically reshaped by the reservoir. The access point is **Brides' Pool** which is served by bus #75R on Sundays and holidays between 8.30 am and 6.40 pm. Alternatively you can take a taxi from Tai Po KCR station. This area is very popular in the summertime as a glance at the map will show, for there are two nature trails and lots of barbeque pits clustered together. Paths lead up to the encircling ridge to the north, or to the eastern edge of the park. The main path leads to **Sam A Chung**, then at beach level across to **Lai Chi Wo** before moving up onto the ridge, or along the valley, before crossing to **Luk Keng**. The China border is just across the water here, one of the few places where you can see the village of Shau Tau Kok which is divided in half by the international border between Hong Kong and China. This is a good day's walk in hot weather of around 15 kilometres.

The easternmost side of the park is almost always deserted. Walk from **Tei Mei Tuk** across the two-kilometre-wide dam and along the narrow spit of causeway by the reservoir. The distance to the far end at **Bluff Head** is around 15 kilometres and never rises above 200 metres. The views of the islands like Kat O Chau and Double Island are a spectacular antidote to the city. Be warned: the shortest hike round the reservoir is 18 kilometres and exceedingly hard going in hot weather. The ridge path from Tai Mei Tuk rises about 200 metres further down the road on the left from the bus stop. It traverses the eastern end of the ridge heading north before doubling back to gain the heights at **Hsien Ku Fung** at 500 metres. It then heads west for about five kilometres at this height to **Ping Fung Shan.** This is very exposed in hot weather but offers a commanding view of Tolo Harbour to the south and Starling Inlet to the north.

The adventurous can make their own pilgrimage to look at the border at **Robin's Nest**. Get off bus #78K, or minibus 55K, at milestone 4 on the Sha Tau Kok Rd. The path is indistinct and rises to almost 500 metres. If you hit the barbed wire you've gone too far; watch out for the helicopter patrols. Use a map as this border area is heavily supervised and the border zone itself is out of bounds.

NEW TERRITORIES–LANTAU ISLAND: MAP 3 IN THE 'COUNTRYSIDE SERIES'

Lantau island is a walker's paradise, or at least it will be for a year or so until the construction of the new airport and associated developments along the northern shore swallow up the island of Chek Lap Kok and destroy the island's rural feel. Lantau's present advantage for walkers is that it is very accessible from Central. Ferries run to Mui Wo, also known as Silvermine Bay, and hydrofoils commute to and from the suburban community of Discovery Bay. It also has the most satisfying of the territory's long walks: the trek along the three peaks' ridge that covers the length of the island. This is also an easy mountain ridge to get off in a hurry as all routes running south eventually hit the main road and the ridge it-self is cut in two by the road to Tung Chung.

Step off the ferry at Mui Wo quickly to get a seat on the bus to **Po Lin monastery**—you have to change to a smaller bus halfway because the road is too narrow—and look for the pathway through the tea plantation. The route passes under an enormous wooden Chinese arch and is clearly visible stepping its way up the mountain to **Lantau Peak** at 934 metres, a rise of almost 400 metres in just 1.5 kilometres up more than 1,400 steps, an exhilarating beginning to the walk. The view from the top is magnificent, gazing south over Cheung Chau and the Soko islands. Other shapes further south can be vaguely discerned which are actually inside Chinese territorial waters. Jetfoils to Macau flit by soundlessly and the scene is baking hot in summer. Don't linger too long because it's a long walk home. The knee-killer is the drop the path makes to around 350 metres as it crosses the Tung Chung Rd, rising again to 800 metres beneath **Sunset Peak**. The huts below here were used by British escapees during the Japanese occupa-tion. If you're a true 'peak bagger' you'll see the summit is only another 50 metres away! The path skids north of the ridge and skirts **Yi Tung Shan** (748 m) before dropping to the road about two kilometres from the ferry. It's only about a 10-kilo-metre walk but packs in about 1,100 metres of steep climbing. You can come off the mountain further north after taking in Lin Fa Shan at 756 metres, but the way down isn't so clear as the light fades and you disappear into a maze of irrigated fields behind Mui Wo village. I've never discovered the way up the hill here and so have never done the walk in reverse. Hot weather precautions are essential and you must start early to do all three peaks in a day.

The northern shore of Lantau is hard to traverse and beyond **Tung Chung** the path in part disappears. However, the route round the southwestern end from **Tai O** village is a lovely walk. It stays mainly on the level and stops off at two deserted beaches ideal for skinny-dipping as the Guangzhou-bound freighters and fishing vessels loom on the horizon. The 12-kilometre walk takes about three or four hours, depending on whether you're dallying or not, and finishes along a water catchment channel to join the road above Shek Pik reservoir.

Shorter walks are possible from **Mui Wo** over the hill to the north to the **Trappist Haven Monastery** where you can buy fresh milk and return to Peng Chau island by *kaido* before connecting with a ferry either to Cheung Chau or direct back to Central. Another quite pleasant path heads south to circle the **Chi Ma Wan peninsula**, cutting back to the ferry either on a ridged path or by the road.

The commuter paradise of **Discovery Bay** also has some tempting walks. March up the hill to the right from the ferry pier and in among the newest blocks on the left you'll find a way up onto the ridge at **Yi Pik Au**. From there you can go left onto the hill tops at about 450 metres and back down to the reservoir, a circular walk of about two or three hours at a slow pace. Alternatively you can bear right until you reach the edge of the island. **Yam O Wan bay** is full of logs destined for local sawmills and the dockyards of Aberdeen. A *kaido* pauses regularly at **Yam O Tuk** and returns across the water past the floating dry docks to Tsing Lung Tau where you can catch a minibus back to Mongkok. The last *kaido* leaves at 17.00. The knoll at the far end of the peninsula at **Fa Peng Teng** makes a good walk but the path is easy to miss.

Cheung Chau and Lamma have some pleasant walks. These are included in the relevant section of the 'Bearings' chapter as none of them are longer than half an hour and are really just afternoon strolls!

MACAU

HISTORY

PORTUGAL'S GREAT EXPLORERS

The Portuguese enclave on the opposite side of the Pearl River delta from Hong Kong is the oldest surviving European colony in Southeast Asia. It dates from the era of Portugal's great explorers, men like Vasco da Gama, who reached India at the end of the 15th century, and Jorge Alvares, who landed in southern China in 1513. No treaty was ever signed to legitimate Macau's founding. Portuguese traders struck a deal with authorities in Canton around the year 1557 to pay dues and fees in return for the use of Macau's inner and outer harbours. The anchorages were vital for Portuguese trade with Japan as the Ming emperor had expressly forbidden Chinese merchants permission to trade directly. Filling this gap, Macau quickly became the entrepôt for the entire China coast, transhipping European luxuries, exotic goods from Africa and the other major Portuguese colonies in India and Brazil, as well as spices and sandalwood from the East Indies. The Portuguese shipped and bartered Japanese silver and gold for Chinese silk in a lucrative trade constantly menaced by Japanese pirate attacks and violent typhoons.

THE MISSIONARIES

With the traders came the missionaries, the second arm of the West's colonising influence. When the Pope's envoy to the Far East, St Francis Xavier, passed through the new Indian colony of Goa and the Malayan spice port of Malacca in 1547 he heard accounts of a new country called Japan. The co-founder of the Jesuit order spent three years in Japan, leaving only in 1552 to proselytize the Chinese. His personal mission closed, however, in December that year when he succumbed to a fever in a town called Sheung Chuen about 80 km up the coast from Macau. Jesuit scholars, however, patiently earned places at the court in Peking after demonstrating their skill in

Western astronomy, the first real cross-fertilisation of Western and Chinese ideas on Chinese soil.

Faced with the rapidly growing European presence in Macau the Chinese authorities were uncertain how to react. Instinctively they elected to try and contain it, in 1573 building the Porto do Cerco wall across the isthmus on which Macau stands. This was closed except for trade twice a month. Two years later, Portuguese merchants were allowed into Canton for the first time to buy raw white silk destined for Japan and Europe. In 1576, 20 years after the first settlers arrived, Macau's bishopric was established which covered all China and Japan. In those days the city was ruled by a cabal of merchants and the Captain-Major of the Japan Voyage, a Portuguese sea captain granted a monopoly of trade by the Portuguese monarch.

THE DUTCH ATTACK

Portugal fell under Spanish domination after the last son of the great King Joao III, Dom Sebastiao, perished in a chaotic and futile attack against Muslim infidels in Morocco in 1580. Though Philip II of Spain was accepted as Portugal's new ruler in 1581, half a world away Macau defiantly continued to fly the royal Portuguese flag throughout the next 60 years of Spanish rule. Trade benefitted by Spanish rule. The route from Macau to the Spanish ports of Manila in the Philippines and Acapulco in Mexico became the most profitable in the world. Ill-garrisoned in deference to orders from the Chinese, the Portuguese were increasingly attacked by their arch-rival in Asian trade, the Dutch, who were based in the spice islands of Indonesia and Java. The Portuguese routed the Dutch finally in 1622, aided by accurate cannon fire directed by Jesuit priests from the Monte Fort, and the desperate butchery of their Negro slaves.

SLOW DECLINE

Despite this victory, Macau's slow decline had already begun by the early 17th century as Dutch ships continued to harass the Portuguese from their new base in Japan. In 1639 the Japanese closed the last of their ports open to the Portuguese and trade between the two effectively ended. The

Dutch, having turned the Japanese against the Portuguese, tried the same ploy with the Chinese but failed. The restoration of the Portuguese monarchy in 1640, and the 1644 victory of the Manchus over the Ming dynasty in China, did not arrest Macau's slow decline, which its 5,000 European citizens did little to reverse.

Several opportunities were missed. In 1705 a papal envoy sent to Peking reversed the traditional Macanese and Jesuit tolerance of Chinese customs, some of which had been incorporated into the Catholic rite. This intemperate act lost them the good favour of the emperor whose broad-minded father had allowed Adam Schall to reform the Chinese calendar and introduce Western optics to China. In a further act of commercial folly, Macau twice refused the emperor's wish to move the European trading houses downstream from Canton to Macau. Despite a brief period of four years in the mid-18th century when Macau dominated the new tea trade, it lapsed into a series of administrative quarrels with Chinese envoys who were eager to suppress Christianity among the Chinese population both in the mainland and in Macau. The city's decline was accelerated by the expulsion of the Jesuits in 1762, part of a private vendetta within the Portuguese court to curtail their power and influence.

In the late 18th century Macau served as the jumping off point for a series of foreign missions to the Chinese court in Peking, including the ill-fated attempt by Lord Macartney in 1794 to gain trading port concessions for the British. Macau gradually opened its doors to all foreign traders and became a polyglot watering hole with a large American contingent. In fact, the tea dumped in Boston's harbour that signalled the beginning of the American Revolution was shipped through Macau.

Its internationalization could not save Macau from becoming caught up in the opium-trade quarrel between the British and the Chinese. By 1839, the drug trade had grown so large that it underpinned the solvency of the British empire in India. In that year the Chinese commissioner in Canton, Governor Lin Zexu, moved to suppress the opium trade. The British commander, Captain Charles Elliot, was forced to journey upriver from Macau to mediate for the release of the British traders and their return to the safety of the Portuguese enclave. Later that year they were compelled to leave Macau and were exiled to the inhospitable island of Hong Kong. Governor Lin's triumph was short-lived. The British returned to test China's strength, extracting reparations and new trade promises, and gaining Hong Kong island under the Treaty of Nanjing in 1842.

The fighting broke China's resistance to Western incursions. Other European powers, including France and Germany, seized treaty ports along the China coast during the 19th century. The Americans, too, made a trade treaty with China in 1844. The signing took place in Macau's Kun Iam Temple only five years after Commissioner Lin had been fêted in the streets after the expulsion of the British. Macau did not prosper from the expansion of the other European powers. A new governor, a tough-minded sailor called Joao Ferreira do Amaral, decided to establish Portugal's sovereignty over Macau, a fact which had purposefully been left vague for several centuries, by expelling the two important Chinese customs officials based in the enclave. Seven assassins from Canton stabbed him to death in 1849 in retaliation, cutting off his head and his left hand to claim a reward. The admiral's statue had stood for 50 years when Lu Ping, the Director of the Chinese Macau Affairs Office stated in 1990 that it must be removed because it "symbolized colonialism" and would be unacceptable to China after 1999. In autumn 1992 it was dismantled from its base and shipped to Lisbon.

DR SUN YAT-SEN

A formal treaty signed granting Portuguese sovereignty over Macau was only signed in 1887. The founder of the Chinese republic, Sun Yat-sen, was born in the neighbouring Zhongshan county and passed through Macau several times, en route to study in Hawaii, and later to learn medicine in Hong Kong where he was also baptised a Protestant. Dr Sun worked as a doctor in Macau in 1882–4 before going into exile in London and Tokyo. The anti-Manchu rebellion he yearned for eventually began whilst he was en route from the USA in 1911.

MODERN TIMES

The twentieth century has offered Macau's chequered history little respite. Nearly starved into submission by a Chinese blockade in the 1930s, neutral Macau was swamped by refugees from Hong Kong and Japanese-occupied China during the World War II, and then again during Mao's abortive Great Leap Forward campaign in the 1950s. During the Cultural Revolution in the late 1960s, Macau was threatened with an insurrection stimulated by Mao's Red Guards, youthful and anarchistic thugs licenced to disrupt in the name of ideology. After a series of violent riots in which several people were killed by Portuguese troops, the colony's governor diverted Chinese attention towards Hong Kong by threatening to evacuate the enclave.

When a revolution in Lisbon in 1974 installed a left-wing government, Portugal offered to hand Macau back to China, which refused the deal for fear of panicking Hong Kong. However, in 1987, exactly a century after China formally ceded Macau, an agreement was reached similar to Britain's arrangement over Hong Kong, to hand Macau back to China, this time on 20th December 1999. The one key difference is that Macau's half-a-million citizens will be entitled to hold a Portuguese passport after 1999, enabling them to return to Portugal or elsewhere in the EEC if they wish, including Britain. This is in stark contrast to the British policy which carefully left the 5.8 million citizens of Hong Kong without the right to move to Britain after 1997.

GAMBLING MECCA

It was a stroke of genius to reverse Macau's slow slide as a trading enclave with a new lease on life as a gambling den, resolving its financial insolvency by licensing vice. Today the tax on betting accounts for a massive proportion of all Macau government revenues, not to mention the attendant gains from prostitution, pawnbroking, hotels and transportation. Though sea pirates were finally vanquished from the waters of the Pearl River in 1910, many visitors return from Macau with empty pockets nonetheless! Of the 6 million tourist arrivals last year—twelve times Macau's actual population—around one million held Western passports. The rest were Hong Kong gamblers. Piggybacking on Hong Kong's industrial growth, Macau's factories today earn about US$1.5 billion from exports.

Despite a proliferation of high-rise buildings, Macau is only slowly throwing off its air of genteel decline. The newest chapter is being written out on the mudflats where a US$450 million airport will rise from the sea off Taipa island, connected to the outer harbour by a US$47 million bridge. This massive project, scheduled for completion around 1994, may destroy Macau's old-world sleepiness forever. Despite its lack of an airport, Macau already figures twice in the history of aviation, firstly as the landing point of the first scheduled crossing of the Pacific Ocean, made by a Pan Am flying boat in 1937; and secondly as host to the world's first hijack, in 1948, when four pirates shot the pilot of a Cathay Pacific Airways Catalina flying boat bound for Hong Kong which crashed into the delta, killing all but one of the 26 persons on board.

A stroll down the side-streets will stimulate echoes of earlier days when missionaries and traders vied over centuries to see which could be the first group to penetrate China. The two have always gone hand in hand. Since the economic reforms were ushered in by Deng Xiaoping in 1976, trade along the coast has boomed. And despite almost four decades of communist rule, China has many, often secret, Christian communities throughout the country, especially in Guangzhou and along the coast towards Shanghai. China has always been more interested in trade, yet when the history of its integration with the West is finally written, Macau will rightfully be able to claim that first chapter for itself.

PRACTICALITIES

GETTING THERE (A–Z PAGE 232)

The easiest way is by the 24-hour **jetfoil** shuttle service run by the Far East Jetfoil Company. This operates from the Shun Tak Centre above Sheung Wan MTR station and next to the Victoria Hotel on Hong Kong island. A jetfoil leaves on the one-hour, 60-kilometre journey every 15 minutes between 7 am and 5.30 pm, then every half-hour until 1.30 am and infrequently through the night at 2.30 am, 3.30 am and 6.30 am. This service is used by 75 percent of travellers to and from Macau so it gets booked up, especially at weekends. The worst choke points are Friday evenings and Saturdays on the outbound journey, and Sundays and Monday mornings on the return to Hong Kong. First class is only marginally more expensive than second class and offers a much better view. Prices also vary according to the departure time during the day within the range $110–145. Illegal ticket scalpers have been operating outside the ferry terminal in the past, especially at bank holidays, but if you are tempted be careful to check that the tickets are valid.

There are also **jetboat** and **hydrofoil** services running from the same centre. These are about 15 minutes slower and offer a much less frequent service. There is also a new **jumbo-cat** service which is slightly quicker. All of these are operated by the Hong Kong Macau Hydrofoil Company and cost $102 weekdays and $110 at weekends. A high-speed ferry runs 5–6 times daily from the Shun Tak Centre, outbound beginning 8 am and closing at 8 pm, the return run operating between 10.30 am and 10.30 pm. Fares range between 52–96 for the 100-minute journey. A more majestic rust-bucket that made a sedate three-hour ride across the delta was scrapped in 1990.

Hydrofoil and jetcat services also operate from the China Ferry Terminal on the Kowloon side, with slightly less frequency. The main Shun Tak Centre is easier to use as it is clearly signposted inside and purpose-built for Macau traffic. A **hoverferry** service operates twelve times daily from the China Ferry Terminal, but this isn't nearly so pleasant a ride as any of the above.

You can also take an 18-minute **helicopter** ride on **East Asia Airlines** at a cost of $982 one-way on weekdays with a $100 surcharge at weekends. There are six flights a day, the first from Hong Kong leaving at 10 am and the last returning from Macau at 4.30 pm. For bookings in Hong Kong, telephone 8593359; in Macau 572983.

Entry formalities are kept to a minimum. Holders of United States, Canadian, Australian, New Zealand, Japanese, Thai, Philippine, Malaysian and most European passports can enter free of charge without a visa and stay for up to 90 days. Brazilians can stay for six months. Commonwealth citizens who are not Hong Kong residents can stay 20 days. All required visas can be purchased on arrival—it's just a simple stamp in the passport as you pass through immigration—except for those countries not maintaining diplomatic relations with Portugal, for which a visa must be applied for in advance.

Customs are straightforward. Only dangerous items are banned and there are no restrictions on money or goods brought into or out of Macau. The **currency** of *patacas* (abbreviated Ptc) and *avos* is valued at a slight discount (around three percent) against the Hong Kong dollar, which is why you'll be offered patacas as small change for your Hong Kong dollar bills! There is no need to change money as the Hong Kong dollar circulates freely. Note, however, that it is almost impossible to convert *patacas* even in a bank when back in Hong Kong. If you want to **change money**, the casinos are open 24-hours and don't levy hidden commissions as in Hong Kong. Banks are open during normal hours.

Latest **information**, addresses of hotels, banks and other services can be found in the Macau Tourist Office's brochures from their offices in Hong Kong or at the ferry port in Macau on arrival. They have an attractive set of leaflets describing Macau's temples, gardens, churches, fortresses, outlying islands and restaurants.

GETTING AROUND

Macau is divided into the main peninsula and two islands, **Taipa** and **Coloane**, linked in a chain by a bridge and a causeway. The mainland is very easy to get around. The best way is by foot, once you've made your way into the town centre. Taxis are usually plentiful by the ferry terminal; check that the flag is down as the journey starts. There is a Ptc5 and Ptc10 surcharge, for outward trips only, to Taipa and Coloane islands respectively. Pedicabs are extortionate and can be troublesome at the ferry terminal. Fares should be around Ptc20 for a ride into the town. Buses operate until midnight: #3, 3A & 10 go to the centre via the Metropole Hotel; #28C goes to the border gate via the Royal Hotel; #28A crosses to Taipa and the Hyatt Regency. There are also minibuses.

Once in town, think about hiring a moke (miniature car) for the day. This is by far the best way to explore the narrow streets of Taipa and the country trails on the two outer islands. The minimum age limit is 21 with a driving licence recognized in Portugal, or an international licence. If you have a larger group (but less than nine persons) you can hire a miniature replica of a 1920 London bus. Bicycles can be hired only next to the Taipa bus terminal for around Ptc8 per hour. These are extremely good fun for exploring the islands but not recommended for the cobbled and hilly city.

Tours are offered by a selection of travel agencies at prices capped by government fiat. A half-day coach tour covering all the major sights with lunch is around Ptc70. A two-hour tour by car costs Ptc160 each for a maximum of four people. The cost is a fraction of this if you go by coach. Harbour tours run from Pier Number One regularly between 9.30 am and 3.30 pm. A half-hour or hour-long tour priced Ptc30–55 includes one drink. A dusk cruise departs at 5 pm for Ptc85 inclusive with unlimited champagne. The truly adventurous can take a 10-minute low altitude flying tour by ultra-light plane for around HK$300. These can be booked on 307343 in Macau.

Hotels are easy to find (A–Z page 242). Macau has several international standard first-class hotels and a wide range of mid-priced hotels and guest houses. The much-loved Bela Vista has been renovated and upgraded. It is easy to find rooms anywhere if you're staying midweek—discounts of around 20 percent are offered or can be asked for—but it's best to book in advance for any time between Friday to Sunday as Macau is flooded with weekend trippers, especially in summer.

The most exclusive of the new hotels are the **Hyatt Regency** on Taipa island and the **Macau Mandarin Oriental** close to the ferry pier. The Hyatt Regency offers cut-price fitness packages during midweek for access to its health club and outdoor pool. The **Royal** and the **Pousada Ritz** are also first-class hotels. Macau's most appealing hotel is the 25-room **Pousada de São Tiago** with its 17th-century foundations, dining terrace and wonderful views over the estuary. Of the mid-price hotels the most interesting is the **Pousada de Coloane**, a family hotel on the furthest island of Coloane surrounded by pine trees overlooking Macau's cleanest beach. In town the **Metropole**, which has a good Western restaurant, the **Mondial**, which still has an interesting if spartan old-fashioned wing, the **Presidente** and the **Sintra** are acceptable. Recently renovated, the **Bela Vista** reopened with only eight rooms under the management of the Mandarin Oriental group and certainly rates a preferential vote. Of the budget hotels the **East Asia**, the **Peninsula**, the **Ko Wah** and the **London** are recommended. A full list of hotels and guesthouses is included in the A–Z section.

There are some great little **restaurants** and bars tucked away in Macau. Some serve exclusively Portuguese colonial dishes, a blend of European and African styles. Others offer a range of European dishes, including Italian. Macau also has excellent Vietnamese and Thai restaurants. A decent meal can come in at under Ptc100 per head while the service tends to be slower than the standard Hong Kong hustle. One of the great joys of Macau is the availability of vinho verde, the young green Portuguese wine that is both cheap and highly drinkable. Lunches are later and dinners taken earlier than in Hong Kong. Few restaurants stay open late midweek even if they advertize that they do. Credit cards are accepted in all but the smallest places.

A **Lorcha**, **Estrela do Mar**, **A Galera**, **Afonso's**, **Portugues**, **Galo**, and **Mocambique** all offer excellent Macanese food. For those looking for something a little different, **Fernando's** on Hac Sa beach has a shifting idiosyncratic menu, a mad chef and superb food in an informal setting among the sheds lining the strand. **Pinocchio's** in Taipa village isn't as quiet as it was in its heyday, but the **Pousada de Coloane** still has its spacious terrace overlooking the sea. The **Riqueixo** in the town centre is as wonderful as ever, its food delivered from private kitchens every morning, with low prices and very cheap wine. Many of the best dishes are quickly exhausted so arrive early. First-class meals are also to be had at the homely Italian-style **Leong Un**, the upmarket **Flamingo** in the Hyatt Regency, and the magnificent **Fortaleza Grill** in the Pousada São Tiago, priced accordingly.

With the influx of Thai girls working Macau's massage parlours and nightclubs has come a range of spicy Thai restaurants, including **Banthai** and **Nova Koka**. The best Vietnamese in town is the **Golden Bull** in the Presidente Hotel. For Japanese, try **Furosato** in the Lisboa Hotel and **Ginza** in the Royal. The **Presidente** also has a good Korean restaurant and the Lisboa has the well-known **Chiu Chow**.

Macanese cuisine takes the basic ingredients of southern Chinese and Portuguese styles and spices them up with influences drawn from Lisbon's other former overseas possessions in South America, India and Africa. The Chinese introduced ginger and soy sauce to the Europeans as well as exotic lychees and a small citrus fruit we know as a tangerine. The Portuguese were the first Europeans exposed to the Chinese tea drinking habit, which they passed on to the English with massive consequences for world history. In return the Portuguese brought chillies from India, peanuts, yams and kidney beans from Brazil, and a variety of green and salad vegetables from Europe. In the resulting confusion what we know as Chinese watercress was named *patao choi,* Portuguese vegetable.

Macanese cuisine isn't regimented but a mélange of influences, ideas and coincidences. Popular are a three-meat stew with prawns in a lemon and chilli sauce known as *arroz gordo,* literally 'plump rice'. Pan-fried minced pork with potatoes cooked swiftly in soy sauce is called *minchi.* Both African chicken and Goanese chicken appear on local menus, chilli-hot dishes rivalling spicy prawns in their potency. There's also a Portuguese chicken, a curry cooked in saffron with black olives, and a Brazilian stew of pork, sausage and beans called *feijoada.* Other colonies are represented too, like the Angolan matapa, a mix of spinach, shrimps and saffron. Fish dishes are common, including *bacalhau a bras,* or broiled codfish. For dessert the Macanese have a partiality for fig and pumpkin compote, mango mousse or a *batatada* of coconut, eggs and potatoes. The Chinese influence can be seen in the cages outside many restaurants: rare animals, often endangered species like owls or cats, destined for an exotic and unnecessary dish.

THE SIGHTS OF MACAU

Macau's principal sights are either strategic or religious. The stout fortifications are now turned to other uses though the massive churches for the Roman Catholic faithful are still very much in use.

When the Portuguese first settled here in the mid-16th century, Chinese authorities forbade them to fortify the new colony. But the depredations of the Dutch, who had the strongest fleet on the high seas and threatened every part of the worldwide Portuguese empire, forced them to erect a series of forts to protect the already wealthy city of Macau. The French king Louis XIV's military designer Vauban placed the forts close to the hillside with upward slanting walls. Portuguese builders used a special mortar made of earth, straw, lime and oyster shells packed between planks of wood called *chunambo* to secure them. The cannon on the ramparts were made locally in a foundry at Bocarro which also supplied the Chinese emperor and the king of Siam.

The five forts and batteries—on the Monte and Penha hills, on Barra Point, at Bomparto and St Francis—were all begun at this time, though they weren't finished until after the great Dutch attack in 1622. They were completed by Macau's first governor, Dom Francisco de Mascarenhas, who also began constructing the Guia fortress and the city walls connecting them. He then booted the Jesuits out of the **Forteleza do Monte** and turned it into his residence. The Jesuits reclaimed it for a while a century later, but were expelled from Macau altogether in 1762. It was engulfed by the great fire of 1835 that destroyed the Church of São Paulo and 40 years later the original cannon were removed so that what remains is just a reminder of its former imposing strength. **Guia Fort** occupies the highest point in the city and offers great views all round. It was finished in 1638 and is in the form of an irregular pentagon. On top is a lighthouse, the oldest on the China coast (1865), and a whitewashed 17th-century chapel with a reserved atmosphere that served as a hermitage.

The fortress of St James of the Bar, known as the **Barra Fortress** or **São Tiago da Barra**, was only completed in 1629, seven years after the Dutch had been vanquished. The fort's walls are two metres thick at the base and supported a garrison of 60 men and two dozen cannon which lay unused for over three centuries until they were sold to buy rice for refugees during World War II, when the fort was a sanctuary for hundreds who fled from Hong Kong. The chapel to St James was built in 1740. A legend has it that the saint used to patrol the wall at night and was found in the morning with mud on his boots. Parts of the fortress were pulled down after the war and the remainder converted into Macau's most gracious hotel, the Pousada de São Tiago. The garrison's old cistern was turned into the fountain on the café terrace, an old water trough bearing the date of 1629 now graces the entrance, and the whole enterprise faithfully creates the air of a stately home of two centuries ago.

The **fortress of Mong-Ha** was begun in 1849, with a second fortress on the Dona Maria hill, after relations with China declined in the aftermath of the Opium Wars between Britain and China. Both face north and never came under attack. The Mong-Ha fort was really used only once, when relations with China declined to a point where an attack was threatened after the assassination of governor Amaral. A group of 36 Portuguese volunteers surprised a Chinese force almost 20 times stronger and routed them. The border gate, the **Portas do Cerco**, was built then too. These days the Macau authorities don't even man it, a casualness that belies its name which literally means 'the gate of the siege'.

The **Fort of St Francis** used to stand on a promontory on the north shore of Praia Grande Bay. Like the Barra fort, it was only completed after the Dutch invasion attempt, but filled an important role linking the city wall to the fort on Monte Hill and the inner harbour. It was also home to a chapter of a Spanish house of Franciscan monks from the Philippines. It was all demolished in 1864, only to be rebuilt later close to the Lisboa Hotel. The **barracks of St Francisco** was the last major military installation to be built in Macau. The rose-coloured building was later converted into the police headquarters and a military museum. Of the rest of Macau's fortifications few traces remain. The fort on Penha Hill has disappeared beneath the bishop's palace, Bomparto's walls survive as the buttressing for the Bela Vista hotel, and the Dona Maria has been reincarnated as a wicked bend on the Grand Prix racing circuit.

On the ecclesiastical side, the noblest monument is the ruined façade of the **Church of São Paulo**, the most visible landmark in Macau. At the time of its consecration in 1603, Portuguese power was on the ascendent and Macau a precious possession. Designed by an Italian Jesuit and constructed by exiled Japanese Christian converts, the façade mixes faiths with representations of the Japanese chrysanthemum and the fleur-de-lys among the statues of four Jesuit saints and the Virgin Mary. This, alas, is all that remains. After the Jesuits were expelled in 1767 the neighbouring college, where the great China missionaries Matteo Ricci and Adam Schall studied astronomy and mathematics, was turned into an army barracks. In 1835 a typhoon fire in the kitchens destroyed it and the neighbouring church.

The Church of São Domingo, the most beautiful baroque church east of Goa, is decorated with Ionic columns and teak and oak doors. The altar and side panels with their carved statues in wood and ivory of the Madonna and Child, and several saints also executed by local artists, are exceptionally beautiful. The church was founded in the late 16th century and has a chequered past marred by violence. In the rioting during the celebration of the restoration of the Portuguese monarchy in 1642 an officer seeking sanctuary from the mob was stabbed to death in front of the altar during mass. During the Rites Controversy in the early 18th century, the Dominicans took a fundamentalist line and sided with the papal legate against the Jesuits and Macau's bishop who wanted Catholic religious ceremonies to be changed slightly so as to appeal more to their educated Chinese converts. After the order was excommunicated, several friars were arrested after fights with troops. Then in 1834 the Portuguese government ordered all religious orders to close their monasteries and sell their property, leaving only the church standing. The main entrance is often only open in the afternoon. To gain access at other times, ring the bell by the green gate at the side entrance.

The **Church of Santo Agostinho** has the oldest foundations of any surviving in Macau. It dates back to 1586, though the building now on the site was completed in 1814. The figure of Christ bearing the Cross is the centrepiece of the Nosso Senhor dos Passos procession just before Easter. Legend has it that the image was washed up on Macau's shores one day and that every time it was removed from the Augustinians' church to the Cathedral it mysteriously made its way back there. Tombstones at the foot of the altar house the remains of early China missionaries. Also inside is the tomb of Maria de Moura, an orphaned 16th-century beauty who married at age 13 an admirer who had lost his right arm from gangrene following a fight with another suitor. The unfortunate girl died in childbirth, by then still aged only 17, and is buried with her baby son and her husband's severed arm. The widower, Antonio D'Albuquerque Coelho, never married again but later became governor of Macau and of Timor, a Portuguese possession in eastern Indonesia.

The **Church of São Jose** is part of the old Jesuit seminary founded in 1728 to train Chinese priests which only closed in 1966. The church, built in 1746–58, has a very peaceful atmosphere, resonant acoustics, some fine statues and interiors, and a quaint domed roof. The cloisters shelter a small garden with a well at its centre. The seminary, while not officially open to the public, does part its doors to interested visitors of Father Manuel Teixeira, the colony's resident patriarch. The seminary's collection includes early 17th-century paintings by Japanese Christian exiles and part of the library of the church of São Paulo rescued from the great typhoon fire and the arm bone of St Francis Xavier, moved here in early 1991 from the chapel of St Francis Xavier in Coloane. The relic came by a peripatetic route, spending 15 years in Japan and another 50 in the church of São Paulo, then periods in the Church of St

Antony, the Cathedral, St Joseph's seminary and in the special-ly consecrated chapel in Coloane from 1978 to 1991. Church and garden are open daily, except Wednesdays, between 10 am and 4 pm.

The double-towered **Church of São Laurenço** is Macau's most fashionable religious setting with a double staircase and shady courtyard. The interior has a fine turquoise painted wooden ceiling and an altar statue of St Lawrence as a young man. The church is not usually open, but the curious visitor can take a discreet look during mass and climb the grand ornamental stairs. Macau's Cathedral, the **Largo da Sé**, occu-pies the same site as the original cathedral built in 1576 which served all of China and Japan in its diocese. However, the pre-sent church constructed in 1850 has little to detain the visitor save some fine stained-glass windows.

Secular Macau is graceful and relaxed, like the banyan trees on the waterfront, more than a century old and originally planted by the one-armed Governor Amaral's successor, who also built the sea wall along Praia Grande and city's sewage system. Amaral's statue stands in the centre of the waterfront to this day, though a senior Chinese communist cadre recently demanded it be removed as an out-moded colonial insult to Chinese sovereignty; the Portuguese agreed, and it will soon make its way to Lisbon.

The bright pink **Leal Senado** houses the government offices and legislature. In Macau's earliest days leading citizens were appointed for life, nominally to assist the Captain-Major of the Japan Voyage, and later the governor, and were very influential. Today the council deals with municipal affairs and is actually more democratic than Hong Kong. The main building dates from only 1875, but the interiors open to the public are worth investigating, including a secluded garden, the excellent library and the art gallery off the foyer. The name translates as 'loyal senate', reference to Macau's isolation in the 17th-century when it ignored the 60-year-long Spanish occu-pation of the Portuguese throne. The action won the city its motto—*nao ha outra mais leal,* 'there is none more loyal'—as the most faithful city in the Portuguese empire.

The **Old Protestant Cemetery** is divided into two parts. The oldest was established in 1820, not 1814 as the inscription over the entrance says. A brief tour offers heart-rending glimpses of the past in the memorials of those who died far from home, sailors who fell from the rigging, missionaries and many young children who succumbed to fevers, Swedish and American traders, and British officers wounded in skirmishes during the Opium Wars outside Canton. George Chinnery, the famous China coast watercolourist, lies here, as does Robert Morrison, the great 19th-century missionary who translated the bible into Chinese, and his wife Mary who died in childbirth. Robert Adams, grandson of George Washington, is interred here with some of those who accompanied Commodore Perry in 1853 when he delivered the American ultimatum to Japan demanding it open its ports to foreign trade. The second section lies in a site in the northern part of the city. The **Catholic cemetery of St Michael** houses the remains of several Macanese families, often in tombs mixing Catholic and Chinese styles and symmetry, including the tomb of the man who saved Macau from the Chinese attack of 1849, Lieutenant Mesquita.

One modern building of note in Macau is the gaudily pretentious **Hotel Lisboa**, opened in 1970. The roof resembles a giant roulette wheel and the mustard-coloured exterior leaves the building looking like a melted candle. The towering Bank of China building stands immediately opposite.

Macau's Chinese temples are often quite pretty. The **Temple of A-Ma** stands on the inner harbour at Barra Point overlooking Lappa island, a former burial ground of Jesuit priests and picnic place for Portuguese families. By tradition, Macau's foundation is a story of retribution: a beautiful girl, refused passage by some rich merchants, was aided by a poor fisherman who was the only one saved when a typhoon suddenly swept by. Fujian fishermen already worshipped here when the Portuguese arrived in 1553. Pleasantly situated, the temple has four shrines. The lower three are dedicated to A-Ma and her four attendants—Kam Tung, the golden boy—Yok Noi, the jade maiden—Tei Chong Wong, the king of hell—and Wai To, the guardian of the law. The uppermost shrine is dedicated to Kun Iam, the Buddhist Goddess of Mercy. A nearby bamboo grove is covered with paper prayers and small dolls placed by women imploring the gods to assist them in conceiving children. The shrines are set among paths, moon gates and rocks carved with red Chinese characters praising A-Ma's powers and grace.

Kun Iam Temple was built in 1627 but may date back to the 14th century. The first prayer hall is dedicated to the three Precious Buddhas, the second in the open courtyard to the Buddha of Longevity. The main hall is dedicated to Kun Iam, a princess whose father murdered her following her conversion to Buddhism and who returned to earth as the Goddess of Mercy to cure him of an illness. The story is told in the calligraphy hangings on the antechamber walls. Special celebrations are held on the 19th day of the second, sixth, ninth and eleventh lunar months. The garden contains a giant banyan formed of four interwoven trunks nicknamed the 'Lovers' tree' and a large stone table where the American plenipotentiary, Caleb Cushing, signed the first Sino-American treaty with the Viceroy of Canton in 1844. This gave the Americans the same trading rights that the British had won through the First Opium War. The American consulate for China stayed in Macau until 1885 when it was transferred to Peking.

Lin Fong Miu, known also as the Temple of the Lotus, hides an exquisite courtyard behind an unprepossessing exterior. The eaves and lintels are covered with ceramic tableaux of birds, flowers and human figures in a style popular in Canton a century and a half ago. The only temple of Taoist origin in Macau, it was renovated a decade ago and completely cleaned and refurbished. Images of Tin Hau and Kwan Tai lead the way to the main hall dedicated to Kun Iam. The lotus motif in the porcelain mural in the central courtyard derives from the temple's origins in 1592 on what was then a narrow isthmus connecting mainland China with Macau. The statue of Commissioner Lin Zexu commemorates his visit in 1839 after snuffing out the opium trade in Canton, just days before Britain declared war to re-establish it. For centuries it was the overnight resting place of mandarins travelling between the enclave and Canton.

Tai Soi Miu, the Temple of the Sleeping Buddha, is set in the hillside behind St Paul's Church with an entrance on the Rua da Figueroa. A narrow stairway leads between prayer halls set at different levels, beginning with the Taoist god of justice, a series of goddesses invoked for pregnancy and child care, and the Buddhist Kun Iam. The main hall contains a reclining Buddha and the upper hall a shrine to Chung Kwei, patron of literature and exorcism, otherwise known as the controller of demons.

The temple of the bazaar, **Hong Kong Miu**, is much more earthy, set in the heart of the open-air marketplace on one side of the Largo do Matapau. Hong Kong, entirely unrelated to the colony of the same name, was a courageous Han-dynasty general whose flight from an unsuccessful battle was disguised by a flock of ducks. His followers eagerly abstain from eating duck one day of the year, on the seventh day of the seventh moon. The carved altar table supports the three figures of the general, of Hong Seng, a god of the sea, and Sai San Hau Bong, another martial performer.

The 17th-century Temple of the Stream of Mourning, **Lin Kai Miu**, off the Estrada do Repouso, is worth investigating. The main hall, unrenovated and darkened with age, is given over to Wah Kwong, a protector against fire and the patron of Cantonese opera troupes. The walls have some fine clay folk art figures and an interesting set of 60 gods, one for each year in the cycle, in the chapel opposite. Another hall is dedicated to the mischievous Taoist deity, the Monkey God. The temple's main festival day is the 28th day of the ninth month.

Macau has a larger concentration of old **shop-houses** and terraces than have survived in Hong Kong. The shop-house tenements are grouped in two main areas: around the Rua das Lorchas by the inner harbour, and in the group of streets tucked below the Monte Hill, for example Rua das Estalgens and Rua da Tercena. The São Lazaro district has the best collection of old **terraced houses** near the Rua Sanches de Miranda and the Calcada-Igreja de São Lazaro. The Avenida do Conselheiro Ferreira de Almeida also has several houses with restored façades, balustrades, arched verandahs and painted exteriors.

Macau has several lovely gardens. The **Camões garden** is a quiet corner to relax in amid giant banyan trees drooping long trails of lianas. Legend has it the epic poet Luis Camões composed part of his famous poem of Portuguese exploration, **Os Lusiados**, in Macau, though no formal record exists. In the 18th century it was the rest garden adjoining the British East India Company house next door and once had an observatory that was used by the French astronomer and explorer, Count La Perouse, who paused here during his search for the Northwest Passage as a possible route back to Europe.

The Chinese garden of **Lou Lim Iok** on the Estrada de Adolfo Loureiro has a different atmosphere. It was built in the last century by a wealthy merchant, whose son subsequently lost the family fortune, on a model of the famous gardens of Suzhou. Like traditional Chinese gardens, it presents an idealisation of nature recreated in miniature. It has neither the gravity or enigma of a Japanese garden with its finely raked pebble 'seas', nor the profusion of a Western flower garden, nor the majesty of a wide park or formal garden. In fact there's something rather smug about the miniature landscape of mountains, forests and lakes, as if it's simply an extension of the mind. The pathway to the central pavilion is crooked to deter evil spirits, who are only able to travel in straight lines, and the central pond is filled with fat ornamental carp and lotus plants.

Other gardens worth exploring are the **Flora Gardens** on the Avenida de Sidonio Pais next to the zoo and the more secluded wooded **Garden of Montanha Russa** on the Estrada Ferreira do Amaral.

MUSEUMS IN MACAU

The **Luis de Camões Museum**, Macau's most famous museum, was housed in the 18th-century headquarters of the British East India Company in Macau and had the best collection of historical, artistic and archaeological items in the colony. It has been converted into a charitable foundation and the building is being gutted. The museum will not reopen for the foreseeable future.

Macau's **Maritime Museum** stands in a new building on Wharf Number One and houses a wide-ranging collection including traditional fishing gear and a mud-skimming sled used by shrimp-catchers. It also has a highly informative historical section with copies of the 15th-century charts used by early Portuguese navigators, early Chinese astrolabes used to measure the altitude of the stars and other nautical navigation equipment. There's also a copy of a **lorcha**, a sleek vessel used to chase pirate war junks. Out in the harbour are floating replicas of a tug boat and a Chinese 'flower boat', a mobile brothel, opium den and bar long since redundant. The museum is open daily except Tuesdays, 10 am–6 pm; entrance Ptc5.

The recently opened **Post Office Museum** contains a number of philatelic rarities, including the special 'chops' postmasters used to direct mail to Europe by train via Siberia or via America by packet boat. This is one of the most idiosyncratic museums in Asia and includes an old postman's bicycle, a 1930 telephone exchange in working order, and several bits of old radio equipment. Housed on the second floor of the General Post Office, Avenida de Almeida Ribeiro. Open weekdays, 3–5 pm.

The **Military Museum** is very tiny and most of its pieces date from World War I. However, there are some Portuguese colonial relics including African spears and Japanese samurai swords. The centrepiece is a cannonball from a trading ship, the *Mae de Deus,* which its captain blew up rather than surrender to Japanese war junks in Nagasaki harbour in 1610. Open weekdays, 2–5 pm, in the São Francisco Barracks, Praia Grande, behind the Lisboa Hotel.

Serious students of history should spend time in Macau's **Historical Archives**, a fascinating collection of manuscripts, books and letters relating to Portuguese exploration, diplomatic missions and Catholic outreach throughout Asia. It also covers the history of Japan, China and Southeast Asia over the last four centuries. Many items are microfilmed and the collection is well catalogued. It is housed in a restored mansion on the Avenida de Conselheio Ferreira de Almeida and is open Monday to Saturday, 9.30 am–5.30 pm, closing a half-hour earlier on Saturdays.

The **Leal Senado library** contains a large collection of newspapers dating back to 1820 and a rare book collection housed on teak shelves, possibly the most comprehensive and eclectic body of 19th- and 20th-century reminiscences, diaries, biographies, academic papers and gossip on China and oriental trade anywhere in Asia. Open Monday to Saturday, 1–7 pm. Note, however, that some stacks don't open until 3 pm.

Macau also has a memorial to the father of the 1911 Chinese revolution, **Sun Yat-sen**, who lived in Macau for two years from 1892. The collection, housed inside a gaudy hall on the Rua Ferreira do Amaral, is poorly laid out but is worth a visit if you're passing by. This isn't the leader's original home, which blew up during the war whilst being used as an ammunition dump. Open weekdays except Tuesday, 10 am– 1 pm; Saturday and Sunday, 3–5 pm.

Exhibitions of photographs, paintings and sculpture are sometimes mounted in the **Leal Senado Gallery**, other private art galleries in the city, and the Lou Lim Iok Garden pavilion.

On Taipa Island, the **Taipa House Museum** looks out over an old tea clipper anchorage and the waterfront praia. The house itself is a middle class Macanese home about 80 years old and has a small furniture collection complete with Chinese tile games. Open 10 am–5 pm daily.

SHOPPING

Macau is a great place to look for small **antiques** and cheap gold. However, fewer valuable heirlooms make their way onto the market these days and Macau never created a distinctive furniture style like Cape Dutch or even Goanese. It's best to look for plain Ming ceramic pieces, coins and bric-a-brac like snuff bottles and other mementoes which can be found quite easily. Most shops seem to stock mainly modern porcelain, figurines and blackwood furniture that lacks appeal. Watch for modern reproductions of antique pieces. **Gold** is retailed in Macau at just about the cheapest prices anywhere in the world, a product of low overheads and modern communications. Twenty-four-carat gold is weighed in taels, a Chinese measure equal to 1.2 troy ounces. Precious metals and gemstones are imported duty-free. Jewellery is usually set in 18-

carat gold. Most shops take credit cards and have English-speaking staff who tend to be a good deal more forthcoming than their Hong Kong counterparts.

The best antiques shops are the **Veng Meng** and the **Wing Tai**, both on the Avenida de Almeida, and **The Antique Shop** on Avenida de Coronel Mesquita. The **Rua de São Paulo** is worth browsing through for antiques and the **Avenida de Almeida Ribeiro** for gold shops. Stalls off Leal Senado Square near the **São Domingos market** and along **Rua Cinco de Outubro** are good for designer clothing overruns and separates. Pawnshops, distinguished by the sign of a gourd outside, are also good places to look out for used electrical goods and the like. Obviously there are no guarantees but prices are often competitive as the gamblers who had to hock their gear were probably in no position to get a good bargain.

GAMBLING

Macau is not Monte Carlo. There is no high society, few floor shows and much more kitsch than glitz. Macau's casinos are for straight-forward hardened gamblers only. Rule number one: don't bet more than you can afford to lose. Gamblers play because of an inner urge verging on obsession. Owners play for the built-in percentages, which is why they win in the long run, which in Macau means one man, Stanley Ho, a legendary multi-millionaire whose company, STDM—Sociedade de Turismo e Diversoes de Macau—provides around half of all of the Macau government's tax revenues! This must rank as the most lucrative franchise in the world. STDM first won it in 1962 and the current one runs until 1999.

The legal age for gambling is 18 for foreigners, 21 for residents. The most upmarket venue is the **Mandarin Oriental Hotel**. The most famous is the **Hotel Lisboa**, which also wins the prize as one of the gaudiest buildings in the East! Both have tables with blackjack, roulette and baccarat, whilst the Lisboa also offers boule, *fan tan* and *dai siu*. The seediest are the **Kam Pek** and the **Macau Palace**, a triple-deck ferry and a former floating restaurant. The **Hyatt Regency** also has a gaming room open 11 am–2.15 am daily. For the last-minute gambler there's the casino next to the ferry terminal which has an entire room of slot machines to swallow up your loose change.

Caveats abound. All of the above, except the Hyatt, are open 24 hours a day. Do *not* try and take photos anywhere: you will be dealt with instantly. Note too that Macau operates a few variations on international rules. For example, anyone side-betting more than the caller in blackjack can demand the cards. Naturally, these variations do not enhance your chances of escaping the table unsqueezed.

Blackjack is a simple card game also known as twenty-one. The dealer offers cards to the players who must collect as close to a face value of twenty-one points as possible. You lose if you exceed twenty-one even if the dealer forfeits too. If you win you get your money back plus 50 percent. Dealers stand on or above 17 and use mixed multiple decks to foil even the sharpest card-counters which takes the element of skill away entirely. **Baccarat** occupies the classier end of the social spectrum. A hand each is dealt to the player and the bank; bets are laid on which hand, when revealed, will total the closest to nine points. Casinos set a minimum bet level. Players can bet on either the dealer's or player's hand, but the house takes a percentage if the bank's hand wins.

Roulette isn't so popular, though it's an easy game to understand. The croupier spins a ball which comes to rest in one of 37 holes. If you guess correctly the payout is 35 times your bet. You can also bet on a red or black—an odd or even—number winning, which proportionally gives you a better chance of success than going for the jackpot. **Boule** is basically the same as roulette but played with a bigger ball and fewer numbers, which gives the bank a greater advantage than even with roulette. **Keno** is a lottery usually held every half hour. It was originally introduced to the West by Chinese labourers building America's railroads in the 19th century. Twenty numbers are drawn from a pool of 80 and you can bet on four or more that you predict will be among those about to be drawn.

Neither **poker** nor **craps** are now played in Macau; the poker table closed a few years back due to lack of interest. However, several other games are played that are unique to

Macau. **Fan tan** involves scooping a cup into a pile of buttons and betting on the number remaining after multiples of four have been removed. You can also bet on whether it will be a specific number or whether it is odd or even. **Dai siu** is very popular. Punters bet on whether three dice in a covered container will come up showing a big number (10-18 is *dai*, 'big') or small (*siu*, 3-9). The catch is that if the numbers are identical then you lose, unless you bet on the triple. **Pai kao** is Chinese dominoes where the house takes a percentage from the winnings for providing the services.

Slot machines are as dumb as they look, designed to offer infrequent small payouts and an ever-elusive jackpot. The Cantonese call them 'hungry tigers'. The casino often seduces the unwary with a huge readout linking a row of machines that speculates on the size of the next jackpot. The mechanics of the beast are simply random so even the degree of skill with which you manipulate the lever doesn't make a damn bit of difference. The odds of hitting a jackpot of three in a row are 1:8,000. Chances of getting four identical symbols are 1:160,000 whilst a row of five is a massive 1:3.2 million.

NIGHTLIFE

Like the gambling circuit in Macau, the **nightclubs** are here to service the thousands of Hong Kong Chinese visiting the enclave. Most of the clubs are stylistic clones of the big ones in Hong Kong. As there, the drinks are expensive and the prices for chatting to a sequinned and often bored girl are exorbitant, though slightly below those in Hong Kong. The **China City**, located near the ferry terminal, has a dance floor and a live band. Conversation costs HK$180 per hour with a minimum drinks charge of HK$200. The **Paris Night Club** in the Estoril Hotel is more friendly towards foreigners and also has a dance band. The girls there are predominantly Thai and charge only Ptc60 per hour for conversation; the minimum drinks costs are also sharply lower than in China City. **The Skylight** in the Presidente Hotel is closer to a European-style nightclub with a great view of the harbour and occidental strippers as featured in the floor show. The **Portas do Sol** has more of a dinner dance atmosphere, better food and occasional performances of Portuguese folk-dancing.

Macau's most famous erotic attraction is the **Crazy Paris Show**, a soft-porn revue launched by STDM in 1979 and a runaway success amongst tour groups of all nationalities and, they claim, both sexes. The routines fall short of art but are often inventive. There are, as the French producers might say, many ways to undress a showgirl, but the can-can chorus line and the underwater mermaid dance are old favourites. Performances are held nightly at the **Mona Lisa Hall** in the Hotel Lisboa at 8.30 pm and 10 pm with an extra showing at 11.30 pm on Saturdays, price Ptc90–100.

The two best **discos** in town are the **Mikado** in the Lisboa Hotel and the slightly higher-tech **Guia** hotel disco. Both run until 4 am and charge a small entrance fee. The **Royal Hotel** operates Macau's first Japanese-style **karaoke** lounge, open until 2 am. The **Guia Hotel** also has a number of rooms with sound systems in its own karaoke bar.

MASSAGE PARLOURS

Hong Kongers like to come to Macau because the Thai and Filipina girls are supposed to be even more fun than Cantonese and Taiwanese girls. This is massage Bangkok-style, with all sorts of extras at previously agreed prices. The parlours range from the gloriously upmarket to the downright seedy. There's not much romance here compared to the old name for a brothel—flower house—but I doubt much demand either. The most luxurious venues are the Estoril, Lisboa, Presidente and Sintra hotels. Parlours are generally open from midday until 4 am or 6 am.

SPORT

Macau is best known for the **greyhound racing**. The canidrome is close to the border gate. Races are run Tuesdays, Thursdays and Saturdays. Most of the trainers are either Irish or Australian so the place has an air of professionalism. The minimum bet is Ptc5 with a full range of exotic bets to complement it. The Macau Jockey Club opened for **horse racing** in 1989 and races twice weekly from September until May. Though a poor relation to the Hong Kong version, it boasts similar facilities and a slightly quieter atmosphere. The old **trotting club** has been disbanded.

The big sports event of the year is the **Macau Grand Prix**, a formula 3 race with side events for motorcycles and production cars. The 6.1-kilometre circuit is a killer of hairpin bends and narrow chicanes that weaves through the enclave's crowded streets before leading down to the one straight stretch along the harbour frontage. The key vantage points on the straight are by the Mandarin Oriental and Lisboa hotels, though rooms are booked months in advance and anyone not involved in the race is advised to steer well clear of Macau that weekend in late November. The **Macau marathon** is held in December and circles the city before heading out over the causeway bridge and around the islands of Taipa and Coloane.

Macau's favourite home-grown sport is a Portuguese invention, **hockey on roller-skates**, introduced by a priest just 30 years ago and still popular. The Macau Forum has the best playing surface for viewing as well as participating. The arena for playing the older form of pelota, or **jai alai**, has now been closed. **Tennis** and **squash** courts can be hired at the Mandarin Oriental and Hyatt Regency hotels. You can fight the locals for a table in the Lisboa Hotel or at the Jai Alai Stadium.

FESTIVALS

Macau runs the full calendar of Chinese festivals as in Hong Kong, though the **Lunar New Year** celebrations are much more lively because Macau has never banned the use of firecrackers. The flower market behind the Lisboa is lavish. The **Dragon Boat festival** falls on the fifth day of the fifth moon, usually in July or August. Races are held in front of the Praia Grande Bay with a spectacular international fireworks display. The autumn **Festival of Hungry Ghosts** is more involved than that in Hong Kong. Opera performances, as well as burnt offerings to those who died without a proper burial, culminate in a parade behind the image of Dai Si, the guardian of the gates of hell, which is itself later ceremonially burned.

Macau differs from Hong Kong because it also observes the feastdays of the Catholic calendar too. The main Easter

parade, the **Procession of Our Lord of Passos**, is held in
Macau on the first day of Lent, not on Good Friday as everywhere else in the world. The image of Christ on the Cross is
carried from the Cathedral past the twelve stations of the cross
to the church of St Augustine, accompanied by crimson-robed
clergy and a maiden dressed in white to represent St Veronica.

TAIPA ISLAND

Taipa was originally two islands, until the channel between
them silted up. In the 18th century it was a convenient
place for boats and ocean-going clippers to tranship their
cargoes before proceeding upriver to Canton. The village still
boasts many traditional crafts, including firecracker factories
which have been banned in Hong Kong for several decades.
The large modern building is the University of East Asia. The
racetrack at the back of the island is Macau's answer to the
corporate might of the Royal Hong Kong Jockey Club. Race
details can be had from the Macau Tourist Office.

There are one or two sights in Taipa worth looking for
if you're wandering around the town. The **Taipa House Museum** has some fine furniture in its collection fitting to its status
as a 1920s home of a middle class merchant. **Pou Tai Un temple** is a Buddhist foundation about a century old and offers
excellent vegetarian food from a café on a quiet verandah, and
even beer and soft drinks. The **Tin Hau temple** next to the bus
station has a beautifully ornate central hall. It was built in the
1820s and most of its buildings are now used as a school. The
Church of Our Lady of Carmel is set between Taipa village
and the restored praia waterfront. It has a fine garden in front
with a vine-covered bower and fountain. Unfortunately, the
church is often closed.

COLOANE ISLAND

Until 1910, Coloane was a refuge for pirates who preyed upon the delta trade routes. It is still a quiet place, even more restful than the main city. There are beaches at Cheok Van, close to the Pousada de Coloane hotel, and at Hac Sá, which literally means 'black sand beach'. **Tam Kong temple** sits on the waterfront facing the Chinese mainland and is dedicated to the god of seafarers, a child-god unique to Macau and Hong Kong revered for his weather-controlling powers. It has a pretty terracotta roof and two prize possessions, a whalebone carving of a model dragon boat with its rowers dressed in bowler hats and the snout of a shark caught in local waters.

The **chapel of St Francis Xavier** is dedicated to the saint who died in southern China in 1552, but the famous arm bone of the great Jesuit is now in the Seminary of St Joseph (São Jose). The shrine is a place of pilgrimage for Japanese couples who remember St Francis as the first to bring Western ideas to Japan. Also commemorated are the bones neatly laid out in cabinets in the sanctorium, of some of the 26 European and Japanese martyrs crucified by the shogun of Nagasaki in 1597. Other bones belong to early 17th-century martyrs from Vietnam. The **Chapel of Our Lady of Sorrows** on the other side of the island was built in 1966 to serve the survivors of the nearby leper colony of Ka Ho.

Coloane Park has a walk-in aviary with more than 200 species set in a designated country park area criss-crossed with hillside dirt trails. There are also some playground attractions for children and a restaurant playfully called **1999**, the date Macau is handed back to China. The park is open 9 am–7 pm. Buses #21A and 25 go direct to the park from the Hotel Lisboa. Other buses to Taipa and Coloane leave regularly from the terminus next to the A-Ma Temple and stop in front of the Hotel Lisboa before crossing the causeway bridge.

GETTING BACK TO HONG KONG

Leave some extra time to fight your way through the Macau jetfoil terminal which is in no way as organised as the Hong Kong end. Don't forget to bring a bottle of duty-free Portuguese white wine at a fraction of its price in Hong Kong.

Check with the Macau Tourist Board for details of ferry services to Canton and Kaohsiung in Taiwan.

MAINLAND CHINA

Hong Kong is the most convenient jumping off point in Asia for day-trips or long explorations of China. Here are a few suggestions for places that are close to the territory which are worth exploring as day trips or including in longer itineraries.

SHENZHEN

Day trips over the border to the most successful of China's Special Economic Zones can be easily arranged through China Travel Service (CTS). They can also arrange a visa at short notice. If you want to go on your own rather than as part of a tour, take the KCR to the border station at Lowu and walk over the border. Citibus also operates a cross-border route that runs several times daily. You can get a visa by entering the upper floor of the building immediately the other side of the river crossing. Check with the HKTA for details, times and the border closing time.

GUANGZHOU

The old port city of Canton, now known as Guangzhou, is a fascinating excursion for an overnight trip or several days' visit. The city has given itself a new lease of life since China opened to the West in 1978 and has an impressive prospect with the wide, muddy sweep of the Pearl River past Shamian island right in the heart of the city. There are monuments to its greatest son, the father of Chinese nationalism, Dr Sun Yat-sen, but it's good just to walk around and soak up the atmosphere of this old trade port. You know you're on the mainland but Guangzhou can't help having a feel of Hong Kong to it, not least because all the taxi drivers listen to Hong Kong radio all day. The back streets resemble Hong Kong 30 years ago, though the main thoroughfares boast high-rise buildings that are designed to impress. Train, hydrofoil and boat services run from Kowloon many times daily. The early morning ride up the upper reaches of the delta is a great way to relax after sleeping on the overnight ferry.

LIANHUASHAN

A hydrofoil traversing the delta calls at Lianhuashan in Panyu county, the delta area booming with a torrent of Hong Kong money from local millionaires returning to feather their ancestral villages with factories and schools. The resort isn't much to write home about, especially if you see it in gloomy, wet weather, but it has a 16th-century Ming-dynasty pagoda and some ruined fortifications that were ineffective in deterring the British during the Opium Wars. It also has some strange rocky scenery, though nothing to compare with Guilin, and some caves. Overnight stays are possible. Call the HKTA for updated travel details.

ZHUHAI AND ZHONGSHAN

Another of China's purpose-built windows on the world, Zhuhai Special Economic Zone is a short hop across the border from Macau. The county of Zhongshan that it lies in now has a population of 1.3 million in what is still an agricultural area of less than 2,000 sq km dotted with duck farms and lychee groves. **Zhongshan** is quite a rich place as many natives of the area who went overseas in the last 150 years have remitted money home. Package tours can be arranged in Hong Kong, or more cheaply in Macau, either for a one-day or three- or four-day visits which include Shiqi, Foshan and Guangzhou. Prices start at around $550.

All tours will inevitably visit the birthplace of Dr Sun Yat-sen in a village called **Cuiheng**, about an hour north of Macau and Zhuhai. **Shiqi** is a pleasant market town with a cantilever bridge over the river which is opened twice a day. This is a good place to see how Hong Kong money has changed a sleepy market town into an energized city within the space of a decade. **Zhuhai** was one of the very first areas of China opened to the West in 1978 and is a popular tourist resort with two 18-hole golf courses, an amusement park and a series of hot springs. Private cars can be hired and plenty of buses move around the delta if you want to go it alone. Hydrofoils from Hong Kong run to Zhuhai three times a day from the Hong Kong China Ferry terminal in Kowloon, price $120 on the boats run by Hong Kong China Hydrofoil Co. Jetcats go four times daily to Zhongshan from the same place, price $110, run by the Chu Kong Shipping Co.

ELSEWHERE IN CHINA

Further afield in southern China, the most popular places for travellers are the southwestern province of **Yunnan** and the picturesque cities of **Kunming** and **Guilin**. Charter flights by Dragonair run from Hong Kong to Guilin daily, and to Kunming on Wednesdays and Sundays. CAAC also flies to these destinations direct and via **Guangzhou**. The two-day train ride can be exhausting, but is really much more of a travel experience and should be attempted for that reason alone.

China's second city of **Shanghai** is a world of its own, a total contrast to Peking and very much a busy riverside port. There is a regular boat that plies up the coast from Hong Kong —the trip takes three days and nights—plus regular daily plane and train service. Nearby are the beautiful old cities of **Suzhou** and **Hangzhou**. **Fuzhou** and **Xiamen** (Amoy) are coastal cities well worth seeing on any overland journey up the coast to Shanghai.

Hong Kong is a good place to organise a trip into **Tibet** rather than relying on pot luck or physical endurance once in Chengdu. Several travel agencies offer packages, including Mera Travel. The situation in Lhasa changes without warning. These agents will tell you what they know, which may not be exactly as other travellers may tell you. Tibet was reopened to individual tourists in October 1991.

A–Z DATABASE

USEFUL INFORMATION AND EMERGENCY TELEPHONE NUMBERS

EMERGENCIES

Fire, Police and Ambulance, tel 999
Police Hotline and Taxi Service Complaints, tel 5277177
Police information, tel 8666166
Tropical Cyclone Warning Signal enquiries, tel 8351473
Family Planning Association hotline, tel 5722222

24-HOUR MEDICAL SERVICES

Adventist Hospital . . . 港安醫院	40 Stubbs Rd, Happy Valley, tel 5746211 跑馬地司徒拔道40號
Matilda's Hospital . . . 明德醫院	41 Mt Kellett Rd, The Peak, tel 8496301 山頂加列山道41號
Queen Elizabeth Hospital 伊利沙伯醫院	Wylie Rd, Yaumatei tel 7102111 九龍油蔴地衛理道
Queen Mary Hospital 瑪利醫院	Pokfulam Rd, Pokfulam, tel 8192111 香港薄扶林道

Samaritans 24-hour helpline, tel 8343333

VISITOR AND CONSUMER INFORMATION

HKTA information, tel 8017177 (daily 8 am–6 pm)
HKTA shopping hotline, tel 8017278 (daily 9 am–5 pm)
HKTA Mandarin-speaking hotline, tel 8017133
Community Advice bureau, tel 5245444
Consumer Council, tel 8563113
Arts Centre Box Office, tel 7342009
City Hall enquiries, tel 5229928
Urbtix enquiries, tel 7237713; bookings tel 7349009

TRANSPORT (PAGE 56)

Taxi Cab booking numbers, 5747311, 5276324, 5278524, 8611011

Ace Car Hire, tel 8930541

Avis Car Hire, tel 8906988

Holiday Rental, tel 7130113

Police Hotline and Taxi Service Complaints, tel 5277177

Transport Advisory Committee Complaints Hotline, tel 5776866

Airport buses information, tel 7454466

Star Ferry information, tel 3662576

Hong Kong and Yaumatei Ferry Company timetable information, tel 5423081

KCR, tel 6027799

KCRC Light Rail Transit, 4687788

MTR, tel 7500170

Peak Tram, tel 5220922

Hong Kong Tramways, tel 5598918

Heliservices, tel 5258817

MACAU TRANSPORT (PAGE 205)

East Asia Airlines, tel 5406806

Far East Jetfoils, tel 8593333

Hong Kong & Macau Hydrofoils, tel 5232136

Macau Jumbocats, tel 5599255

Macau High-speed Ferries, 8153043

Macau Hoverferries, tel 7361387

Macau microlight tour bookings, tel (853) 307343

COMMUNICATIONS

INTERNATIONAL TELEPHONE

Hong Kong Telecom International, Rm 102A, Exchange Square, Tower I, Central (24 hrs)

香港國際電訊 中環交易廣場第一座102A室

Hong Kong Telecom International, Hermes House, 10 Middle Rd, Tsimshatsui, (24 hrs)

香港國際電訊 尖沙咀中間道10號國際電訊大廈

Hong Kong Telecom International, Telecom House, 3 Gloucester Rd, Wanchai (8 am–9 pm weekdays, 8 am–3 pm Saturdays)

香港國際電訊 告士打道 3 號電訊大廈

Hong Kong Telecom International, Shop D37, Kai Tak Airport Terminal Bldg (daily 8 am–11 pm)

香港國際電訊 啓德機場主樓

Hong Kong Telecom International, 761 Nathan Rd, Mongkok (Monday–Saturday 8 am–8 pm)

香港國際電訊 旺角彌敦道761號

Hong Kong Telephone, Shop 102C, HK Convention & Exhibition Centre, 1 Harbour Rd, Wanchai (daily 9 am–6 pm)

香港電話公司 灣仔港灣道 1 號香港會議展覽中心

Hong Kong Telephone, Telecom Service Centre, 3 Hennessy Rd, Wanchai (Monday–Friday 9 am–6 pm, Saturdays 9 am–4 pm)

香港電話公司 灣仔軒尼詩道 3 號

Hong Kong Telephone, Shop 14, Lower Ground floor, Hilton Towers, 96 Granville Rd, Tsimshatsui (Monday–Saturday 11am–7 pm, Sundays and public holidays 2–7 pm)

香港電話公司 加連威老道96號希爾頓大廈地庫14室
International calls can also be made from 20 Hong Kong CSL shops during working hours.

24-HOUR FAX

Cable & Wireless, 37th Floor, Exchange Square Tower Two, Central, tel 8882888

香港電訊 中環交易廣場第二座37樓

TELEPHONE USAGE

Hong Kong telephone directory enquiries, tel 1081 (English), 1083 (Chinese)

International telephone directory enquiries, tel 013

International fax directory enquiries, tel 014

Telephone fault report line, tel 109

International Direct Dialing (IDD) code in Hong Kong is 001

International fax direct dialing code is 002
Operator-assisted international calls, tel 010
International collect calls, tel 011
Operator-assisted calls to most cities in China, tel 012
Time and temperature information, tel 18501

Home Direct Numbers allow callers from any phone in Hong Kong to speak directly to an overseas operator in the following countries and charge the call to the overseas number. For locations of several dedicated home direct phones and countries online in Hong Kong, call 013. Countries online in 1992 were: Australia 800 1611, Canada 800 1100, Finland 800 1358, Netherlands 800 1311, New Zealand 800 1641, Singapore 800 1651, South Korea 800 1821, Thailand 800 1661, UK 800 1441, USA 800 1111 (Alaska 800 1121).

UTILITIES
Hong Kong Electric Co Ltd fault report line, tel 5554000
China Light & Power Co Ltd fault report line, tel 7288333
Hong Kong & China Gas Co Ltd fault report line,
      tel 3345345
Water Supplies Dept: Hong Kong and Outer Islands,
      tel 8110788
Water Supplies Dept: Kowloon, tel 3960210

IN MACAU
Police emergencies, tel 333
Ambulance, tel 3300

HONG KONG ACCOMMODATION

KOWLOON: MORE THAN US$200 PER NIGHT
Kowloon Shangri-La . . . 64 Mody Rd, Tsimshatsui East,
香格里拉大酒店   tel 7212111, fax 7238686
                         尖沙咀麼地道64號

Peninsula . . . . Salisbury Rd, Tsimshatsui,
半島酒店   tel 3666251, fax 7224170
                         尖沙咀梳士巴利道

Nikko . . . . 72 Mody Rd, Tsimshatsui East,
日航酒店   tel 7391111, fax 3113122
     尖沙咀麼地道72號

Ramada Renaissance . . . 8 Peking Rd, Tsimshatsui,
華美達麗新酒店   tel 3751133, fax 3116611
     尖沙咀北京道 8 號

Regent . . . . 18 Salisbury Rd, Tsimshatsui,
麗晶酒店   tel 7211211, fax 7394546
     尖沙咀梳士巴利道18號

Sheraton Towers . . . . 20 Nathan Rd, Tsimshatui,
香港喜來登酒店   tel 7326781, fax 7393579
     尖沙咀彌敦道20號

HONG KONG ISLAND:
MORE THAN US$200 PER NIGHT

Conrad . . . . Pacific Place, 88 Queensway,
港麗酒店   Admiralty, tel 5213838
     金鐘道88號太古廣場

Grand Hyatt . . . . 1 Harbour Rd, Wanchai,
君悅酒店   tel 5881234, fax 8020677
     灣仔港灣道 1 號

Hilton . . . . 2 Queens Rd, Central,
希爾頓酒店   tel 5233111, fax 8452590
     中環皇后大道中 2 號

Island Shangri-La . . . . Pacific Place, 88 Queensway, Ad-
港島香格里拉大酒店   miralty, tel 8773838, fax 5218742
     金鐘道88號太古廣場

Mandarin Oriental . . . . 5 Connaught Rd, Central,
文華東方酒店   tel 5220111, fax 5297978
     中環干諾道中 5 號

Marriott . . . . Pacific Place, 88 Queensway, Ad-
萬豪酒店   miralty, tel 8108366, fax 8450737
     金鐘道88號太古廣場

Victoria . . . . Shun Tak Centre,
海港酒店   200 Connaught Rd, Central,
     tel 5407228, fax 8583398
     中環干諾道中200號信德中心

KOWLOON: MORE THAN $150 PER NIGHT

Holiday Inn Golden Mile
金域假日酒店

46-50 Nathan Rd, Tsimshatsui,
tel 3693111, fax 3698016
尖沙咀彌敦道46-50號

Holiday Inn Harbour View
海景假日酒店

70 Mody Rd, Tsimshatsui East,
tel 7215161, fax 3695672
尖沙咀麼地道70號

Hyatt Regency . . . . . .
香港凱悅酒店

67 Nathan Rd, Tsimshatsui,
tel 3111234, fax 7398701
尖沙咀彌敦道67號

Miramar . . . .
美麗華酒店

130 Nathan Rd, Tsimshatsui,
tel 3681111, fax 3691788
尖沙咀彌敦道130號

Omni Hong Kong . . . .
奧麗香港酒店

Harbour City, 3 Canton Rd,
Tsimshatsui, tel 7360088,
fax 7360011
尖沙咀廣東道3號海港城

Omni Marco Polo . . . .
奧麗馬哥孛羅酒店

Harbour City, Canton Rd,
Tsimshatsui, tel 7360888,
fax 7360022
尖沙咀廣東道3號海港城

Omni Prince . . . .
奧麗太子酒店

Harbour City, 3 Canton Rd,
Tsimshatsui, tel 7361888,
fax 7360066
尖沙咀廣東道3號海港城

Regal Airport Meridien . .
富豪機場酒店

Sa Po Rd, Kowloon City,
tel 7180333, fax 7184111
九龍城沙埔道

Regal Meridien . . . . . .
富豪九龍酒店

71 Mody Rd, Tsimshatsui East,
tel 7221818, fax 3696950
尖沙咀麼地道71號

Royal Garden . . . .
帝苑酒店

69 Mody Rd, Tsimshatsui East,
tel 7215215, fax 3699976
尖沙咀麼地道69號

Sheraton . . . .
香港喜來登酒店

20 Nathan Rd, Tsimshatsui,
tel 3691111, fax 7398707
尖沙咀彌敦道20號

HONG KONG ISLAND:
MORE THAN US$150 PER NIGHT

Furama Kempinski . . . . 1 Connaught Rd, Central,
富麗華酒店　　　　　　 tel 5255111, fax 8459339
　　　　　　　　　　　 中環干諾道中1號

New World Harbour View 1 Harbour Rd, Wanchai,
新世界海景酒店　　　　 tel 8028888, fax 8028833
　　　　　　　　　　　 灣仔港灣道1號

Park Lane Radisson . . . . 310 Gloucester Rd, Causeway
栢寧酒店　　　　　　　 Bay, tel 8903355, fax 5767853
　　　　　　　　　　　 銅鑼灣告士打道310號

KOWLOON: MORE THAN US$100 PER NIGHT

Ambassador . . . . 26 Nathan Rd, Tsimshatsui,
國賓酒店　　　　　　　 tel 3666321, fax 3690663
　　　　　　　　　　　 尖沙咀彌敦道26號

Concourse . . . . 20-46 Lai Chi Kok Rd,
京港酒店　　　　　　　 Mongkok, tel 3976683,
　　　　　　　　　　　 fax 3813768
　　　　　　　　　　　 旺角荔枝角道20-46號

Eaton. . . . . 380 Nathan Rd, Yaumatei,
逸東酒店　　　　　　　 tel 7821818, fax 7825563
　　　　　　　　　　　 油麻地彌敦道380號

Empress . . . . 17–19 Chatham Rd, Tsimshatsui,
帝后酒店　　　　　　　 tel 3660211, fax 7218168
　　　　　　　　　　　 尖沙咀漆咸道17-19號

Fortuna . . . . 355 Nathan Rd, Yaumatei,
富都酒店　　　　　　　 tel 3851011, fax 7800011
　　　　　　　　　　　 油麻地彌敦道355號

Grand Tower . . . . . . 627-641 Nathan Rd, Mongkok,
雅蘭酒店　　　　　　　 tel 7890011, fax 7890945
　　　　　　　　　　　 旺角彌敦道627-641號

Guangdong . . . . 18 Prat Avenue, Tsimshatsui,
粵海酒店　　　　　　　 tel 7393311, fax 7211137
　　　　　　　　　　　 尖沙咀寶勒巷18號

Imperial . . . . 30–34 Nathan Rd, Tsimshatsui,
帝國酒店　　　　　　　 tel 3662201, fax 3112360
　　　　　　　　　　　 尖沙咀彌敦道30-34號

International 國際酒店	33 Cameron Rd, Tsimshatsui, tel 3663381, fax 3695381 尖沙咀金馬倫道33號
Kowloon 九龍酒店	19–21 Nathan Rd, Tsimshatsui, tel 3698698, fax 3698698 尖沙咀彌敦道19-21號
Kowloon Panda Hotel 九龍悅來酒店	Tsuen Wah St, Tsuen Wan, New Territories, tel 409 1111, fax 4091818 新界荃灣荃華街
Metropole 京華國際酒店	75 Waterloo Rd, Yaumatei, tel 7611711, fax 7610769 油麻地窩打老道75號
Nathan 彌敦酒店	378 Nathan Rd, Yaumatei, tel 3885141, fax 7704262 油麻地彌敦道378號
New Astor 新雅圖酒店	11 Carnarvon Rd, Tsimshatsui, tel 3667261, fax 7227122 尖沙咀加拿芬道11號
New World 新世界酒店	24 Salisbury Rd, Tsimshatsui, tel 7244622, fax 7210714 尖沙咀梳士巴利道24號
Park 百樂大酒店	61–65 Chatham Rd, Tsimshatsui, tel 3661371, fax 7397259 尖沙咀漆咸道61-65號
Ramada Inn Kowloon 九龍華美達軒酒店	73–75 Chatham Rd, Tsimshatsui, tel 3111100, fax 3116000 尖沙咀漆咸道73-75號
Royal Pacific 皇家太平洋酒店	33 Canton Rd, Tsimshatsui, tel 7361188, fax 7361212 尖沙咀廣東道33號
Shamrock 新樂酒店	223 Nathan Rd, Yaumatei, tel 7352271, fax 7367354 油麻地彌敦道223號
Stanford 仕德福酒店	18 Soy St, Yaumatei, tel 7811881, fax 3883733 油麻地豉油街18號

Windsor . . . . 39–43A Kimberley Rd, Tsimshat-
溫莎酒店 sui, tel 7395665, fax 3115101
尖沙咀金巴利道39至43A號

HONG KONG ISLAND:
MORE THAN US$100 PER NIGHT

China Harbour View . . . 189–193 Gloucester Rd, Wanchai,
中華海景酒店 tel 8382222, fax 8380136
灣仔告士打道189-193號

China Merchants . . . . . 160-161 Connaught Rd, Western,
華商酒店 tel 5596888, fax 5590038
西環干諾道西160-161號

City Garden . . . . 231 Electric Rd, North Point,
城市花園酒店 tel 8872888, fax 8871111
北角電氣道231號

Eastin Valley . . . . 1A Wang Tak St, Happy Valley,
東豪酒店 tel 5749922, fax 8381622
跑馬地宏德街1A

Emerald . . . . 152 Connaught Rd, Western,
綠晶酒店 tel 5468111, fax 5590255
西環干諾道西152號

Excelsior . . . . 281 Gloucester Rd, Causeway
怡東酒店 Bay, tel 8948888, fax 8956669
銅鑼灣告士打道281號

Grand Plaza . . . . 2 Kornhill Rd, Quarry Bay,
康蘭酒店 tel 8860011, fax 8861738
鰂魚涌康怡路 2 號

Harbour . . . . 116–122 Gloucester Rd, Wanchai,
華國酒店 tel 5118211, fax 5722185
灣仔告士打道116-122號

Lee Gardens . . . . Hysan Avenue, Causeway Bay,
利園酒店 tel 8953311, fax 5769775
銅鑼灣希慎道33-37 號

Luk Kwok . . . . 72 Gloucester Rd, Wanchai,
六國酒店 tel 8662166, fax 8662622
灣仔告士打道72號

New Harbour . . . . . . 41–49 Hennessy Rd, Wanchai,
星港酒店 tel 8611166, fax 8656111
灣仔軒尼詩道41-49號

Ramada Inn . . . . 61–73 Lockhart Rd, Wanchai,
華美酒店   tel 8611000, fax 8656023
                  灣仔駱克道61-73號

KOWLOON: MORE THAN US$50 PER NIGHT

Bangkok Royal . . . . . 2–12 Pilkem St, Yaumatei,
曼谷貴賓酒店   tel 7359181, fax 7302209
                  油麻地庇利金街2-12號

Booth Lodge . . . . 11 Wing Sing Lane, Yaumatei
  (Salvation Army)   tel 7719266, telex 57091
救世軍卜維廉賓館   油麻地永星里11號

Caritas Bianchi Lodge . . 4 Cliff Rd, Yaumatei,
明愛白英奇賓館   tel 3881111, fax 7706669
                  油麻地石壁道4號

Caritas Lodge . . . . . . 134 Boundary St, Shamshuipo,
明愛賓館   tel 3393777, fax 3382864
                  深水埗界限街134號

Holy Carpenter Hostel . 1 Dyer Ave, Hung Hom,
聖匠賓館   tel 3620301, fax 3622193
                  紅磡戴亞街1號

King's . . . . 473 Nathan Rd, Yaumatei,
高雅酒店   tel 7801281
                  油麻地彌敦道473號

The Salisbury YMCA . . 41 Salisbury Road, Tsimshatsui,
香港基督教青年會   tel 3692211, fax 7399315
                  尖沙咀梳士巴利道41號

YMCA International House 23 Waterloo Rd,
青年會國際賓館   Yaumatei, tel 7719111, fax
                  3885926
                  油麻地窩打老道23號

YWCA Guest House . . . 5 Man Fuk Rd, Waterloo Hill
女青會賓館   Rd, Yaumatei, tel 7139211,
                  fax 7611269
                  油麻地窩打老山道文福道5號

HONG KONG ISLAND:
MORE THAN US$50 PER NIGHT

Noble Hostel . . . . . . Flat C1, 7/F, Paterson Bldg,
高富旅館

	37 Paterson St, Causeway Bay, tel 5766148
	銅鑼灣百德新街37號百德大廈 7 樓 C1
YMCA Harbour View. . . . **International House**	4 Harbour Rd, Wanchai, tel 8020111, fax 8029063

灣景國際賓館（中華基督教青年會） 灣仔港灣道 4 號

KOWLOON: LESS THAN US$50 PER NIGHT

Chungking House. . . . . 重慶招待所	Block A, Chungking Mansion, 4–5/F, 40 Nathan Rd, Tsimshatsui, tel 3665362 尖沙咀彌敦道40號重慶大廈A座4-5樓
STB Hostel . . . . 學聯旅舍	2/F, Great Eastern Mansion, 255–261 Reclamation Rd, Mongkok, tel 3321073, fax 3850153 旺角新填地街255-261號 2 樓

NEW TERRITORIES: LESS THAN US$120 PER NIGHT

Regal Riverside . . . . . 麗豪酒店	Tai Chung Kiu Rd, Shatin, tel 6497878 沙田大涌橋道
Royal Park. . . . . 帝都酒店	8 Pak Hok Ting St, Shatin, tel 6012111 fax 6013666 沙田白鶴汀街 8 號

OUTLYING ISLANDS: AROUND US$30 PER NIGHT

Cheung Chau Star House 長洲星光渡假村	149 Tai Sun Bak St, Cheung Chau, tel 9812186 長洲大新後街149號
Warwick. . . . . 華威酒店	East Bay, Cheung Chau, tel 9810081 fax 9819174 長洲東灣
Han Lok Yuen. . . . . . 閒樂園	Hung Shing Ye Beach, Lamma, tel 9820608 南丫島洪聖爺灣
Lamma Vacation House 南丫渡假屋	29 Main St, Yung Shue Wan, Lamma, tel 9820427 南丫榕樹灣正街29號

Man Lai Wah . . . . . . 文麗華	Main St, Yung Shue Wan, Lamma, tel 9820220 南丫榕樹灣正街
Cheung Sha Resort . . . . 芙蓉閣	Cheung Sha, Lantau, tel 8911161 大嶼山長沙
Jockey Club, Mong . . . . **Tung Wan Hostel** 賽馬會望東灣旅舍	Cheung Sha, Lantau, tel 9841389 大嶼山長沙
Po Lin Monastery . . . . **& Lantau Tea Gardens** 寶蓮寺	Ngong Ping, Lantau, tel 9856854 大嶼山昂平
Sea Breeze Hotel . . . . . 海風酒店	Pui O Beach, Lantau, tel 9847977 大嶼山貝澳
Silvermine Bay Beach . . . 銀礦灣酒店	Mui Wo, Lantau, tel 9848295 大嶼山梅窩
Trappist Haven Monastery 熙篤會神樂院	Lantau, tel 9876286 大嶼山

MACAU ACCOMMODATION (PAGE 207)

OVER US$100 PER NIGHT

Bela Vista . . . . 澳門峯景酒店	8 Rua do Comendador Kou Ho Neng, tel 965333, fax 965588 澳門高可寧新市街 8 號

LESS THAN US$100 PER NIGHT

Hyatt Regency . . . . . . 凱悅酒店	2 Estrada Almirante Marques Esparteiro, Taipa Island, tel 853-321234, fax 853-320595 氹仔史伯泰海軍馬路 2 號
Mandarin Oriental . . . . 文華東方酒店	Avenida da Amizade, tel 567888, fax 594589 友誼大馬路
Pousada de São Tiago . . . 聖地牙哥酒店	Fortaleza de São Tiago, Avenida da Republica, tel 78111, fax 553170 HK bkg 5217413 民國大馬路

Royal . . . . Estrada da Vitoria, tel 552222,
皇都酒店　　　　　　　　　fax 563008 HK bkg 542033
　　　　　　　　　　　　　　得勝馬路

Pousada Ritz . . . . Rua da Boa Vista, tel 339955,
濠璟酒店　　　　　　　　　fax 317826 HK bkg 5406333
　　　　　　　　　　　　　　竹室正街

Lisboa . . . . Avenida da Amizade, tel 577666,
葡京酒店　　　　　　　　　fax 562285 HK bkg 5591028
　　　　　　　　　　　　　　友誼大馬路

LESS THAN US$80 PER NIGHT

Beverly Plaza . . . . Avenida Dr Rodrigo Rodrigues,
富豪酒店　　　　　　　　　tel 337755, fax 308878 HK bkg
　　　　　　　　　　　　　　5406333
　　　　　　　　　　　　　　羅理基博士大馬路

Guia . . . . 1 Estancia Engenheiro Trigo,
東望洋酒店　　　　　　　　Guia Hill, tel 513888,
　　　　　　　　　　　　　　fax 559822 HK bkg 7709303
　　　　　　　　　　　　　　東望洋山松山馬路 1 號

Matsuya . . . . 5 Estancia São Francisco,
松屋酒店　　　　　　　　　tel 575466, fax 568080 HK bkg
　　　　　　　　　　　　　　3686181
　　　　　　　　　　　　　　馬斯欄馬路 5 號

Metropole . . . . 63 Rua da Praia Grande,
京都酒店　　　　　　　　　tel 88166, fax 330890 HK bkg
　　　　　　　　　　　　　　5406333
　　　　　　　　　　　　　　南灣街63號

Mondial . . . . Rua Antonio Basto, tel 566866,
環球酒店　　　　　　　　　fax 514083 HK bkg 5408180
　　　　　　　　　　　　　　巴士度街

Pousada de Coloane . . . . Praia de Cheoc Van, Coloane
竹灣酒店　　　　　　　　　Island, tel 328143, fax 328251
　　　　　　　　　　　　　　HK bkg 7366922
　　　　　　　　　　　　　　路環竹灣

Presidente . . . . Avenida da Amizade, tel 553888,
總統大酒店　　　　　　　　fax 552735 HK bkg 5256873
　　　　　　　　　　　　　　友誼大馬路

Sintra.	Avenida Dom Joao IV,
新麗華酒店	tel 385111, fax 567769 HK
	bkg 5408028
	約翰四世大馬路

LESS THAN US$30 PER NIGHT

Capital	Rua Contantino 3, tel 571782
京華酒店	貢士誕甸奴街
Central	26 Avenida Almeida Ribeiro,
中央酒店	tel 777000
	亞美打利卑盧大馬路
East Asia	1 Rua da Madeira, tel 572631,
東亞酒店	fax 389748 HK bkg 5406333
	新埗頭街 1 號
Estoril	Avenida Sidonio Pais, tel 57208,
愛都大酒店	fax 71215 HK bkg 5221832
	士多烏拜斯大馬路
Grand	146 Avenida Almeida Ribeiro,
國際酒店	tel 579922, fax 511591
	亞美打利卑盧大馬路146 號
Ka Va.	Val Santo Joao 5, tel 574022
嘉華賓館	大堂斜巷 5 號
Kam Loi	Avenida Infante Dom Henrique
金來別墅	34, tel 77608
	殷皇子大馬路
Kuan Heng	Rua Ponte e Horta 4, tel 5733629
羣興賓館	羣興新街 4 號
Ko Wah	Rua Felicidade, tel 75452
高華酒店	福隆新街
London	4 Praca Ponte e Horta, tel 83388
英京酒店	司打街口4- 6 號
Nam Long	Rua Dr Pedro Jose Lobo 30,
南龍別墅	tel 81042
	羅保博士街 30號
Nam Pan.	Avenida Dom Joao IV,
南濱別墅	tel 572289
	約翰四世大馬路

Peninsula . . . .   Rua das Lorchas, tel 318899,
半島酒店   fax 344933 HK bkg 8339300
                           火船頭街

Universal. . . . .   Rua Felcidade 73, tel 573629
世界賓館   福隆新街 73 號

AIRLINES: ON-LINE OFFICES (PAGE 150)

Air France, res 5248145, flt info 7696662

Air India, res 5221176

Air Lanka, res 7697141, 7185359, flt info 7697183

Air Mauritius, res & flt info 5231114

Air New Zealand, res 7471888, flt info 7471234

Air Niugini, res 5242151

Alitalia, res 5237047, flt info 7696448

All Nippon Airways, res 8107100, flt info 7698606

American Airlines, res 8269269

Asiana Airlines, res 5238585, flt info 7697782

British Airways, res 8680303, 3689255, flt info 7698380, 8680768

CAAC/Air China (PRC), res 8610322, flt info 7698571

Canadian Airlines, res 8683123, flt info 7697113

Cathay Pacific, res 7471888, flt info 7471234, 7673888

China Airlines (Taiwan), res 8682299, 3674181, flt info 7698391-5

Dragonair, res 7360202, 8108055, flt info 7697727

Emirates, res & flt info 5267171

Garuda Indonesia, res 8400000, flt info 5229071

Gulf Air, 8680832, flt info 7698337

Japan Airlines, res 5230081, 3113355, flt info 7696524

KLM Royal Dutch Airlines, res 8228111, flt info 7698111

Korean Air, res 3686221, 5235177, 7337111, flt info 7697511

Lauda Air, res 5246178, flt info 7697017

Lufthansa, res 8682313, flt info 7696560

Malaysia Airlines, res 5218181, flt info 7697967

Northwest Airlines, res 8104288, flt info 7697345-7

Philippine Airlines, res 3694521, 5227018, flt info 7698111, 7696253

Qantas, res 5242101, flt info 5256206, 7698571

Royal Brunei Airlines, res 7471888, flt info 7475522, 7673888

Royal Nepal Airlines, res 3659151

Singapore Airlines, res 5202233, flt info 7696387, 5211133

South African Airways, res 8773277, 8680303, flt info 8680768

Swissair, res 5293670, flt info 7698864

Thai International, res 5295601, 7309225, flt info 7697421

United Airlines, res 8104888, flt info 76971155

ART GALLERIES & ANTIQUE SHOPS (PAGE 146)

Alisan Fine Arts Ltd . . . . 315 Prince's Bldg, Central,
藝倡畫廊
tel 5261091
中環太子大廈315室

Altfield Gallery . . . . . 31 Lyndhurst Terrace, Central,
藝苑
tel 5422098
中環擺花街31號地下

Ancient Chinese Antiques 199 Hollywood Rd, Central,
古華鑑 (古美術)
tel 5410183
香港荷里活道 199 號地下

Cat Street Galleries . . . . 38 Lok Ku Rd, Sheung Wan,
嚤囉街中心
tel 5418908
上環樂古道38號

Chan Shing Kee . . . . . . 228–230 Queen's Rd, Central,
陳勝記
tel 5440808
中環皇后大道中228-230號

Artland Gallery . . . . . . 48 Hollywood Rd, Central,
藝林閣
tel 5457376
中環荷李活道48號

Gallerie du Monde . . . . 328–9 The Mall, Pacific Place,
雅高
88 Queensway, Admiralty,
tel 5250529, fax 5254959
金鐘道88號太古廣場328-9號

Hanart TZ Gallery . . . . 5/F Old Bank of China Bldg.
漢雅軒

Bank St, Central,
tel 5269019, fax 5212001
中環德輔道 2A 舊中國銀行大厦 5 樓

Helene Bennett Antiques   7 Hollywood Rd, Central,
tel 5444988
中環荷李活道 7 號

Honeychurch Antiques Ltd   29 Hollywood Rd, Central,
tel 5432433
中環荷李活道29號

Ian McLean . . . .   73 Wyndham St, Central,
tel 5244542, fax 8453471
中環雲咸街73號

Kander's . . . .   G/F, Alexandra House, 15 Des
勝大莊美術館   Voeux Rd, Central, tel 8690812
中環德輔道中15歷山大廈地下

Plum Blossom (Intl) Ltd   306–7 One Exchange Square,
萬玉堂   8 Connaught Place, Central,
tel 5212189, fax 8684398
中環交易廣場 1 座306-7

Pottery Workshop. . . . .   2 Lower Albert Rd, Central,
樂天陶社   tel 5257949
中環下亞厘畢道 2 號

Pok Art House. . . . . . .   18 Granville Rd, Tsimshatsui,
博雅藝術有限公司   tel 3685930
尖沙咀加連威老道18號

San Shi Tang Antiques . .   G/F, 196 Queen's Rd, Central,
三喜堂   tel 8150603
中環皇后大道中196號地下

Susan Chen & Co . . . . .   Rm 1002, Car Po Comm'l Bldg,
18–20 Lyndhurst Terrace, Central,
tel 5415779, fax 8542986
中環擺花街18-20號嘉寶商業大廈1002室

Teresa Colman Fine Arts   37 Wyndham St, Central,
杜麗沙高文   tel 5262450
中環雲咸街39號

T.Y. King . . . .   Swire House, 9 Connaught Rd,
金財記   Central, tel 5236434
中環干諾道 9 號太古大廈

Tong-In Antiques Gallery 5–15 Hankow Rd, Tsimshatsui,
通仁 tel 3691406
尖沙咀漢口道5-15號

AUCTION HOUSES

Christie's Swire . . . . . . Room 2804, Alexandra House,
  Hong Kong Ltd 16-20 Chater Rd, Central,
太古佳士得有限公司 tel 5215396, fax 8452646
中環遮打道16-20號歷山大廈2804室

Sotheby's Hong Kong Ltd Rm 502, Exchange Square II,
蘇富比拍賣行 Central, tel 5248121,
fax 8106238
中環交易廣場第二座502室

AUDIO, CAMERA, HI-FI SHOPS (PAGE 148)

A1 Electronics . . . . Holiday Inn Golden Mile,
Basement Shop 1178, 50 Nathan
Rd, Tsimshatsui, tel 3666552
尖沙咀彌敦道50號金域假日酒店地庫

Akihabara Electronic Centre 7/F, Chung Kiu Centre
秋葉原 47–51Shan Tong St, Mongkok,
tel 7800911
旺角山東街47-51號中僑大廈7樓

Carlton Audio . . . . . . 80D Nathan Rd, Tsimshatsui,
  & Photo Supplies tel 3685097
華爾登影音器材有限公司 尖沙咀彌敦道80號D

Delon Photo & HiFi Centre Shop 323 Ocean Centre,
狄龍影音有限公司 Tsimshatsui, tel 7302756
尖沙咀海洋中心323室

Photo Scientific . . . . . . 6 Stanley St, Central, tel 5221903
攝影科學有限公司 中環士丹利街6號

Rodgers Audio. . . . . . . Shop 232, Prince's Bldg, Central,
  & Video Co Ltd tel 8107828
樂爵士影音公司 中環太子大廈232室

The Sound Chamber . . . 1801Caxton House, 1 Duddell
St, Central, tel 5263431
中環都爹利街1號樂古行1801室

BOOKSTORES (PAGE 151)

Arts Bookshop	2/F, Arts Centre, 2 Harbour Rd, Wanchai, tel 8662182 灣仔港灣道 2 號藝術中心 2 樓
Bookazine	Shop 249 Prince's Bldg, Central, tel 5221785 中環太子大廈249室
Chung Hwa Book Company 中華書局	450-2 Nathan Rd, Tsimshatsui, tel 3856588 尖沙咀彌敦道450-2號
Commercial Press . . . . . 商務印書局	9–15 Yee Wo St, Causeway Bay, tel 8908028 銅鑼灣怡和街9-15號
Hong Kong Book Centre 香港圖書文具有限公司	Basement, On Lok Yuen Bldg, 25 Des Voeux Rd, Central, tel 5227064, 5238847, 5258216 Shop B64, First basement, The Landmark, Central Shop 303, Podium level, One Exchange Square, Central 中環德輔道25號地庫 中環置地廣場 B 64室 中環交易廣場 一座 303室
Joint Publishing (HK) Ltd 三聯書店	9 Queen Victoria St, Central, tel 5230105 中環域多利皇后街 9 號
Kelly & Walsh . . . . 必發圖書有限公司	Two Pacific Place, Admiralty, tel 5227893 金鐘太古廣場第二座
The New Age Shop 	7 Old Bailey St, Central, tel 8108694 中環奧卑利街 7 號
The Professional Bookshop	104A Alexandra House, 10 Chater Rd, Central, tel 5265387, fax 8770755 中環遮打道10號歷山大廈104 A 室

SCMP Family Bookshop 南華早報書店	Star Ferry Concourse, Central, tel 5221012 中環天星小輪大堂
Swindon's . . . . 晨衝	Ocean Terminal, Tsimshatsui, tel 7306877 13 Lock Rd, Tsimshatsui tel 3678789 尖沙咀海運大廈 尖沙咀樂道13號
Wanderlust Books Ltd . .	30 Hollywood Rd, Central, tel 5232042 中環荷李活道30號

CARPETS AND RUGS (PAGE 147)

Aristocrat Rug Co	23 Mody Rd, Tsimshatsui, tel 7234873 尖沙咀麼地道23號
Banyan Tree	2/F, Shop 214, Prince's Bldg, Central, tel 5235561 中環太子大廈2樓214室
Carpet House . . . . 鳴盛行地毯公司	I-30 Lippo Sun Plaza, 28 Canton Rd, Tsimshatsui, tel 3758001 尖沙咀廣東道28號太陽廣場
Carpet World . . . . 地毯世界	G/F, 46 Morrison Hill Rd, Wanchai, tel 8930202 灣仔摩利臣山道46號地下
Chinese Carpet Centre . . 珍藝行地毯公司	Shop 178, Ocean Terminal, Harbour City, Kowloon, tel 7351030 尖沙咀海運中心178室
Chinese Rugs Co . . . . . 中華地毯	3-4 Hanoi Rd, 13/F, Century House, Tsimshatsui, tel 7227713 尖沙咀河内道3-4號世紀商業大廈
Hwa Yee Carpet Co . . . . 華藝地毡有限公司	31–33 King's Rd, North Point, tel 5784928 北角英皇道31至33A1號

Sunny Rug Co . . . . 102 Austin Rd, Tsimshatsui,
tel 3684938
尖沙咀柯士甸道102號

Tai Ping Carpet Salon . . Wing On Plaza, 62 Mody Rd,
太平地毯有限公司 Tsimshatsui East, tel 3694061
尖沙咀麼地道永安廣場

Tribal Arts & Crafts . . . . 37 Wyndham St, Central,
tel 5222682
中環雲咸街37號

CHEMISTS

Manning's . . . . Shop B, 22-23 1st Basement,
萬寧藥房 Landmark Bldg, 12-16A Des
Voeux Rd, Central, tel 5249855

Unit 230, Ocean Galleries,
Harbour City, Phase 4, 3 Canton
Rd, Tsimshatsui, tel 7350841
中環置地廣場第一地庫22-23B 室
尖沙咀海港城第 4 期海洋廊230室

Watson's . . . . G/F, Melbourne Plaza, 33
屈臣氏 Queen's Rd, Central, tel 5230666
Haiphong Mansion 101, Nathan
Rd, Tsimshatsui, tel 3666831
中環皇后大道中33號萬邦行地下
尖沙咀彌敦道101號海防大廈

Nam Pei Hong . . . . . G/F, 117 Des Voeux Rd, Central,
   (Chinese medicine) tel 5436536
南北行 中環德輔道中117號地下

CINEMAS (PAGE 55)

HONG KONG ISLAND

Arts Centre . . . . Lim Por Yuen Theatre, Arts
藝術中心 Centre, Wanchai, tel 5820200
灣仔藝術中心林百欣劇院

Cathay ABC . . . . 125 Wanchai Rd, Wanchai,
國泰戲院 A B C tel 8335677
灣仔灣仔道125號

Cine-Art House . . . . . . Ground floor, Sun Hung Kai
影藝戲院 Centre, Wanchai, tel 8275015
灣仔新鴻基中心地下

Columbia Classics . . . . Great Eagle Centre, Harbour Rd,
新華戲院 Wanchai, tel 8278291
灣仔港灣道鷹君中心

Gala I . . . . Cityplaza, Taikoo Shing,
嘉年戲院 tel 5670421
北角太古城中心

Golden Hung Kai . . . . 483 King's Rd, North Point,
金鴻基戲院 tel 5656328
北角英皇道483號

Palace . . . . 2/F, World Trade Centre, 280
碧麗宮戲院 Gloucester Rd, Causeway Bay,
tel 8951500
銅鑼灣告士打道280號

Park . . . . 180 Tunglowan Rd, Causeway
百樂戲院 Bay, tel 5705454
銅鑼灣道180號

Pearl-Jade . . . . Paterson St, Causeway Bay,
翡翠明珠戲院 tel 5776351
銅鑼灣百德新街

Queen's . . . . 51 Queen's Rd, Central,
皇后戲院 tel 5227036
中環皇后大道中51號

UA Queensway . . . . . . G/F, Pacific Place,
UA 金鐘 88 Queensway, Admiralty,
tel 8690322
金鐘道88號太古廣場地下

KOWLOON AND NEW TERRITORIES

Astor Classics . . . . . . 380 Nathan Rd, Yaumatei,
普慶戲院 Kowloon, tel 7811833
油麻地彌敦道380號

Broadway . . . . 6 Sai Yeung Choi St, Mongkok,
百老滙戲院　　　　　　　tel 3325731
　　　　　　　　　　　　旺角西洋菜街 6 號

Harbour City . . . . . . World Shipping Centre, Canton
海城戲院　　　　　　　　Rd, Tsimshatsui, tel 7356915
　　　　　　　　　　　　尖沙咀廣東道環球航運中心

Ocean . . . . 3 Canton Rd, Tsimshatsui,
海運戲院　　　　　　　　tel 7305444
　　　　　　　　　　　　尖沙咀廣東道 3 號

UA6 Shatin . . . . New Town Plaza, Shatin,
沙田 UA6　　　　　　　　tel 6980651
　　　　　　　　　　　　沙田新城市廣場

UA Whampoa . . . . . . Whampoa Plaza, Hung Hom,
UA 黃埔　　　　　　　　tel 3031041
　　　　　　　　　　　　紅磡黃埔廣場

COFFEE SHOPS AND TEAHOUSES

China Tee Club . . . . . 1/F, Pedder Bldg, Pedder St, Cen-
中國茶會　　　　　　　　tral, tel 5210233
　　　　　　　　　　　　中環畢打街畢打行 1 樓

Finealley . . . . 2 Glenealy, Central, tel 5233595
　　　　　　　　　　　　中環己連拿利街 2 號

Luk Yu Tea House . . . . 24–6 Stanley St, Central,
陸羽茶室　　　　　　　　tel 5235463
　　　　　　　　　　　　中環士丹利街24-6號

Post 97 . . . . Lan Kwai Fong, Central,
　　　　　　　　　　　　tel 8109333
　　　　　　　　　　　　中環蘭桂坊

Queen's Café . . . . . . 7 Tang Lung St, Causeway Bay,
皇后飯店　　　　　　　　tel 8939103
　　　　　　　　　　　　銅鑼灣登龍街 7 號

COMPACT DISCS (PAGE 152)

Delight Music . . . . . . 3/F, Hong Kong Hotel Arcade,
娛樂唱片公司　　　　　　Canton Rd, Tsimshatsui,
　　　　　　　　　　　　tel 7353662
　　　　　　　　　　　　尖沙咀廣東道香港酒店商場 3 樓

Jackie's Music Shop . . . .
怡聲唱片公司
205 Excelsior Plaza , 24–6 East
Point Rd, Causeway Bay,
tel 5768157
銅鑼灣東角道怡東酒店商場

Kai Lai . . . .
佳麗唱片公司
Basement Shop 25A, Man Yee
Bldg, Central, tel 5222782
中環萬宜大廈地庫25A

Megastore . . . .
Radio City, 505-511 Hennessy
Rd, Causeway Bay, tel 8920123
銅鑼灣軒尼詩道505-511號

Samson Co. . . . .
雅達唱片公司
G35 Peninsula Centre, 67 Mody
Rd, Tsimshatsui East,
tel 7236486
尖沙咀麼地道67號半島中心 G35

United Records . . . . .
聯邦唱片有限公司
20A Lan Fong Rd, Causeway Bay,
tel 5778703
Basement Shop 63, Edinburgh
Tower, The Landmark, Central,
tel 5226970
銅鑼灣蘭芳道20A

CONSULATES

Argentina . . . .
阿根廷駐港總領事館
2510 Jardine House, Connaught
Place, Central, tel 5233208
中環怡和大廈2510室

Australia . . . .
澳洲總領事館
23-4/F, Harbour Centre,
25 Harbour Rd, Wanchai,
tel 8278881
灣仔港灣道25號海港中心23-4樓

Austria . . . .
奧地利領事館
Rm 2201 Wang Kee Bldg, 34-7
Connaught Rd, Central,
tel 5228086
中環干諾道34-7號宏記大廈2201室

Bangladesh. . . . .
孟加拉領事館
3807 China Resources Bldg,
26 Harbour Rd, Wanchai,
tel 8274278
灣仔港灣道26號華潤大廈3807室

Belgium . . . .
比利時領事館

9/F, St John's Bldg, 33 Garden Rd, Central, tel 5243111
中環花園道33號聖約翰大廈 9 樓

Brazil . . . .
巴西總領事館

Rm 1504 Dina House, 11 Duddell St, Central, tel 5257002
中環爹利道帝納大廈1504室

Canada . . . .
加拿大領事館

11–14/F, One Exchange Square, 8 Connaught Place, Central, tel 8104321
中環交易廣場一座11-14樓

Chile . . . .
智利領事館

11408 Great Eagle Centre, 23 Harbour Rd, Wanchai, tel 8271826
灣仔港灣道鷹君中心11408室

Colombia . . . .
哥倫比亞總領事館

6A, CMA Bldg, 64-66 Connaught Rd, Central, tel 5458547
中環干諾道廠商會大廈6A

Costa Rica . . . .
哥斯達尼加總領事館

Flat C10 Hung On Bldg, 3 Tin Hau Temple Rd, Causeway Bay, tel 5665181
銅鑼灣天后廟道 3 號鴻安大廈 C10

Denmark . . . .
丹麥領事館

2402B Great Eagle Centre, 23 Harbour Rd, Wanchai, tel 8279737
灣仔港灣道23號鷹君中心2402B

Dominican Republic . . .
多明尼加共和國領事館

Rm 709, Asia Standard Tower, 59-65 Queen's Rd, Central, tel 5212801
中環皇后大道中59-65號泛海大廈709室

Egypt . . . .
埃及領事館

1309 Great Eagle Centre, 23 Harbour Rd, Wan chai, tel 8270668
灣仔港灣道鷹君中心1309室

Finland . . . .
芬蘭領事館

1818 Hutchison House, Central, tel 5255385
中環和記大廈1818室

France . . . . 法國總領事館	26/F, Tower II, Admiralty Centre, 18 Harcourt Rd, Admiralty, tel 5294351 金鐘夏愨道18號海富中心二座26樓
Germany . . . . 德國領事館	21/F, United Centre, 95 Queensway, Admiralty, tel 5298855 金鐘統一中心21樓
Iceland . . . . 冰島領事館	48/F, Hopewell Centre, Wanchai, tel 5283911 灣仔合和中心48樓
India . . . . 印度領事館	16D United Centre, 95 Queensway, Admiralty, tel 5291289 金鐘統一中心16D
Indonesia . . . . 印尼領事館	6-8 Keswick St, Causeway Bay, tel 8904421–8 銅鑼灣敬誠街6-8號
Israel . . . . 以色列總領事館	Rm 702 Tower II, Admiralty Centre, Admiralty, tel 5296091 金鐘海富中心二座702室
Italy . . . . 意大利領事館	Rm 805 Hutchison House, 10 Harcourt Rd, Central, tel 5220033–6 中環夏愨道10號和記大廈805室
Japan . . . . 日本領事館	25/F, Bank of America Tower, 12 Harcourt Rd, Central, tel 5260796 中環夏愨道12號美國銀行中心25樓
Korea . . . . 韓國領事館	5 & 6/F, Far East Finance Centre, 16 Harcourt Rd, Admiralty, tel 5294141 金鐘夏愨道16號遠東金融中心5-6樓
Malaysia . . . . 馬來西亞領事館	24/F, Malaysia Bldg, 50 Gloucester Rd, Wanchai, tel 5270921 灣仔告士打道50號馬來西亞大廈24樓
Mexico . . . . 墨西哥領事館	1809 World Wide House,

	19 Des Voeux Rd, Central, tel 5214365 中環德輔道19號環球大廈1809室
Myanmar (Burma) . . . . 緬甸領事館	Rm 2421–5 Sun Hung Kai Centre, 30 Harbour Rd, Wanchai, tel 8277929 灣仔港道30號新鴻基中心2421-5室
The Netherlands . . . . 荷蘭領事館	3/F, China Bldg, 29 Queen's Rd, Central, tel 5225120 中環皇后大道中29號華人行3樓
New Zealand . . . . . . 新西蘭專員公署	Rm 3414 Jardine House, Connaught Rd, Central, tel 5255044 中環干諾道怡和大廈3414室
Nigeria . . . . 尼日利亞領事館	25/F, Tung Wai Comm'l Bldg, 109–111 Gloucester Rd, Wanchai, tel 8939444 灣仔告士打道109-111號
Norway . . . . 挪威領事館	Rm 1401 AIA Bldg, 1 Stubbs Rd, Happy Valley, tel 5749253 跑馬地司徒拔道1號友邦大廈1401室
Pakistan . . . . 巴基斯坦領事館	Rm 3806, China Resources Bldg, 26 Harbour Rd, Wanchai, tel 8270681 灣仔港灣道華潤大廈3806室
Panama . . . . 巴拿馬領事館	Rm 1008 Wing On Centre, 111 Connaught Rd, Central, tel 5452166 中環干諾道111號永安中心1008室
Peru . . . . 秘魯領事館	10/F, Wong Chung Ming Com- mercial House, 16 Wyndham St, Central, tel 8682622 中環雲咸街16號王仲銘商業大廈10樓
Philippines . . . . 菲律賓領事館	21/F, Wah Kwong Regent Centre, 88 Queen's Rd, Central, tel 8100183 中環皇后大道中88號華光勵精中心21樓

Portugal 葡萄牙領事館	1001–2 Two Exchange Square, 8 Connaught Place, Central, tel 5225789 中環交易廣場二期1001-2室
Singapore 新加坡領事館	901–2 Tower I, Admiralty Centre, 18 Harcourt Rd, Admiralty, tel 5272212-4 金鐘夏愨道18號海富中心一座901-2室
South Africa 南非領事館	27/F, Sunning Plaza, 10 Hysan Avenue, Causeway Bay, tel 5773279 銅鑼灣希慎道10號新寧大廈27樓
Spain 西班牙領事館	8/F, Printing House, 18 Ice House St, Central, tel 5253041 中環雪廠街18號印刷行8樓
Sweden 瑞典領事館	8/F, Hong Kong Club Bldg, 3A Chater Rd, Central, tel 5211212 中環遮打道3A香港會大廈8樓
Switzerland 瑞士領事館	Rm 3703 Gloucester Tower, The Landmark, 11 Pedder St, Central, tel 5227147 中環置地廣場告羅士打大廈3703室
Thailand 泰國領事館	8/F, Fairmont House, 8 Cotton Tree Drive, Central, tel 5216481 中環紅棉路8號東昌大廈8樓
USA 美國領事館	26 Garden Rd, Central, tel 5239011 fax 8451598 中環花園道26號
Uruguay 烏拉圭領事館	501B Crocodile House, 50 Connaught Rd, Central, tel 5440066 中環干諾道50號鱷魚恤大廈501B室

Enquiries concerning UK trade & commerce should be directed to the **British Trade Commission**, 9/F Bank of America Tower, 12 Harcourt Rd, Central, tel 5230176; visa enquiries and passport renewals should be forwarded to the Hong Kong Government, Immigration Department.

英國商貿部 中環夏愨道12號美國銀行大廈9樓
香港人民入境事務處

Chinese visa enquiries to the P.R.C. Visa Office, 5/F Lower Block, 26 Harbour Rd, Wanchai tel 5851794.
中國人民共和國（中國）簽證辦事處 灣仔港灣道26號低座 5 樓

Taiwan visa enquiries to Chung Hwa Travel Service, 4/F, Bond Centre, Admiralty tel 5258315.
中華旅行社 金鐘奔達中心 4 樓

There are **Honorary Consuls** for the following states: Antigua & Barbuda, Barbados, Belize, Bhutan, Cote d'Ivoire, Cuba, Cyprus, El Salvador, Gabon, Gambia, Greece, Guatemala, Guinea, Honduras, Jamaica, Jordan, Liberia, Luxembourg, Malta, Mauritius, Monaco, Mozambique, Nicaragua, Oman, Paraguay, Peru, St Kitts and Nevis, St Lucia, Senegal, Sri Lanka, Togo, Tonga, Trinidad & Tobago, Tuvalu & Venezuela. Their names, addresses and telephone numbers can be found via the government's Protocol Office on 8102230.

COURIER FLIGHTS (PAGE 150)

Jupiter Air	tel 7351946 Rainbow Yip
Line Haul Express	tel 7352012 Matthew
TNT Skypak	tel 3051413 Jeanne Wong

CULTURAL VENUES (PAGE 71)

MAINSTREAM VENUES

Academy for Performing Arts 香港演藝學院	1 Gloucester Rd, Wanchai, tel 8231500 灣仔告士打道 1 號
Arts Centre 香港藝術中心	2 Harbour Rd, Wanchai, tel 5820200 灣仔港灣道 2 號
City Hall 香港大會堂	7 Edinburgh Place, Central, tel 5229928 中環愛丁堡廣場 7 號
Cultural Centre 香港文化中心	10 Salisbury Rd, Tsimshatsui, tel 7342009 尖沙咀梳士巴利道10號

Hong Kong Coliseum...   9 Cheong Wan Rd, Hung Hom,
香港紅磡體育館   tel 7659215
紅磡暢運道 9 號

Queen Elizabeth Stadium   18 Oi Kwan Rd, Wanchai,
香港伊利莎伯體育館   tel 5756793
灣仔愛羣道18號

Sheung Wan Civic Centre   345 Queen's Rd, Central,
上環文娛中心   tel 8532689
中環皇后大道中345號

Sai Wan Ho Civic Centre   111 Shaukeiwan Rd, Shaukeiwan,
西灣河文娛中心   tel 5683721
筲箕灣道111號

Ngau Chi Wan Civic Centre   11 Clearwater Bay Rd, Kowloon,
牛池灣文娛中心   tel 7260854
九龍清水灣道11號

ON THE FRINGE

Alliance Française . . . . .   123 Hennessy Rd, Wanchai,
法國文化協會   tel 5277825
灣仔軒尼詩道123號

British Council . . . . . .   Easey Commercial Bldg, 255
英國文化協會   Hennessy Rd, Wanchai,
tel 8315138
灣仔軒尼詩道255號依時商業大廈

Fringe Club . . . .   2 Lower Albert Rd, Central,
藝穗會   tel 5217251
中環下亞厘畢道 2 號

Goethe Institute . . . . . .   14/F, Arts Centre,
哥德學院   2 Harbour Rd, Wanchai,
tel 8020088
灣仔夏愨道 2 號文化中心14樓

City Contemporary Dance   G/F, 110 Shatin Pass Rd,
Theatre Company   Wong Tai Sin, Kowloon,
城市當代舞蹈團   tel 3289205
九龍黃大仙沙田坳道110號

Institute for the Promotion   Room 1001–5 Shun Tak Centre,
of Chinese Culture   200 Connaught Rd, Central,
香港中華文化促進中心

tel 5594904
中環干諾道200號信德中心1001-5室

CIVIC VENUES IN THE NEW TERRITORIES

Tuen Mun Town Hall . . 3 Tuen Hei Rd, Tuen Mun,
屯門大會堂　　　　　　tel 4527300
　　　　　　　　　　　屯門屯喜路 3 號

Tsuen Wan Town Hall . . Yuen Tun Circuit, Tsuen Wan,
荃灣大會堂　　　　　　tel 4141355
　　　　　　　　　　　荃灣圓墩圍

Tai Po Civic Centre . . . . 1 On Ping Rd, Tai Po,
大埔文娛中心　　　　　tel 6654477
　　　　　　　　　　　大埔安平街 1 號

Shatin Town Hall . . . . . 1 Yuen Wo Rd, Shatin,
沙田大會堂　　　　　　tel 6942536
　　　　　　　　　　　沙田源和路 1 號

North District Town Hall 3 Lung Sun Rd, Sheung Shui,
上水北區大會堂　　　　tel 6714400
　　　　　　　　　　　上水龍琛路 3 號

Lut Sau Town Hall . . . . Tai Wuk Rd, Yuen Long,
元朗大會堂　　　　　　tel 4731393
　　　　　　　　　　　元朗體育路

DEPARTMENT STORES (PAGE 153)

China Arts & Crafts . . . . Shell House, 24–28 Queen's Rd,
中藝　　　　　　　　　Central, tel 5226745
　　　　　　　　　　　Garley Bldg, 233–239 Nathan
　　　　　　　　　　　Rd, Tsimshatsui, tel 7300061
　　　　　　　　　　　中環皇后大道中24-28號亞細亞行
　　　　　　　　　　　尖沙咀彌敦道233-239號嘉利大廈

China Products . . . . . . Lok Sing Centre, 31 Yee Wo St,
中國國貨　　　　　　　Causeway Bay, tel 8908322
　　　　　　　　　　　銅鑼灣怡和街31號樂聲中心

Daimaru . . . . Great George St, Causeway Bay,
香港大丸百貨　　　　　tel 5765222
　　　　　　　　　　　銅鑼灣紀利佐治街

Lane Crawford. . . . . . .   70 Queen's Rd, Central,
連卡佛   tel 5266121

                                    Shop 100, Ocean Terminal,
Harbour City, 3 Canton Rd,
Tsimshatsui, tel 7302393

    1–3/F, Pacific Place,
88 Queensway, Admiralty,
tel 8451838

中環皇后大道中70號
尖沙咀海港城海運大廈100室
金鐘道88號太古廣場第一期商場1-3層

Marks & Spencer . . . . .   Shop 120-229, Pacific Place II,
馬莎百貨   88 Queensway, Admiralty,
tel 5232366

    Shop 102 & 254, Ocean Centre,
Harbour City, 3 Canton Rd,
Tsimshatsui, tel 7303163

金鐘道88號太古廣場第二座120及229室
尖沙咀海港城海洋中心102及254室

Mitsukoshi. . . . .   Hennessy Centre, 500 Hennessy
三越百貨公司   Rd, Causeway Bay, tel 5765222

    Sun Plaza, 28 Canton Rd,
Tsimshatsui, tel 3757272

銅鑼灣軒尼詩道500號興利中心
尖沙咀廣東道28號太陽廣場

Sogo . . . .   East Point Centre, 555 Hennessy
崇光香港百貨   Rd, Causeway Bay, tel 8338338

銅鑼灣軒尼詩道555號東角中心

Uny . . . .   City Plaza 2, 18 Taikoo Shing
生活創庫   Rd, Quarry Bay, tel 8850331

鰂魚涌太古城道18號太古中心第二期

Wing On. . . . .   211 Des Voeux Rd, Central,
永安百貨   tel 8521888

中環德輔道中211號

DISCOS (PAGE 180)

JJ's . . . . Grand Hyatt Hotel, 1 Harbour
Rd, Wanchai, tel 8611234
灣仔港灣道 1 號君悅酒店

Club Berlin . . . . 19 Lan Kwai Fong, tel 8779398
中環蘭桂坊19號

Club 97 . . . . 9 Lan Kwai Fong, tel 8109333
中環蘭桂坊9號

Canton . . . . Canton Rd, Tsimshatsui,
tel 3687939
尖沙咀廣東道

Hot Gossip . . . . Harbour City, Tsimshatsui,
tel 7306884
尖沙咀海港城

FOOD & RESTAURANTS (PAGE 156)

BEIJING
American Restaurant . . . 20 Lockhart Rd, Wanchai,
美利軒   tel 5277277
灣仔駱克道20號

Manhattan . . . . 301 Hennessy Rd, Wanchai,
tel 8240380
灣仔軒尼詩道301號

Peking Garden . . . . . . Excelsior Hotel Arcade, Causeway
北京樓   Bay, tel 5777231
Alexandra House, Chater Rd,
Central, tel 5266456
銅鑼灣怡東酒店商場
中環遮打道歷山大廈

Pine and Bamboo . . . . . Leighton Rd, Causeway Bay,
松竹樓   tel 5774914
銅鑼灣禮頓道

Spring Deer . . . . 42 Mody Rd, Tsimshatsui,
鹿鳴春飯店   tel 3664012
尖沙咀麼地道42號

CANTONESE

Boil & Boil Wonderful . . . Cleveland St, Causeway Bay,
煲煲好菜館   tel 5779788
銅鑼灣加寧街

Dynasty . . . . New World Harbour View Hotel,
滿福樓   Convention Avenue, Wanchai,
tel 8662288
灣仔新世界海景酒店

Flourishing Court . . . . Prudential Centre, 216 Nathan
福陞火鍋酒家   Rd, Tsimshatsui East,
tel 7392308
尖沙咀廣東道瑞園大廈

Flourishing Restaurant . . Shui Heng Yuen Apts, 504–12
福陞閣酒家   Canton Rd, Tsimshatsui, tel
3840358
尖沙咀彌敦道216號恒豐中心

Flower Lounge. . . . . . Lockhart House, 441 Lockhart
香滿樓海鮮酒家   Rd, Wanchai, tel 8937977
3 Peace Avenue, Mongkok,
tel 7156557
灣仔駱克道441號駱克大廈
旺角太平道 3 號

Fook Lam Mu . . . . . 53 Kimberly Rd, Tsimshatsui,
福臨門酒家   tel 3688755
尖沙咀金巴利道53號

Heichinrou . . . . 2/F, Sun Plaza, 28 Canton Rd,
聘珍樓海鮮酒家   Tsimshatsui, tel 7217123
尖沙咀廣東道太陽廣場 2 樓

Jade Garden . . . . 1/F, Swire House, 9 Connaught
翠園酒家   Rd, Central, tel 5239966
中環干諾道太古大廈 1 樓

Lai Ching Heen . . . . . The Regent, Salisbury Rd,
麗晶軒   Tsimshatsui, tel 7211211
尖沙咀梳士巴利道麗晶酒店

Man Wah . . . . Mandarin Oriental, 5 Connaught
文華酒樓   Rd, Central, tel 5220111
中環干諾道 5 號文華東方酒店

Maxim's . . . . World Trade Centre,
美心大酒樓

Gloucester St, Causeway Bay,
tel 5766333
銅鑼灣告士打道世界貿易中心

Ocean City . . . . New World Centre, Salisbury Rd,
海洋大酒樓   Tsimshatsui, tel 3699688
尖沙咀梳士巴利道新世界中心

Orchid Garden . . . . . 37 Hankow Rd, Tsimshatsui,
蘭香閣   tel 7289111
尖沙咀漢口道37號

Shang Palace . . . . Shangri-La Hotel, 64 Mody Rd,
香宮   TST East, tel 7212111
尖沙咀麼地道64號香格里拉酒店

Some Like It Hot . . . . . 7/F, Causeway Bay Plaza,
489 Hennessy Rd, Causeway Bay,
tel 8388303
銅鑼灣軒尼詩道489號銅鑼灣廣場 7 樓

Spring Moon . . . . The Peninsula, Salisbury Rd,
嘉麟樓   Tsimshatsui, tel 3666251
尖沙咀梳士巴利道半島酒店

Steam and Stew Inn . . . . 21–23 Tai Wong St East,
蒸燉炆棧   Wanchai, tel 5293413
灣仔大王東街21-25號

Sunning Unicorn . . . . . Sunning Plaza, 1 Sunning Rd,
麒麟新閣   Causeway Bay, tel 5776620
銅鑼灣新寧道 1 號新寧大廈

Tao Yuan . . . . Great Eagle Centre, 23 Harbour
桃源酒家   Rd, Wanchai, tel 8278080
灣仔港灣道23號鷹君中心

Tai Fat Hau . . . . G/F, Lok Moon Bldg, 29-31
大佛口食坊   Queen's Rd East, Wanchai,
tel 5291286
灣仔皇后大道東29-31號樂滿大廈地下

Yung Kee . . . . 1–4 F, 32-40 Wellington St,
鏞記酒家   Central, tel 5221624
中環威靈頓街32-40號1-4樓

Zen . . . . LG1 The Mall, Pacific Place,
采蝶軒   Admiralty, tel 5257306
中環金鐘太古廣場第 1 期 LG1室

CHIU CHOW

Carrianna
佳寧娜

1/F, 151 Gloucester Rd, Wanchai, tel 5741282

2/F, Hilton Tower, 96 Granville Rd, Tsimshatsui, tel 7244828

灣仔告士打道151號1樓
尖沙咀加連威老道96號希爾頓中心

Chiu Chow Garden
潮江春

Jardine House, Central, tel 5258246

Hennessy Centre, 500 Hennessy Rd, Causeway Bay, tel 5775440

Tsimshatsui Centre, 66 Mody Rd, Tsimshatsui, tel 3687266

中環怡和大廈
銅鑼灣軒尼詩道500號興利中心
尖沙咀麼地道66號尖沙咀中心

City Chiu Chow
潮洲城酒樓

East Ocean Centre, 99 Granville Rd, Tsimshatsui East, tel 7236226

尖沙咀東加連威老道99號東海商業中心

Golden Island Bird's Nest
金島燕窩潮洲酒樓

25–31 Carnarvon Rd, Tsimshatsui, tel 3695211

尖沙咀加拿芬道25-31號

Harbour City Chiuchow
潮港城

2/F, Elizabeth House, 254 Gloucester Rd, Causeway Bay, tel 8336678

銅鑼灣告士打道254號伊利莎伯大廈2樓

Houston Chiu Chow
好時潮洲酒家

Houston Centre atrium, Mody Rd, Tsimshatsui, tel 7242957

尖沙咀麼地道好時中心

Manning Chiu Chow
萬年潮洲酒樓

1/F, Asian House, 1 Hennessy Rd, Wanchai, tel 8612882

灣仔軒尼詩道1號熙信大廈1樓

Pak Lok
百樂潮洲酒家

23 Hysan Avenue, Causeway Bay, tel 5768886

銅鑼灣希慎道23號

Spring Moon
中港嘉麟酒家

China Hong Kong City complex,

Canton Rd, Tsimshatsui,
tel 7362878
尖沙咀廣東道中港城

HANGZHOU
Tien Heung Lau . . . . . .   18 Austin Rd, Tsimshatsui,
天香樓   tel 3662414
尖沙咀柯士甸道18號

HUNAN
Hunan Garden . . . . .   The Forum, Exchange Square,
洞庭樓   Central, tel 8682880
中環交易廣場富臨閣

SEAFOOD
Chung Kong . . . .   China Hong Kong City complex,
中港軒海鮮酒家   Canton Rd, Tsimshatsui,
tel 7301388
尖沙咀廣東道中港城

Chuk Yuen . . . .   Wong Nei Chung Rd, Happy
竹苑   Valley, tel 8931197
跑馬地黃泥涌道

East Ocean Seafood . . . .   East Ocean Centre, 99 Granville
東海海鮮酒家   Rd, Tsimshatsui East,
tel 7238128
尖沙咀東部加連威老道99號東海中心

Hoi Tin Garden . . . . .   53–9 Praya Rd, Lei Yue Mun,
海天花園酒家   tel 3481482
鯉魚門海傍道中53-59號

Fat Siu Lau . . . .   Houston Centre, Mody Rd,
佛笑樓   Tsimshatsui East, tel 3686291
尖沙咀東部麼地道好時中心

New Home . . . .   20 Hanoi Rd, Tsimshatsui,
新客鄉村客粵海鮮酒家   tel 3662989
尖沙咀河内道20號

New Hon Kee . . . .   4 Main St, Tap Mun Island, Tolo
新漢記   Channel, New Territories,
tel 3282428
新界吐露港塔門大街4號

Ocean City Seafood . . . . New World Centre, 20 Salisbury
竹林園   Rd, Tsimshatsui, tel 7225500
尖沙咀梳士巴利道20號新世界中心

Oi Man . . . . 4 Lau Fau Shan Main St,
愛民   New Territories, tel 4721504
新界流浮山大街4號

Palace . . . . 18 Whitfield Rd, Causeway Bay,
迎福樓   tel 5782339
銅鑼灣威菲路道18號

Regal Seafood . . . . . . 2/F, Paliburg Plaza, 68 Yee Wo
豪苑魚翅海鮮酒家   St, Causeway Bay, tel 5761717
銅鑼灣怡和街68號百利保廣場

Sun Tung Lok . . . . 137 Connaught Rd West,
  Shark's Fin Restaurant Central, tel 5462718
新同樂魚翅酒家   中環干諾道西137號

Tai Woo Seafood . . . . 17 Wellington St, Central,
太湖海鮮城   tel 5252960
中環威靈頓街17號

Tin Tin Seafood Harbour Elizabeth House, Gloucester Rd,
天天漁港   Causeway Bay, tel 8336683
銅鑼灣告士打道伊利莎伯大廈

SHANGHAI

Great Shanghai . . . . . 26–36 Prat Avenue, Tsimshatsui,
大上海飯店   tel 3668158
尖沙咀寶勒巷26-36號

Lao Ching Hing . . . . . Kai Chiu Rd, Causeway Bay,
老正興上海菜館   tel 8951781
銅鑼灣啟超道

Shanghai 369 . . . . . . 208 Queen's Rd East, Central,
上海三六九飯店   tel 8938117
中環皇后大道東208號

Shanghai Garden . . . . Hutchison House, Murray Rd,
滬江春   Central, tel 5238322
中環美利道和記大廈

SICHUAN

Cleveland . . . . 6 Cleveland St, Causeway Bay,
加寧川菜館   tel 5763876
                             銅鑼灣加寧街 6 號

Fung Lum Szechuan . . . 23 Granville Rd, Tsimshatsui,
楓林閣   tel 3678919
                             尖沙咀加連威老道23號

Pep'N Chili . . . . 12–22 Bluepool Rd, Happy Valley,
乾坤閣   tel 5738251
                             跑馬地藍塘道12-22號

Pepper Garden . . . . . 6/F, Arts Centre, 2 Harbour Rd,
松軒酒家   Wanchai, tel 8020006
                             灣仔港灣道藝術中心 6 樓

Prince Court Szechuan . . 115–6 Sutton Court, Harbour
太子閣川菜酒家   City, Canton Rd, Tsimshatsui,
                             tel 7303100
                             尖沙咀廣東道海港城秀棠閣115-116號

Red Pepper . . . . 7 Lan Fong Rd, Causeway Bay,
南北樓   tel 5776346
                             銅鑼灣蘭芳道 7 號

Sichuan Garden . . . . . 3/F, The Landmark, Pedder St,
錦江春川菜館   Central, tel 5214433
                             中環畢打街置地廣場 3 樓

TAIWANESE

Ching Yip . . . . Shop C, G/F, Towning Mansion,
青葉菜館   Paterson St, Causeway Bay,
                             tel. 577 8018
                             銅鑼灣百德新街56號唐寧大廈地下C座

Forever Green . . . . . . G/F, 93–95A Leighton Road,
欣葉高級台灣料理   Causeway Bay, tel. 890 3448
                             銅鑼灣禮頓道93-95A號地下

Tin Tin Hot Pot . . . . . 16 Carnarvon Rd, Tsimshatsui,
天天火鍋   tel 3694806
                             尖沙咀加拿芬道16號

VEGETARIAN

Bodhi Vegetarian . . . . . 56 Cameron Rd, Tsimshatsui,
菩提素食   tel 7219991

          381 Lockhart Rd, Wanchai,
          tel 5732153
          尖沙咀金馬倫道56號
          灣仔駱克道381號

Vegi Food Kitchen . . . . 8 Cleveland St, Causeway Bay,
香齋廚素食館   tel 8906603
          銅鑼灣加寧街 8 號

Woodlands (Indian). . . . 8 Minden Avenue, Tsimshatsui,
          tel 3693718
          尖沙咀棉登徑 8 號

ASIAN

Spices . . . . 109 Repulse Bay Rd, Repulse
          Bay, tel 8122711
          One Pacific Place, Wanchai,
          tel 8454798
          淺水灣淺水灣道109號
          金鐘道88號太古廣場一期

BURMESE

Rangoon . . . . 265 Gloucester Rd, Causeway
仰光南洋餐廳   Bay, tel 8932281
          銅鑼灣告士打道265號

FILIPINO

Cinta . . . . 41 Hennessy Rd, Wanchai,
金蒂餐廳   tel 5271199
          灣仔軒尼詩道41號

Mabuhay. . . . . 11 Minden Avenue, Tsimshatsui,
菲律賓餐廳   tel 3673762
          尖沙咀棉登徑11號

INDIAN

Bombay Palace. . . . . . . G/F, Far East Finance Centre,
帝殿印度餐廳

16 Harcourt Rd, Admiralty, tel
5270115, takeaways 5293562
金鐘夏慤道16號遠東金融中心地下

Greenlands India Club . . 1/F, 64–6 Wellington St, Central,
tel 5225607
中環威靈頓街64-6號1樓

Gunga Din's . . . . 59 Wyndham St, Central,
雅適閣 tel 5231276
中環雲咸街59號

Indian Curry Club . . . . 3/F, Flat M, Windsor Bldg,
Wing Wah Land, Lan Kwai
Fong, Central, tel 5232201
中環蘭桂坊榮華里溫莎大廈3樓M座

Jo Jo Mess Club . . . . . 86 Johnston Rd, Wanchai,
tel 5273776
灣仔莊士頓道86號

Shalimar Club . . . . . . 28A Stanley St, Central, tel
沙士亞會所 5228489
中環士丹利街28號A

Tandoor . . . . 1/F, Carfield Comm'l Bldg, 75–7
Wyndham St, Central,
tel 5218363
中環雲咸街75-7號1樓

Viceroy of India . . . . . Sun Hung Kai Centre, Harbour
華仕萊苑 Rd, Wanchai, tel 5727227
灣仔港灣道新鴻基中心

Woodlands International . G/F, 8 Minden Avenue
Tsimshatsui, tel 3693718
尖沙咀棉登徑8號

INDONESIAN

Java Rijsttafel . . . . . . 38 Hankow Rd, Tsimshatsui,
爪哇餐廳 tel 3671230
尖沙咀漢口道38號

New Indonesian . . . . . 500 Lockhart Rd, Causeway Bay,
印尼餐廳 tel 8920328
銅鑼灣駱克道500號

JAPANESE

Ah-So . . . .   Harbour City, Canton Rd
阿蘇餐廳   Tsimshatsui, tel 73522
                              尖沙咀廣東道海港城

Benkay . . . .   First Basement, The Landmark,
弁慶日本餐廳   Central, tel 5213344
                              中環置地廣場地庫

Ginza . . . .   The Regent Hotel arcade,
銀座日本餐廳   Salisbury Rd, Tsimshatsui,
                              tel 3686138
                              尖沙咀梳士巴利道麗晶酒店商場

Hanagushi . . . .   1/F, California Entertainment
花串日本料理   Bldg, 34-6 D'Aguilar St, Central,
                              tel 5210868
                              中環德忌立街34-6號加樂大廈1樓

Hooraiya . . . .   Food St, off Kingston St,
鐵板燒   Causeway Bay, tel 5771183
                              銅鑼灣京士頓街口食街

J & F . . . .   12C Sing Woo Rd, Happy
日本食店   Valley, tel 5730872
                              跑馬地成和道12號C

Nadaman . . . .   Shangri-La Hotel, 64 Mody Rd,
灘萬   Tsimshatsui, tel 7212111
                              尖沙咀麼地道64號香格里拉酒店

Paper Moon . . . .   Sunning Plaza, Hysan Avenue,
日本餐廳   Causeway Bay, tel 8901882
                              銅鑼灣希慎道新寧廣場

Sagano . . . .   Hotel Nikko, 72 Mody Rd,
嵯峨野   Tsimshatsui, tel 7391111
                              尖沙咀麼地道72號日航酒店

Sui Sha Ya . . . .   G/F, Lockhart House, 440 Jaffe
水車屋日本料理   Rd, Causeway Bay, tel 8381808
                              Hecny Tower, 9 Chatham Rd,
                              Tsimshatsui, tel 7225001
                              銅鑼灣謝斐道440號駱克大廈地下
                              尖沙咀漆咸道9號地下

KOREAN

Arirang . . . . Sutton Court, Harbour City,
阿里朗韓國餐廳 Canton Rd, Tsimshatsui,
tel 7350789

76 Morrison Hill Rd, Happy
Valley, tel 5723027
尖沙咀廣東道海港城秀棠閣
跑馬地廟利臣山道76號

Silla Won . . . . Southland Bldg, 47 Connaught
新羅園餐廳 Rd, Central, tel 5458873
中環干諾道47號南源商業大廈

MALAYSIAN

Cosmo . . . . 80 Kwong Fuk Rd, Tai Po
高士墓餐廳 Market, Tai Po, tel 6507056
大埔大埔墟廣福道80號

Malaya . . . . 23A Granville Rd, Tsimshatsui,
馬來餐廳 tel 3678550

15B Wellington St, Central,
tel 5251675
尖沙咀加連威老道23A
中環威靈頓街15B

SRI LANKAN

Club Sri Lanka . . . . . . 17 Hollywood Rd, Central,
tel 5266559
中環荷李活道17號

THAI

Chili Club . . . . 88 Lockhart Rd, Wanchai,
tel 5272872
灣仔駱克道88號

Chilli and Pepper . . . . . 11A Bonham Rd, Mid-Levels,
tel 8572412
半山般含道11A

Golden Elephant . . . . . G/F, Barnton Court, 9 Canton
金象苑 Rd, Tsimshatsui, tel 7350733
尖沙咀廣東道海港城班桃閣地下

Golden Poppy . . . . . . 5/F, Henan Bldg, 90–2 Jaffe Rd,
Wanchai, tel 5283128
灣仔謝斐道海德中心 5 樓

Heng Thai . . . . 68 Kai Tak Rd, Kowloon City,
慶珍珍餐廳 tel 3839159
九龍城啟德道68號

Sawadee . . . . 6 Ichang St, Tsimshatsui,
泰國餐廳 tel 3763299
尖沙咀宜昌街 6 號

Silks . . . . 4–6 On Lan St, Central,
泰國餐廳 tel 5242567
中環安瀾街4-6號

Supatras . . . . 46 D'Aguilar St, Central,
美味泰國菜 tel 5225073
中環德己立街46號

Thai Delicacy . . . . . . 44 Hennessy Rd, Wanchai,
泰禾美食 tel 5272591
灣仔軒尼詩道44號

Thai Kitchen . . . . . . 6/F, Goldmark Bldg, 1–3 Jardine's
泰皇泰國菜 Bazaar, Causeway Bay,
tel 5770018
銅鑼灣渣甸街1-3號黃金廣場 6 樓

VIETNAMESE

Café de la Paix Vietnamese Hillwood Rd, Yaumatei,
和平館越南菜館 tel 7212582
油麻地山林道

Golden Bull . . . . New World Centre, 18 Salisbury
金牛苑 Rd, Tsimshatsui, tel 3694617
尖沙咀梳士巴利道18號新世界中心

Paterson's . . . . Paterson St, Causeway Bay,
百德越菜館 tel 8908288
銅鑼灣百德新街

Perfume River . . . . . . 89 Percival St, Causeway Bay,
香河越南餐館 tel 5762240
銅鑼灣波斯富街89號

Professional Musicians Club 7–8 Tak Hing St, Yaumatei,
職業樂師同樂會 tel 3671400
油麻地德興街7-8號

Yin Ping . . . . 24 Cannon St, Causeway Bay,
燕萍 tel 8329038
銅鑼灣景隆街24號

AUSTRIAN
Mozart Stub'n . . . . . . 8 Glenealy, Central, tel 5221763
中環己連拿利 8 號

FRENCH
Café de Paris. . . . . . . California Tower, 30-2 D'Aguilar
St, Central, tel 5247521
中環德己立街30-2號

Gaddi's. . . . . The Peninsula, Salisbury Rd,
吉地士餐廳 Tsimshatsui, tel 3666251
尖沙咀梳士巴利道半島酒店

La Rose Noire . . . . . . 1/F, 8–13 Wo On Lane, Central,
黑玫瑰 tel 5265965
中環和安里8-13號 1 樓

Le Restaurant de France . Regal Meridien Hotel, 71 Mody
法國餐廳 Rd, Tsimshatsui, tel 7221818
尖沙咀麼地道71號富豪酒店

Le Tire Buchon . . . . . 9 Old Bailey St, Central,
tel 5235459
中環奧卑利街 9 號

Margaux . . . . Shangri-La Hotel, 64 Mody Rd,
瑪高餐廳 Tsimshatsui, tel 7212111
尖沙咀麼地道64號香格里拉酒店

Pierrot . . . . Mandarin Oriental, 5 Connaught
法國餐廳 Rd, Central, tel 5220111
中環干諾道 5 號文華東方酒店

Plume . . . . The Regent, Salisbury Rd,
布倫餐廳 Tsimshatsui, tel 7211211
尖沙咀梳士巴利道麗晶酒店

Stanley's . . . . 86–8 Stanley Main St, Stanley,
赤柱法國餐廳 tel 8138873
赤柱大街86號

The Verandah . . . . . . 109 Repulse Bay Rd, Repulse
露臺餐廳 Bay, tel 8122722
淺水灣道109號

GERMAN
The Baron's Table. . . . . Holiday Inn Golden Mile,
男爵扒房 50 Nathan Rd, Tsimshatsui,
tel 3693111
尖沙咀彌敦道50號金域假日酒店

ITALIAN
Capriccio. . . . . Ramada Renaissance Hotel,
8 Peking Rd, Tsimshatsui,
tel 3751133
尖沙咀北京道 8 號華美達麗新酒店

Grappa's Ristorante Toscana Two Pacific Place, Admiralty,
tel 8680086
金鐘太古廣場

Grissini. . . . . Grand Hyatt Hotel, One
意大利餐廳 Harbour Rd, Wanchai,
tel 5881234
灣仔港灣道 1 號君悅酒店

Il Mercato . . . . 126 Stanley Main St, Stanley,
tel 8139090
赤柱赤柱大街126號

Italian Tomato . . . . . Kornhill Plaza, Taikoo Shing,
tel 8860131
太古城康怡廣場

La Taverna. . . . . Shun Ho Tower, 24–30 Ice
House St, Central, tel 5238624
中環雪廠街24-30號

Niccholini's . . . . Conrad Hotel, Pacific Place,
意寧谷 Admiralty, tel 5213838
金鐘太古廣場港麗酒店

SWISS

Chesa. . . . . The Peninsula, Salisbury Rd,
瑞樵閣 Tsimshatsui, tel 3666251
尖沙咀梳士巴利道半島酒店

UP-MARKET

Bentley's Seafood . . . . . Prince's Bldg, 3 Des Voeux Rd,
& Oyster Bar Central, tel. 8680881
中環德輔道中 3 號太子大廈

Brown's Wine Bar. . . . . 206 Podium level, Exchange
Square II, Central, tel 5237003
中環交易廣場第二座高臺206

Dan Ryan's Chicago Grill Pacific Place, Admiralty,
芝加哥餐廳 tel 8454600
Ocean Terminal, Canton Rd,
Tsimshatsui, tel 7356111
金鐘太古廣場
尖沙咀廣東道海運大廈

Duddell's . . . . 1 Duddell St, Central,
tel 8452299
中環都爹利街 1 號

Landau's . . . . Sun Hung Kai Centre,
蘭杜餐廳 30 Harbour Rd, Wanchai,
tel 8277901
灣仔港灣道30號新鴻基中心

The Mandarin Grill . . . . The Mandarin Oriental,
文華扒房 5 Connaught Rd, Central,
tel 5220111
中環干諾道中 5 號文華東方酒店

Michelle's . . . . Fringe Club Bldg, 2 Lower Albert
藝穗會餐廳 Rd, Central, tel 8774000
中環下亞厘畢道 2 號藝穗會

Portico . . . . L/G Floor, Citibank Plaza,
3 Garden Rd, Central,
tel 5238893
中環花園道 3 號萬國寶通銀行大廈地下

San Francisco Steak House 101 Barnton Court, 9 Canton Rd
三藩市牛扒屋 Tsimshatsui, tel 3761576
尖沙咀廣東道 9 號海港城班桃閣101室

LESS UP-MARKET

Revolving 66 . . . . 62/F, 183 Hopewell Centre,
旋轉66   Queen's Rd East, Wanchai,
           tel 8626166
           灣仔皇后大道東183號合和中心62樓

BARS

Asahi Super Dry . . . . . . G/F, Bank of America Tower,
朝日餐廳   12 Harcourt Rd, Admiralty,
          tel 5210309
          金鐘夏愨道12號美國銀行大廈地下

Beaches . . . . 29A Stanley Main St, Stanley,
海堤餐廳   tel 8137313
          赤柱赤柱大街29A

Biergarten . . . . 8 Hanoi Rd, Tsimshatsui,
          tel 7212302
          尖沙咀河內道 8 號

Bottom's Up . . . . 14 Hankow Rd, Tsimshatsui,
露臀夜總會   tel 3675696
          尖沙咀漢口道14號

Cactus Club . . . . 13 Lan Kwai Fong, Central,
          tel 5256732
          中環蘭桂坊13號

Club 64 . . . . 12–14 Wing Wah Lane, Central,
          tel 5232801
          中環榮華里12-14號

Finealley . . . . 2 Glenealy, Central, tel 5233595
          中環己連拿利街 2 號

Joe Bananas . . . . 21–25 Luard Rd, Wanchai,
          tel 5291811
          灣仔盧押道21-25號

King's Arms . . . . 6/F, 9–11 Sunning Plaza,
          Causeway Bay, tel 8956557
          銅鑼灣新寧廣場9-11號 6 樓

Le Jardin . . . . 10 Wing Wah Lane, Central,
          tel 5262717
          中環榮華里10號

Godown . . . . G/F, Admiralty Centre,
Admiralty, tel 8661166
金鐘海富中心地下

Hardy's . . . . 35 D'Aguilar St, Central,
tel 5224448
中環德忌立街35號

Mad Dog's . . . . 8 Wyndham St, Central,
tel 8101000
32 Nathan Rd, Tsimshatsui,
tel 3012222
中環雲咸街8號
尖沙咀彌敦道32號

Post 97 . . . . 9 Lan Kwai Fong, Central,
tel 8109333
中環蘭桂坊9號

Schnurrbart . . . . 29 D'Aguilar St, Central,
tel 5234700
中環德忌立街29號

Ueno . . . . 6 Hart Avenue, Tsimshatsui,
tel 7239827
尖沙咀赫德道6號

The Wanch . . . . 54 Jaffe Rd, Wanchai,
tel 8611621
灣仔謝斐道54號

Yin Yang Club . . . . . . 24–30 Ice House St, Central,
陰陽   tel 8684066
中環雪廠街24-30號

TRENDY PLACES, DELIS AND CLUBS

Al's Diner . . . . 27–39 D'Aguilar St, Central,
tel 8691869
中環德忌立街27-39號

Beverley Hills Deli . . . . 21 Lan Kwai Fong, Central,
百富利餐廳   tel 5265809
中環蘭桂坊21號

Beverley Hills Deli . . . . Level 2, New World Centre,
百富利餐廳　　　　　　55 Salisbury Rd, Tsimshatsui,
　　　　　　　　　　　tel 3698695
　　　　　　　　　　　尖沙咀梳士巴利道55號新世界中心

The Big Apple . . . . . . Unit 111 Ruttonjee Centre,
大蘋果餐廳　　　　　　Duddell St, Central, tel 8107103
　　　　　　　　　　　中環都爹利街律敦治大廈1字樓111室

California . . . . 30 Lan Kwai Fong, Central,
　　　　　　　　　　　tel 5211345
　　　　　　　　　　　中環蘭桂坊30號

Graffiti . . . . 17 Lan Kwai Fong, Central,
　　　　　　　　　　　tel 5212202
　　　　　　　　　　　中環蘭桂坊17號

Mecca 97 & Post 97 . . . G/F, 9 Lan Kwai Fong, Central,
　　　　　　　　　　　tel 8109333
　　　　　　　　　　　中環蘭桂坊9號地下

USA Deli & Restaurant . . Hop Hing Centre, 8-12
美國餐廳　　　　　　　Hennessy Rd, Wanchai,
　　　　　　　　　　　tel 8653278
　　　　　　　　　　　灣仔軒尼詩道8-12號合興中心

CAFES

La Rose Noire . . . . . . 3/F, Pacific Place, Admiralty,
黑玫瑰餐廳　　　　　　tel 8770118
　　　　　　　　　　　金鐘太古廣場3樓

Peak Café . . . . 121 Peak Rd, Hong Kong,
山頂餐廳　　　　　　　tel 8497868
　　　　　　　　　　　香港山頂道121號

Queen's Café . . . . . . 39–41 Lee Garden Rd, Causeway
皇后飯店　　　　　　　Bay, tel 5762659
　　　　　　　　　　　銅鑼灣利園山道39-41號

24-HOUR FOOD

McDonald's . . . . Tsimshatsui Star Ferry Terminal
麥當奴　　　　　　　　and Granville Rd, Tsimshatsui
　　　　　　　　　　　尖沙咀加連威老道
　　　　　　　　　　　尖沙咀天星小輪碼頭

Wally Matt Bar . . . . . . G/F, 9 Cornwall Ave,
好朋友酒吧   Tsimshatsui, tel 3676874
                       尖沙咀康和里 9 號地下

FAST FOOD

Gomenbo (Japanese) . . . . 8 Wyndham St, Central,
御麵坊   tel 5253737
                     中環雲咸街 8 號

Ueno sushi bar. . . . . . . 22 Minden Avenue, Tsimshatsui,
紅葉   tel 7216101
                    尖沙咀棉登徑22號

TAKE-OUT PIZZA

Marco Polo Pizza Gourmet 23 Lan Kwai Fong, Central,
                          tel 8681013
                          中環蘭桂坊23號

FRENCH BAKERY

Point Chaud . . . . Chiu Lung Bldg, 15 Chiu Lung
法國餅店   St, Central, tel 5254280
                      中環昭隆街15號昭隆大廈

MACAU RESTAURANTS (PAGE 208)

PORTUGUESE/INTERNATIONAL

A Galera . . . . 3/F, New Wing, Lisboa Hotel,
葡京扒房   tel 577666 x1103
                      葡京酒店 3 樓

A Lorcha . . . . Rua do Almirante Sergio 289,
船屋餐廳   tel 313193
                      海邊新街289號

Afonso's . . . . Hyatt Regency Hotel, Taipa
亞豐素餐廳   Island, tel 321234
                      氹仔凱悅酒店

Barra Nova . . . . 287A Rua do Almirante Sergio,
                      tel 512287
                      海邊新街287A

Estrela do Mar . . . . . . Rua Direita Carlos Eugenio 12,
海星餐室　　　　　　 Taipa Island, tel 320843
　　　　　　　　　　 氹仔施督憲正街12號

Fernando's . . . . Hac Sa beach, tel 328264
法蘭度餐廳　　　　　 黑沙灣

Flamingo. . . . . Hyatt Regency Hotel, Taipa
紅鶴餐廳　　　　　　 Island, tel 321234
　　　　　　　　　　 氹仔凱悅酒店

Fortaleza Grill . . . . . . Pousada da São Tiago, Avenida
　　　　　　　　　　 Republica, tel 378111
　　　　　　　　　　 聖地牙哥酒店

Galo . . . . Rua do Cunha 47, Taipa Island,
公雞餐廳　　　　　　 tel 327318
　　　　　　　　　　 氹仔官也街47號

Henri's Galley . . . . . . Avenida Republica 4, tel 556251
美心餐廳　　　　　　 民國大馬路 4 號

Metropole . . . . Hotel Metropole, Rua da Praia
京都餐廳　　　　　　 Grande 63, tel 388166
　　　　　　　　　　 南灣街63號京都酒店

Mocambique. . . . . . . Rua dos Clerigos 28, Taipa village,
莫三鼻給餐廳　　　　 tel 321475
　　　　　　　　　　 氹仔木鐸街 28 號

1999 . . . . Coloane Island, tel 328291
1999餐廳　　　　　　 路環石排灣郊野公園

Nova Koka. . . . . Ferreira do Amaral 21, tel 568993
東望洋街21號

Panda . . . . Rua Carlos Eugenio 4–8, Taipa
熊貓餐廳　　　　　　 Island, tel 327338
　　　　　　　　　　 氹仔施督憲正街4-8號

Pele. . . . . 25 Rua São Tiago da Barra,
比利餐廳　　　　　　 tel 965624
　　　　　　　　　　 媽閣上街25號地下

Pinnochio's . . . . Rua do Sol 4, Taipa village,
木偶餐廳　　　　　　 tel 327128
　　　　　　　　　　 氹仔日頭街 4 號

Portugues . . . . 葡國餐廳	Rua do Campo, tel 375445 水坑尾街
Pousada de Coloane . . . . 竹灣海景餐廳	Praia de Cheoc Van, Coloane Island, tel 328144 路灣竹灣
Praia Grande. . . . . 美麗灣餐廳	Praca Lobo d'Avila, No. 10A, Rua da Praia Grande, tel 973022 南灣燒炭爐10A
Riqueixo 	Park 'N Shop, Sidonio Pais 69, tel 76294 士多紐拜斯大馬路
Safari . . . . 金池餐廳	Patio do Cotovelo 14, Avenida de Ribeiro, tel 574313 新馬路德隆新街14號
Solmar . . . . 沙利文餐廳	Rua da Praia Grande 11, tel 574391 南灣街11號
Vasco da Gama . . . . . 華士古餐廳	Royal Hotel, Estrada da Vitoria, tel 552222 得勝馬路皇都酒店

CHINESE

Chiu Chow . . . . 葡京潮州酒樓	Lisboa Hotel, tel 377666 葡京酒店
Dynasty . . . . 萬歲廳	Mandarin Oriental Hotel, tel 567888 文華東方酒店
Fat Siu Lau. . . . . 佛笑樓	Rua da Felicidade 64, tel 573585 福隆新街64號
Fook Lam Moon . . . . 福臨門魚翅海鮮酒家	Avenida da Amizade 63, tel 86883 友誼大馬路63號
Shanghai 456 . . . . . . 上海456荣館	New Wing, Lisboa Hotel, tel 388474 葡京大酒店 2 樓

ITALIAN
Leong Un . . . .   Rua de Cunha 46, Taipa village,
氹苑意大利餐廳   tel 327387
      氹仔官也街46號

JAPANESE
Furosato . . . .   Lisboa Hotel, tel 577666
富士餐廳   葡京酒店

Ginza. . . . .   Royal Hotel, tel 568412
銀座餐廳   皇都酒店

THAI
Banthai. . . . .   Rua de Henrique de Macedo,
泰屋餐廳   tel 344663
      馬大臣街

KOREAN
Korean. . . . .   Presidente Hotel, Avenida da
總統韓國菜館   Amizade, tel 569039
      總統酒店

JEWELERS (PAGE 149)

Chaumont . . . .   10/F, Metropole Bldg,
旋曼地公司   57 Peking Rd, Tsimshatsui,
      tel 3687331
      尖沙咀北京道57號國都大廈10樓1003室

Made in Hong Kong Ltd   1/F, Block J, Kaiser Estate,
港貨店   51 Man Yue St, Hunghom,
      tel 3344415
      紅磡民裕街51號凱旋工商中心1樓J座

Opal Mine Ltd . . . . . .   Burlington House, 92 Nathan
澳之寶有限公司   Rd, Tsimshatsui, tel 7219933
      尖沙咀彌敦道92號華敦大廈

Win Sun Jewelery Ltd. . .   Shop B6, 15/F, Hankow Centre,
榮生珠寶有限公司   4A Ashley Rd, Tsimshatsui,
      tel 3692380
      尖沙咀亞士厘道4A號漢口中心15樓B6

Yee On Gems and . . . . .   G/F, Unit 4, Block A,
    Jewellery Fty Co Ltd   Focal Industrial Centre, 21 Man
怡安寶石首飾廠有限公司   Lok St, Hunghom, tel 3650366-7
    紅磡民樂街21號富高工業中心A座地下

JUNK HIRE

AML . . . .   11/F, Flat K, 8 Johnston Rd,
  Wanchai, tel 5271511
  灣仔莊士頓道 8 號11樓K室

De Tours Ltd . . . .   161 Wong Nai Chung Road,
  44 Sport Mansion, Happy Valley
  tel 8519601
  香港跑馬地黃泥涌道 161 號 4 樓

Standard Boat Service . . .   B37, Seven Seas Shopping
    Company   Centre, 121 King's Road,
  North Point
  tel 5701792
  北角英皇道121號七海商業中心B37室

MUSEUMS (PAGE 68)

Art Gallery . . . .   Institute of Chinese Studies,
藝術廊   Chinese University, Shatin,
  tel 6097416
  沙田中文大學中國文化研究所

Flagstaff House . . . . . .   Hong Kong Park, Cotton
    Museum of Tea   Tree Drive, Central, tel 5299390
旗桿屋茶具文物館   中環紅棉路香港公園

Fung Ping Shan Museum   University of Hong Kong,
馮平山博物館   94 Bonham Rd, Mid-Levels,
  tel 8592114
  半山區般含道94號香港大學

Hong Kong Cultural . . .   Salisbury Rd. Tsimshatsui,
    Centre Art Museum   tel 7342009
香港文化中心藝術館   尖沙咀梳士巴利道

Hong Kong Museum of Art   14 Salisbury Rd, Tsimshatsui,
香港藝術館   tel 7342167
  尖沙咀梳士巴利道14號

Hong Kong Science Museum
香港科學館
2 Science Museum Rd, Tsimshatsui East, tel 7323232
尖沙咀東科學館道 2 號

Hong Kong Space Museum:
Space Theatre and
Exhibition Hall
香港太空館：天象廳及展覽廳
10 Salisbury Rd, Tsimshatsui, tel 7342722
尖沙咀梳士巴利道10號

Hong Kong Police Museum
香港警察博物館
27 Coombe Rd, The Peak, tel 8497019
香港山頂甘道27號

Hong Kong Railway . . . Museum
香港鐵路博物館
On Fu Rd, Tai Po, tel 6533339
大埔安富道

Law Uk Folk Museum . .
羅屋民族博物館
14 Kut Shing St, Chai Wan, tel 8967006
柴灣吉勝街14號

Lei Cheng Uk . . . .
李鄭屋
41 Tonkin St, Lei Cheng Uk Resettlement Estate, Shamshuipo, tel 3862863
深水埗李鄭屋村東京街41号

Museum of Chinese . . . .
Historical Relics
中國文物展覽館
1/F, Causeway Centre, 28 Harbour Rd, Wanchai, tel 8274692
灣仔港灣道銅鑼灣中心 1 樓

Museum of History . . . .
歷史博物館
Kowloon Park, Haiphong Rd, Tsimshatsui, tel 3671124
尖沙咀海防道九龍公園

Sam Tung Uk Museum . .
三棟屋博物館
Kwu Uk Lane, Tsuen Wan, tel 4112001
荃灣古屋里

Sheung Yiu Folk Museum
上窰民俗文物館
Pak Tam Chung Nature Trail, Sai Kung, tel 7926365
西貢北潭自然教育徑

Tsui Museum of Art . . .
徐氏藝術館
10/F, Rediffusion House, 822 Laichikok Rd, Laichikok, Kowloon, tel 7852101
九龍荔枝角道822號麗的呼聲大廈10樓

NIGHTCLUBS AND HOSTESS CLUBS (PAGE 179)

China City Night Club . . 4/F, Peninsula Centre, 67 Mody
中國城夜總會
Rd, Tsimshatsui East,
tel 7230388
尖沙咀東麼地道67號半島中心 4 樓

Club Boss . . . . Lower Ground floor, Mandarin
大富豪夜總會
Plaza, 24 Museum Rd, Tsimshatsui East, tel 3692883
尖沙咀東新文華商業中心低層

Club Metropolitan . . . . Lower Ground floor, Chinachem
大都會夜總會
Golden Plaza, 77 Mody Rd,
Tsimshatsui, tel 3111111
尖沙咀東部麼地道77號華懋黃金廣場

New Tonnochy Night Club 1–5 Tonnochy Rd, Wanchai,
新杜老誌夜總會
tel 5754376
灣仔杜智台1-5號

Ocean City Restaurant . . New World Centre, Level B,
and Nightclub
22 Salisbury Rd, Tsimshatsui,
海城大酒樓夜總會
tel 3699688
尖沙咀梳士巴利道22號新世界中心

Ocean Palace Restaurant 4/F, Ocean Centre, Harbour
and Nightclub
City, Tsimshatsui, tel 3677111
海洋皇宮大酒樓夜總會
尖沙咀海港城海洋中心 4 樓

PHOTOCOPYING AND PRINTING

Alphagraphics . . . . . . 810 Block B, Sea View Estate,
雅快圖
Watson Rd, North Point,
tel 5703432
北角屈臣道海景大廈B座810室

Prontaprint . . . . Far East Finance Center,
速達店
Admiralty, tel 8657525
金鐘遠東金融中心

RELIGIOUS SERVICES

St. John's Cathedral . . . . 4–8 Garden Rd, Central,
(Anglican)
tel 5234157
聖約翰大教堂
中環花園道4-8號

St. Joseph's Church . . . . . 37 Garden Rd, Central,
(Roman Catholic)   tel 5223992
聖約瑟聖堂   中環花園道37號

United Jewish Congregation PO Box 6083, Hong Kong,
                           tel 4638156, fax 4563450
                           香港郵箱6083號

Hindu Temple . . . .   Wong Nai Chung Rd, Happy
                           Valley, tel 5725284
                           跑馬地黃泥涌道

SAUNAS, MASSAGE AND NATUROPATHS

Frederique's . . . .   4/F, Wilson House, 19–27
樊德禮美容院   Wyndham St, Central,
                           tel 5223054
                           中環雲咸街19-27號威信大廈 4 樓

New Paradise Health Club   414–30 Lockhart Rd, Wanchai,
新瀛宮芬蘭館   tel 5748807
                           灣仔駱克道414-30號

Sunny Paradise . . . .   339 Lockhart Rd, Wanchai,
新瀛閣桑拿   tel 5722561
                           灣仔駱克道339號

Vital Life Centre . . . . . .   12/F, 6 Duddell St, Central,
                           tel 8778206
                           中環都爹利街 6 號12樓

Acupressure and Massage   Dragon Seed Building,
 Centre for the Blind   Queen's Rd Central, tel 8106666
失明人按摩中心   皇后大道中龍子行

SHOEMAKERS (PAGE 149)

Kow Hoo Shoe Co . . . .   Shop 24, 1/F Hilton Hotel
高和皮鞋公司   Shopping Arcade, 2 Queen's Rd,
                           Central, tel 5230489
                           中環皇后大道中 2 號希爾頓酒店商場

Mayer Shoe Co . . . . . .   M-23, Mandarin Oriental Hotel,
美雅公司   5 Connaught Rd, Central,
                           tel 5243317
                           中環干諾道中 5 號文華東方酒店 M-23 室

SOUVENIRS (PAGE 152)

Amazing Grace Elephant Company	1/F, Excelsior Hotel, Causeway Bay, tel 8902776 Shop 249, Ocean Terminal, Harbour City, Tsimshatui, tel 7305455 308 City Plaza II, Taikoo Shing, tel 5673180 銅鑼灣告士打道281號怡東酒店購物商場 尖沙咀海港城海運大廈249室 鰂魚涌英皇道1111號太古城中心308室
Design Selection	39 Wyndham St, Central, tel 5248819 中環雲咸街39號
Fook Ming Tong Tea Shop 福茗堂茶莊	G/F, Pedder Building, 8 Theatre Lane, Central, tel 5210337 中環戲院里畢打行地下
Mitsukoshi Department Store 三越	Basement, One Hennessy Centre, Causeway Bay, tel 8952728 銅鑼灣軒尼詩道500號興利中心地庫1樓
Hong Kong Rattan Art Craft and Ware Ltd 香港藤器工藝中心有限公司	G/F, 33 Wing Lok St, Central, tel 5437508 中環永樂街33號地下
Mountain Folkcraft 高山文藝	12 Wo On Lane, Central, tel 5232817 中環和安里12號

SPORTS

Go-Kart racing 高卡賽車	Mai Po race track, New Territories, tel 8070576 新界米埔賽車徑
Horse Racing 賽馬	Royal Hong Kong Jockey Club, 2 Sports Rd, Happy Valley, tel 8378111 跑馬地體育路2號英皇御准賽馬會

Swimming . . . . 游泳	Victoria Park Pool, Causeway Bay, tel 5704682 Kowloon Park Pool, Tsimshatsui, tel 7243344 銅鑼灣維多利亞公園泳池 尖沙咀九龍公園泳池
Tennis . . . . 網球	Victoria Park Tennis Courts, tel 5706186 維多利亞公園網球場
YMCA's . . . . 中華基督教青年會	YMCA of Hong Kong, 41 Salisbury Rd, Tsimshatsui, tel 3692211 YMCA International House, 23 Waterloo Rd, Yaumatei, tel 7719111 Garden View International House (YWCA), 1 Macdonnell Rd, Central, tel 8773737 Harbour View International House, 4 Harbour Rd, Wanchai, tel 5201111 尖沙咀梳士巴利道41號中華基督教青年會 油麻地窩打老道23號青年會國際賓館 中環麥當勞道1號花園國際賓館 灣仔港灣道4號灣景國際賓館 （中華基督教青年會）

TAILORS (PAGE 148)

A. Man Hing Cheong . . . 亞民興昌洋服	Mandarin Oriental, Central, tel 5223336 中環文華東方酒店
Ascot Chang . . . . 新星	The Peninsula, Tsimashatui, tel 3662398 The Regent, Tsimshatsui, tel 3678319 尖沙咀半島酒店

Ash Samtani	Burlington Arcade, 92–4 Nathan Rd, Tsimshatsui, tel 3674285 尖沙咀彌敦道92-94號華敦大廈
Bobby's Fashions	Mirador Mansions, 5 Carnarvon Rd, Tsimshatsui, tel 7242615 尖沙咀加拿芬道 5 號美麗都大廈
Jimmy Chen . . . . 陳占美	Hong Kong Hotel Arcade, Tsimshatsui, tel 7305045 尖沙咀奧麗香港酒店商場
David's Shirts . . . . . . 大偉製衣	Wing Lee Bldg, 33 Kimberley Rd, Tsimshatsui, tel 3684368 Mandarin Oriental, Central, tel 5242979 尖沙咀金巴利道33號永利大廈地下
Nita Fashions	9A Bristol Avenue, Tsimshatsui, tel 3683020 尖沙咀碧仙桃路 9 號A
Sam's Tailor	94 Nathan Rd, Tsimshatsui, tel 3679423 尖沙咀彌敦道94號
Shanghai Custom Tailoring 上海洋服	Sheraton Hotel, Tsimshatsui, tel 3686980 尖沙咀喜來登酒店
W.W. Chan & Sons . . . . Tailoring	2/F, Burlington House, Block A2 94 Nathan Rd, Tsimshatsui, tel 3669738 尖沙咀彌敦道94號華敦大廈 2 樓 A2室
Ying Tai . . . . 永泰	The Peninsula, Tsimshatsui, tel 7230404 尖沙咀半島酒店

TRAVEL AGENTS

China Travel Service . . . **(HK) Ltd** 香港中旅社	2/F, China Travel Bldg, 77 Queen's Rd, Central, tel 5252284 中環皇后大道77號中旅大廈 2 樓

China Travel Service . . .   1/F, Alpha House, 27–33 Nathan
 (HK) Ltd   Rd, Tsimshatsui, tel 7211331
香港中旅社   尖沙咀彌敦道27-33號良士大廈1樓

Concorde Travel. . . . . .   1/F, 8–10 On Lan St,
協調旅行社   Central, tel 5263391
  中環安瀾街8-10號1樓

Hong Kong Student Travel   1/F, 499 Hennessy Rd, Causeway
香港學聯旅遊   Bay, tel 8339909
  Room 901, Wing On Central
  Bldg, Des Voeux Rd, Central,
  tel 8107272
  銅鑼灣軒尼詩道499號1樓
  中環德輔道永安中心大廈901室

Kingsway Travel. . . . . .   19/F, Ho Lee Bldg,
威信旅遊   30–44 D'Aguilar St, Central,
  tel 8456696
  中環德忌立街好利商業大廈19樓

Mera Travel . . . .   Room 1307–9 Argyle Centre,
凱達旅運   688 Nathan Rd, Yaumatei,
  tel 3916892
  油麻地彌敦道688號旺角中心1307-9室

INDEX

Hong Kong

CHINA
GUANGDONG PROVINCE

Shenzhen

Sheung Shui

Deep Bay

Shekou

Mai Po Marshes

Yuen Long   Kam Tin

Tai Mo Shan
▲ 957

N E W

583 ▲
Castle Peak   Tuen Mun

LUNG KWU
CHAU

Tai Lam
Chung   Tsuen Wan

PEARL
ISLAND

MA WAN

TSING YI

THE BROTHERS

STONECUTTERS
ISLAND

CHEK LAP
KOK   CHEK LAP
KOK

KOW

Proposed site
for new airport   Discovery
Bay   Discovery
Bay

GREEN
ISLAND

Ken
To

KAU YI
CHAU

Vict

Tai O   PENG CHAU

Mui Wo

LANTAU ISLAND   869
Sunset Peak

933
Lantau Peak

SUNSHINE
ISLAND

East Lam

HEI LING
CHAU

CHI MA WAN
PENINSULA

Yung Shue
Wan

CHEUNG
CHAU

LAMMA ISLAND

FAN LAU

Lantau Channel

West Lamma Channel

Sok Kwu
Wan

SHEK KWU
CHAU

SOKO ISLANDS

South China Sea

CROOKED ISLAND

PING CHAU

Sha Tau Kok

Starling Inlet

CRESCENT ISLAND

Mirs Bay

DOUBLE ISLAND

Wong Leng
639 △

Plover Cove
Reservoir

Tolo Channel

TAP MUN CHAU

Po

Tolo Harbour

Sharp Peak
△ 468

Ma Liu Shui

Ma On Shan
702 △

Tai Long Wan

R I T O R I E S

Sai Kung

High Island Reservoir

Sha Tin

KAU SAI CHAU

HeBe Haven

SHARP ISLAND

△ Rock

Kowloon Peak
602 △

Port Shelter

SHELTER ISLAND

Kai Tak Airport

Hang Hau Town

TIU CHUNG CHAU

BASALT ISLAND

Hung Hom

Kwun Tong

Rennie's Mill

North Point

Junk Bay

arbour

Shau Kei Wan

Causeway Bay

JUNK ISLAND

Clear Water Bay

NINEPIN GROUP

ONG ISLAND

Chai Wan

Tathong Channel

Big Wave Bay

TUNG LUNG CHAU

Repulse Bay

Shek O

Tai Tam Wan

Stanley

BEAUFORT ISLAND

PO TOI ISLANDS

WAGLAN ISLAND

SUNG KONG

△ PO TOI

Legend

Country Park

Main Road

Secondary Roads

Railway

Mass Transit Railway

Light Railway

Ferry

N

| 0 | 2 | 4 | 6 | 8 | 10 km |

| 0 | 2 | 4 | 6 miles |

© The Guidebook Company Ltd

Ferry to Jordan Road

Hoverferries to Tuen Mun & Discovery Bay

Ferries to Lamma Island Tai Kok Tsui & Sham Shui Po

Ferries to Lamma & Cheung Chau Islands

Hoverferry to Tsuen Wan

Hoverferries to Lantau & Cheung Chau Islands

Victoria Harbour

Government Pier

Outlying Islands Ferries Pier

Vehicular Ferry Pier

Blake Pier

Watertours

← To Macau Ferry Terminal

← To Western District

Central Waterfront Promenade

Connaught

Exchange Square Bus Terminus

Exchange Square

General Post Office

Student Travel Bureau

China Travel

Des

Road

CENTRAL DISTRICT

Jardine House

H.K. Tourist Association

Wing On Street

Jubilee Street

Voeux

Victoria

Street

Road

Central

Jubilee Street

Central Market

Queen

Street

China Travel

Pottinger

Li Yuen Street West

Li Yuen Street East

HK Book Centre

Swire House

Queen's

Chinese Emporium

Road

Queen's Cinema

Alexandra House

Wellington

Stanley

Street

Street

Luk Yu Teahouse

Street

Central

The Landmark

Peddar Street

MARKET AREA

Peel

Graham

Gage Street

Cochrane

Terrace

Pottinger

Street

King's Cinema

Wyndham Street

China Arts & Crafts

American Express

Lyndhurst

Hollywood

Road

Wanderlust Books

The Guidebook Co. Ltd.

D'Aguilar

Wyndham

Arbuthnot

Lan Kwai Fong (Restaurants & Bars)

Foreign Correspondent's Club

Ice

House

Duddell Street

Street

Staunton

Street

Bailey

Street

Prison

MID-LEVELS

Mad Dogs Pub.

Fringe Club Theatre

Street

Shelley

Old

Caine

Road

Road

© The Guidebook Company Ltd

↓ To Zoological Gardens

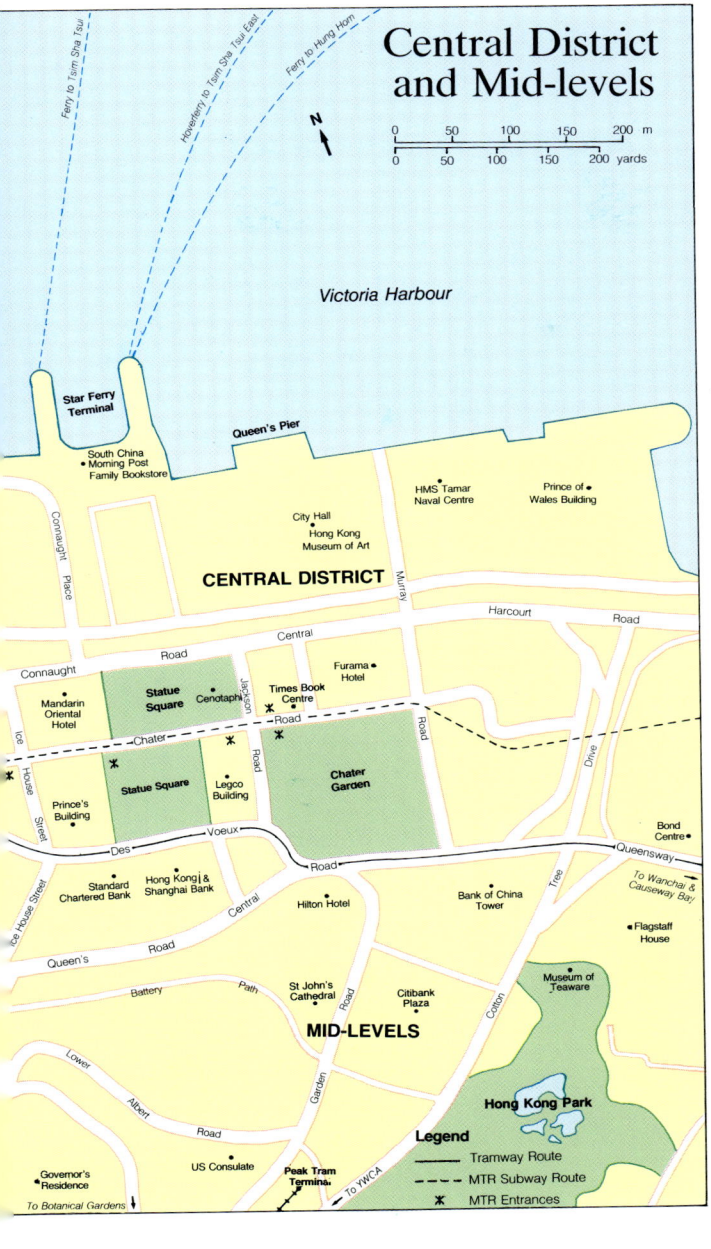

Central District and Mid-levels

0   50   100   150   200 m

0   50   100   150   200 yards

N

Victoria Harbour

Ferry to Tsim Sha Tsui

Hoverferry to Tsim Sha Tsui East

Ferry to Hung Hom

Star Ferry Terminal

Queen's Pier

South China
Morning Post
Family Bookstore

HMS Tamar
Naval Centre

Prince of
Wales Building

City Hall
Hong Kong
Museum of Art

Connaught Place

CENTRAL DISTRICT

Murray

Harcourt   Road

Road

Connaught   Road

Central

Furama
Hotel

Statue
Square   Cenotaph

Jackson

Times Book
Centre

Mandarin
Oriental
Hotel

Chater

Road

Chater
Garden

Ice House

Prince's
Building

Statue Square   Legco
Building

Voeux

Des

Road

Road

Bond
Centre

Queensway

To Wanchai &
Causeway Bay

Ice House Street

Standard
Chartered Bank

Hong Kong &
Shanghai Bank

Central

Road

Hilton Hotel

Bank of China
Tower

Tree

Drive

Flagstaff
House

Queen's   Road

Battery   Path

St John's
Cathedral

Road

Citibank
Plaza

Cotton

Museum of
Teaware

MID-LEVELS

Lower

Albert

Road

Garden   Road

Hong Kong Park

Legend

—— Tramway Route

--- MTR Subway Route

✳ MTR Entrances

Governor's
Residence

To Botanical Gardens

US Consulate

Peak Tram
Terminal

To YWCA

Wanchai and Causeway Bay

N

| 0 | 100 | 200 | 300 | 400 m |

| 0 | 100 | 200 | 300 | 400 yards |

Victoria Harbour

To Kowloon Star Ferry Pier

To Hung Hom

Wanchai Ferry Pier

Convention Avenue

Bus Station

Grand Hyatt Hotel & JJs

Hong Kong Convention & Exhibition Centre

New World Harbour View Hotel

Columbia Classics Cinema

Great Eagle Centre

Sports Centre and Swimming Pool

Road

Hong Kong Arts Centre

YMCA

Harbour

China Resources Building and Hong Kong Exhibition Centre

Sun Hung Kai Centre

Hong Kong Academy for Performing Arts

Cable and Wireless Building

New Supreme Court/ Gov't Houses

Museum of Chinese Historical Relics

Cine Ar House

Gloucester Road

Harbour Hotel

Arsenal Street

The Wanchai Pub.

Joe Bananas

WANCHAI

Road

Fenwick Street

Ramada Inn

Jaffe

Lockhart

O'Brien

Fleming

Road

Road

Lockhart Road Market

Stewart

Road

To Pacific Place, Conrad Hotel & Marriott Pacific Place Hotel

Queensway

American Peking Restaurant

New Harbour Hotel

Chili Club

Old China Hand Pub.

Hennessy

Road

Sailors & Soldiers Home

Luard

Road

Southorn Playground

Thomson

Road

Wanchai Road

Johnston

Road

Cathay Cinema

Imperial Cinema

Wood

Queen's Road East

Wanchai Market

Tang Shiu Hospit

Kennedy

Tai Wong Temple

Cross Street

Wanchai Market

Ruttonjee TB Sanatorium

Queen's Road East

Road

Hopewell Centre

Old Wanchai Post Office

Bowen

Kennedy

Road

Stubbs

Ro

Bowen

Road

— Tramway Route

- - - MTR Subway Route

✳ MTR Entrances

© The Guidebook Company Ltd

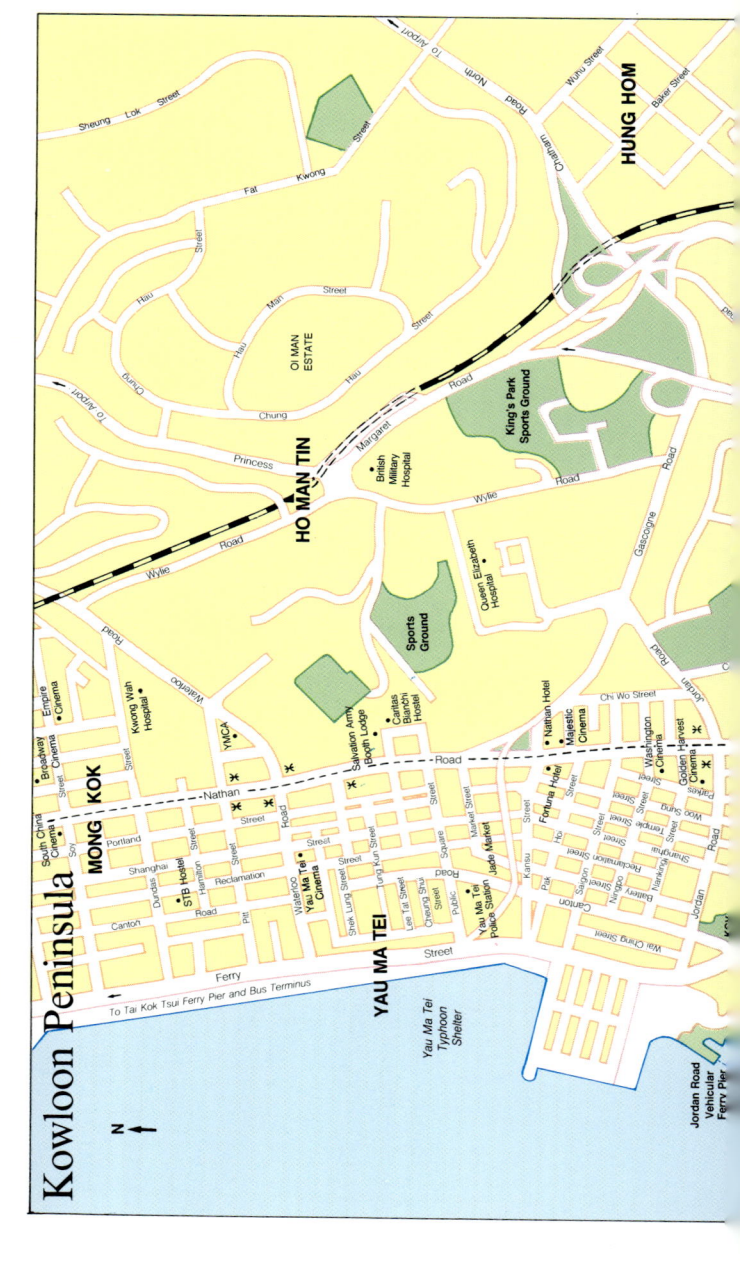

Kowloon Peninsula

HUNG HOM

Wuhu Street
Baker Street
Gillies

To Kai Tak Airport
North

King's Park Sports Ground

HO MAN TIN

OI MAN ESTATE

Hau

Man Street

Chung

Princess Margaret

Road

British Military Hospital

Wylie

Queen Elizabeth Hospital

Gascoigne Road

Road

Sheung Lok Street

Fat Kwong Street

Street

Hau

Hau

To Kowloon

Wylie

Road

Sports Ground

Waterloo

Kwong Wah Hospital

Salvation Army

Booth Lodge

Caritas Bianchi Hostel

Nathan Hotel

Chi Wo Street

Washington Cinema

Golden Harvest Cinema

Majestic Cinema

Fortuna Hotel

Wo Shing

Gordon

Nathan

Road

YMCA

Empire Cinema

Broadway Cinema

MONG KOK

South China Cinema

Sau

Portland

Shanghai

Street

Hamilton

Street

Dundas

Reclamation

Canton Road

STB Hostel

Pitt

Pak Hoi Street

Kansu

Saigon Street

Pak Hoi

Reclamation Street

Shanghai Street

Temple Street

Battery Street

Nanking Street

Ning Po Street

Hankow

Carnarvon

YAU MA TEI

Waterloo

Yau Ma Tei Cinema

Tong Kun Street

Shek Lung Street

Cheung Sha

Public Square Street

Jade Market

Yau Ma Tei Police Station

Kansu Street

Canton Road

Wui Cheng Street

Jordan Road

Ferry Street

To Tai Kok Tsui Ferry Pier and Bus Terminus

Yau Ma Tei Typhoon Shelter

Jordan Road Vehicular Ferry Pier

N

LAND UNDER
RECLAMATION

Hung Hom KCR Station

Hong Kong Coliseum

Cross Harbour Tunnel

Ferries from Hung Hom to Wanchai and Central

© The Guidebook Company Ltd

400 m
400 yards

Hong Kong Polytechnic

Yuk Choi Road

Hong Chong Road

Cheong Wan Road

Tak Shing Street

Cricket Club

Road

Rosary Church

Austin Road

Observatory Road

Royal Observatory

Hillwood Road

Kimberley Street

Kimberley Road

Carnarvon Road

Cameron Road

Austin Road

London Cinema

St. Andrew's Church

TSIM SHA TSUI

Miramar Hotel

Tin Hau Tok Joji
Tinfoo International Hotel

Lucky Guest House

Humphrey's Ave

Park Hotel

TSIM SHA TSUI EAST

China Chem Centre

Empire
Isimura
Museum

Royal Garden Hotel

Imperial Hotel

Regal Hotel

Holiday
Garden

Guangdong Hotel

Chatham Road

Nanyo Road

Prat Ave

Grand Hotel

Astor Hotel

Shanghai Road

Hunghom Waterfront Promenade

Kowloon Park

Hong Kong Museum of History

Park Lane Shopper's Blvd.

Islamic Centre
Kowloon Mosque

Nathan Road

Thomas Cook

Mody Road

Chungking Mansions

Holiday Inn Golden Mile

New World Centre

Empress Hotel

Black Head Point Garden

Salisbury Road

New World Hotel

Regent Hotel

Lock Road

Swindon's Books

Haiphong Road

Ned Kelly's

Hankow Road

Ashley Road

Peking Road

Middle Road

Kowloon Hotel

The Peninsula

Sheraton

Hong Kong
Cultural Centre

Space Museum
Planetarium

Hong Kong Hotel

YMCA

Ramada Renaissance Hotel

Marine Police Head Quarters

Ocean Cinema

Old KCR Station

Clock Tower

HKTA Centre

Kowloon Pier

Star Ferry Pier

Ferry to Central

Ferry to Wanchai

Canton Road

Omni Prince Hotel

China Hong Kong City

Harbour City

Canton Hotel

Omni Marco Polo Hotel

Ocean Centre

Watertours Pier

The Hong Kong Hotel

China Ferry Terminal

Pier Observation Deck

Ocean Galleries

Ocean Galleries

Ocean Galleries

Ocean Galleries

Ocean Terminal

Victoria Harbour

Ferry to Central

Legend

KCR

MTR Subway Route

MTR Entrances

Macau

N ←

Border Gate

Estrada Marginal do Hipodromo

Iao Hon

Rua da Fabrica

Ilha Verde

Avenida do Conselheiro Borja

Areia Preta

Avenida de Venceslau de Morais

Lin Fong Temple

Mong-Ha Fort

Canidrome

Av. General Castelo Branco

Kun Iam Temple

Pateira

Balichao

Riquexo

Sun Yat-sen Memorial Home

Mondial

Cabral

Avenida do Coronel Mesquita

Xavier

Francisco Xavier Pereira

Avenida do Ouvidor Arriaga

Costa

Avenida de Horta e Costa

Rua de Almeida

Avenida Sidonio Pais

Avenida de Almirante Lacerda

Lou Lim Ieoc Gardens

Rua Marinho Monteverde

Amaral

Rua de

Coelho

Estrada do Repouso

Rua

Camões Gardens and Grotto

Old Protestant Cemetery

Inner Harbour

Outer Harbour

© The Guidebook Company Ltd

| 0 | 200 | 400 | 600 | 800 m |
| 0 | 200 | 400 | 600 | 800 yards |

Legend

★ = Hotel
■ = Restaurant
† = Church
● = Other

Arrivals/Departures Terminal

Jai Alai Stadium

Mandarin Oriental

Macau Forum

Kingsway

Guia Fort & Lighthouse

Matsuya

Guia

New World

Royal

Avenida de Rodrigo Rodrigues

Vasco da Gama Park

Presidente

Beverly Plaza

Lisboa

Estrada St Francisco

Avenida do Dr Rodrigo Rodrigues

Rua Nova Guia

Avenida Amizade

Avenida Infante de Henrique

Avenida de João IV

Avenida Amizade

Macau-Taipa Bridge

(Under Reclamation)

St Paul's Ruins

Monte Fort

Rua Pedro Nolasco da Silva

Rua Palha

Grand

East Asia

Rua das Estalagens

St Dominic's

Central

G.P.O.

Leal Senado

Avenida Almeida Ribeiro

St Augustine's

† St Joseph's

Rua Gamboa

Rua Central

Government Palace

Praia Grande

Peninsula

Macau Palace (Floating) Casino

Rua das Lorchas

Rua do Almirante Sérgio

St Lawrence's †

Calçada da Barra

Penha Hill

Pousada Ritz

★ Bela Vista

Henri's Galley

Praia Grande

Rua da Praia Grande

A Lorcha

A-Ma Temple

Rua da Barra

Maritime Museum

Governor's Mansion

Pousada de São Tiago

Avenida da República